The Psychology of Terrorism

Recent Titles in Psychological Dimensions to War and Peace

Perpetration-Induced Traumatic Stress: The Psychological Consequences of Killing
Rachel M. MacNair

Memory Perceived: Recalling the Holocaust
Robert N. Kraft

The Psychological Impact of War Trauma on Civilians: An International Perspective
Stanley Krippner and Teresa M. McIntyre, editors

The Psychology of Terrorism

◆

Volume IV
Programs and Practices
in Response and Prevention

Edited by Chris E. Stout
Foreword by Klaus Schwab

Psychological Dimensions to War and Peace
Harvey Langholtz, Series Editor

PRAEGER

Westport, Connecticut
London

Library of Congress Cataloging-in-Publication Data

The psychology of terrorism / edited by Chris E. Stout ; foreword by Klaus Schwab.
    p. cm.—(Psychological dimensions to war and peace, ISSN 1540–5265)
    Includes bibliographical references and index.
    ISBN 0–275–97771–4 (set)—ISBN 0–275–97865–6 (vol. I)—ISBN 0–275–97866–4
(vol. II)—ISBN 0–275–97867–2 (vol. III)—ISBN 0–275–97868–0 (vol. IV)
    1. Terrorism—Psychological aspects. 2. Terrorists—Psychology. 3.
Terrorism—Prevention. I. Stout, Chris E. II. Series.
HV6431 .P798 2002
303.6'25—dc21   2002072845

British Library Cataloguing in Publication Data is available.

Library of Congress Catalog Card Number: 2002072845
ISBN: set: 0-275-97771-4
        v.I: 0-275-97865-6
        v.II: 0-275-97866-4
        v.III: 0-275-97867-2
        v.IV: 0-275-97868-0
ISSN: 1540-5265

First published in 2002

Praeger Publishers, 88 Post Road West, Westport, CT 06881
An imprint of Greenwood Publishing Group, Inc.
www.praeger.com

Printed in the United States of America

The paper used in this book complies with the
Permanent Paper Standard issued by the National
Information Standards Organization (Z39.48-1984).

10 9 8 7 6 5 4 3 2 1

To my parents, Carlos L. and Helen E. (Simmons) Stout,
to my wife and soulmate, Dr. Karen Beckstrand, and
to my children and heroes, Grayson Beckstrand Stout and
Annika Beckstrand Stout.

You all have taught and continue to teach me so very much.

Contents

Foreword

First of all, I want to note the impressive collection of academics, thinkers, activists, and clinicians congregated in this set of volumes. Through their active engagement, the result is a series of works that crosscut an immense range of related factors—historical contexts; group dynamics; social psychological aspects; behavioral, forensic, psychopathological, evolutionary theory, peace-building, and conflict resolution perspectives; as well as the political, clinical, and social aspects of prevention, intervention, and security issues. Global perspectives vis-à-vis understanding, empathy, bias, prejudice, racism, and hate are also represented.

This group of authors offers a unique combination of talents and viewpoints rarely seen in the worlds of academia or activism. Their work and voices move knowledge and understanding forward in a way that will serve as a framework and catalyst for readers to consider ways in which to respond to terrorism in its various displays. Dr. Stout has fostered a self-organizing environment that has enabled this work to be a collaboration of ideas that goes beyond the traditional and almost complacent; instead it is realistically erudite and even provocative in some instances.

I suspect that the readership will likewise be broad and crosscutting—including academics and departments of psychology, political science, religious studies, military sciences, law enforcement, public health, sociology, anthropology, social work, and law, as well as the lay public and the media, policy makers, elected government officials, leaders of nongovernmental organizations, ambassadors and diplomats, military leaders, law enforcement professionals, the intelligence community, and members of think tanks and private and public policy institutes and centers.

Such integration of diversity in thought and perspective parallels our "Forum Plus" strategy at the World Economic Forum. This strategy aims to advance critical issues on the global agenda through the creation of task forces and initiatives that integrate business, governments, international organizations, civil society, academics, and technical experts.

Similarly, Dr. Stout has been successful in gathering some of the greatest thinkers on this topic from around the world, including Fulbright scholars, a Kellogg International fellow, a Pulitzer Prize winner, a Beale fellow (Harvard), a *boursier de la Confédération Suisse*, a Medical Research Council fellow, American Psychological Association fellows, a Royal College of Physicians fellow, an American College of Psychiatrists fellow, American Psychiatric Association fellows, and a Regents scholar. Authors represent a wide array of academic institutions: the University of Pennsylvania; Harvard Medical School; Rutgers University; Princeton University; Northwestern University Medical School; Mount Sinai School of Medicine; Nelson Mandela School of Medicine, University of Natal, South Africa; George Mason University; University of Massachusetts; University of Michigan; Civitan International Research Center at the University of Alabama; Institute for Mental Health Initiatives at George Washington University; Marylhurst University; Portland State University; Southwest Texas State University; Al Aksa University in Gaza; University of Lagos, Akoka-Yaba, Lagos, Nigeria; University of Wisconsin; Northern Arizona University; Bryn Mawr College; Randolph-Macon College; Illinois State University; University of South Florida; Elmhurst College; Howard University; University of Texas Health Science Center; Texas A&M College of Medicine; University of California; Saybrook Graduate School and Research Center; New School University; and New York University. Authors also represent the United Nations (a Humanitarian Affairs Officer, an Assistant to the Under-Secretary-General for Peacekeeping, and an Assistant to the Special Representative of the Secretary-General to the former Yugoslavia and to NATO), the Disaster Mental Health Institute; the Comprehensive Medical Center in Dubai, United Arab Emirates; GGZ Den Bosch/Outpatient and Daytreatment Centre for Refugees in the Netherlands; the Human Sciences Research Council in South Africa; Delta Psychiatric Teaching Hospital in Poortugaal, the Netherlands; Maagalim–Institute of Psychotherapy and Counseling in Tel Aviv; the United Nations Development Program for Women; the USAID Rwanda Rule of Law Project; and the Christian Children's Fund.

Many of the authors are also current or past officers of a wide variety of professional associations and other organizations: the World Psychiatric Association on Urban Mental Health; the Commission on Global Psychiatry of the American Psychiatric Association; the South African Institute for Traumatic Stress; Solomon Asch's Center for Ethno-Political Conflict at the University of Pennsylvania; the American Psychological Association Committee on Global Violence and Security within Division 48; the Society for the Study of Peace, Conflict, and Violence; the Association for Humanistic Psychology; the Non Governmental Organizations Executive Committee on Mental Health—UN; Psychologists for Social Responsibility; the Conflict Resolution Action Committee; the Conflict Resolution Working Group (of Division 48 of the American Psychological Association); the Philadelphia Project for Global Security; the American Academy of Psychiatry and the Law; the National Council of State Medical Directors; the Board of Presidents of the Socialist Countries' Psychiatric Associations in Sofia, Bulgaria; the Society for the Study of Peace, Conflict and Violence: Peace Psychology Division of the

American Psychological Association (APA); the International Society for Political Psychology; the Committee for International Liaisons for the Division of International Psychology (APA); and the Common Bond Institute.

Dr. Stout has also assembled some of the best and the brightest to serve as his Editorial Advisory Board: Terrance Koller, Dana Royce Baerger, Malini Patel, Ron Levant, and Stephen Kouris.

The rapid growth of global communications, information technology, and international business in the second half of the twentieth century increased the need for a common platform where the stakeholders of society could be brought together to consider and advance the key issues on the global agenda. The World Economic Forum's goal is to provide that platform, asking a mix of individuals to articulate the major problems facing the world and to find solutions. Works like this are catalytic to our thinking and dialogue.

It is our hope at the Forum to support the global public interest and to improve the state of the world. I believe this series adds to such a mission by its integration of thinking and facilitation of dialogue among different stakeholders and across different regions and intellectual disciplines. This series promotes progress by expanding common ground and developing new approaches.

Klaus Schwab
Founder and President
World Economic Forum

Acknowledgments

A project such as this one—with authors from all over the world covering a breadth and depth of examination of such a complex topic—can only happen as the result of a team effort. As such, I would like first of all to thank my family. Annika, Grayson, and I have sacrificed many a weekend of playing together; and I have also missed time with my very supportive partner and wife, Dr. Karen Beck-strand. Debora Carvalko, our editor at Greenwood, has been the crucial link in this project. She has worked with herculean effort to keep things organized and work-ing. In fact, it is thanks to her that this project was even undertaken. The Editorial Advisory Board worked diligently, reading and commenting on many more manu-scripts than those seen herein. The work of Terrence Koller, Malini Patel, Dana Royce Baerger, Steven P. Kouris, and Ronald F. Levant was impeccable and key to ensuring the quality of the chapters. I am also indebted to the council of Hedwin Naimark for invaluable help and thinking.

Professor Klaus Schwab has been a valued resource to me over the years and he was kind enough to provide the foreword. Harvey Langholtz has been an ongoing source of inspiration and mentorship to me. He is without a doubt the most diplo-matic of all psychologists I know (it must have been all those years at the United Nations). And, this project would have been no more than an idea without the intellectual productivity of the contributing authors. We were fortunate to have more submissions than we could use in the end, but even those whose works were not used surely had an impact on my thinking and perspective, and I am very grateful. Finally, behind-the-scenes thanks to Ralph Musicant, Lawrence W. Osborn, Phillip Zimbardo, Patrick DeLeon, and Michael Horowitz.

I am markedly indebted to you all at a level that I shall never be able to repay. My sincere thanks to each of you.

Introduction

In thinking about the words to write here, I am struck with the vast array of ironies.

I had been writing and presenting talks on issues of terrorism for a while before September 11, 2001. In June 2001, I had submitted a proposal dealing with issues of terrorism for a clinical practice conference in November 2001, and I cannot help but suspect that the proposal could easily have been rejected because of a busy agenda and other competing topics that would have been considered more important to attendees. Instead, the proposal was accepted and it was the largest crowd I have ever addressed. Standing room only, and the only presentation over the course of a three-day conference that was videotaped. Sad, indeed, how some things change. I now often find myself reminding audiences that terrorism existed before September 11, 2001. In fact, that was what my talk was about. Terrorism in Japan, in Lebanon, in Ireland. In the world. In our world. For many of us who are U.S. citizens, the term "our world" now has a new and different meaning.

I have presented and written a fair amount on terrorism, and war, and trauma, and civilian casualties. I've worked with children who have been tortured, talked with traumatized refugees, broken bread with former political prisoners, and worked with a center offering pro bono clinical services to refugees who are victims of torture. I've seen the aftermath of atrocities—exhumed corpses, mass graves, and murdered infants. I have gone on medical missions to far-off places around the world. I have slides and statistics, bar graphs and citations; I can quote numerous facts and figures. But prior to September 11, 2001, all of that was done with a certain degree of clinical detachment. I would go somewhere else, and then come home. I have not ever been in an active war zone, nor have I been a victim of a terrorist attack. After September 11, I feel a bit different.

More people now know what is meant by a "dirty bomb," or what anthrax and Cipro are, than knew before September 11. I'm not sure if that is a good thing or not. I work in Chicago, the city that again has title to the tallest building in the United States. Who could have ever imagined such an odd occurrence? The reclaiming of such a title as the result of a kiloton of destructive force toppling the towers of the World Trade Center, all for the price of a plane ticket and a box cutter. Unbelievable.

I cannot help but wonder what might have been different if the West/North had dealt before September 11 with brewing, yet largely ignored, issues—from an intelligence perspective, a psychological perspective (in all its varieties, forms, and flavors), a diplomacy and foreign policy perspective. I wonder what might have been achieved in tackling the larger dynamics of both the good and the bad that accompany globalization. All of this juxtaposed with issues of religious fundamentalism and politics. I'd like to believe things would have been better, but perhaps they would not.

Terrorism is a complex issue that does not respond well to reductionism. I apologize in advance if somehow this project looks as if it tries to simplify the complexities. My objective is not to teach the reader everything he or she ever wanted to know about terrorism in four easy lessons, but rather to offer a sampling of diverse and rich thought. Perhaps this can be the spark that starts a dialogue or a debate. That is OK by me. I have been amazed at the diversity, if not downright division, of some of the opinions and resultant debates following September 11. There are arguments regarding violent and aggressive responses versus forgiveness and passivism, evil versus good, behavioral reinforcement versus social psychology theories, isolationism versus globalism, "we are victims" versus "we brought this on ourselves," and my favorite dichotomy—"this is a start of the end" versus "this is the start of a new beginning." I think back to the horrible nature of the Oklahoma City bombing. That event was not at the same level as the New York and D.C. attacks in terms of the loss of life, damage, destruction and, frankly, vast media coverage. But the horror may also be mitigated by the fact that it was done by a McVeigh, not a bin Laden.

Everything is a political act, it simply cannot be escaped. A lack of political participation (such as not voting) or a lack of political activism (such as not supporting a cause) is still a political act (as in support of a status quo). As you will see, some of our authors are academics, some are clinicians, and some are activists. Try as we all do to check our political biases at the door, they surely squeak in, and most likely in ways that are difficult to see. I hope that an Editorial Advisory Board makes it more difficult to miss these biases, but I still suggest that readers, like all good academics, seek to understand by questioning assumptions and looking for empirical evidence wherever possible. Certainly this topic may often not comply with such methods, but we have all tried our best to present good scholarship herein.

This project started out as one book. It quickly grew to four volumes. Many more chapters went unused due to space limitations, duplication, or other technical reasons. There simply is no singular psychology of terrorism, no unified field theory if you will. None of the chapters is a stand-alone work; they are best understood in the greater context of the book, and then likewise in the wider context of the series. In some instances, the reader may see differences of perspectives or tensions between viewpoints. None of the books is a homogenized or sterile rendition of information. Personally, I find it difficult to talk about terrorism without also talking about war. And it's hard to discuss war without getting into issues of torture. Similarly, it's difficult to discuss torture without also discussing violence, and so forth. Thus, in this project on terrorism, readers will see discussions concerning such various related issues, because none of these issues can easily or correctly be dis-integrated from terrorism. Thus these four books emanated from an organic, self-organizing developmental process, resulting in:

I. The Psychology of Terrorism: A Public Understanding

II. The Psychology of Terrorism: Clinical Aspects and Responses

III. The Psychology of Terrorism: Theoretical Understandings and Perspectives (with a special section on the Roles and Impacts of Religions)

IV. The Psychology of Terrorism: Programs and Practices in Response and Prevention

While there is no unifying perspective per se, I hope that these books may act as a unified source of perspectives. Also, they are incomplete. Individuals representing even more perspectives had hoped to contribute, but the realities prevented them from doing so. Certainly there will be continued interest, and I hope to see much more on these issues as we all become more aware and wise.

Volume I—A Public Understanding—provides an overview of issues in a way to help the public, in general, better understand the various issues involved. Volume II—Clinical Aspects and Responses—is an adequately telling title and offers much in the way of dealing with the emotional impacts of such traumas. Volume III—Theoretical Understandings and Perspectives—offers various perspectives of psychological understanding and theory intertwined with culture, context, politics, globalization, and social injustice as well as diplomatic processes. This volume also has a special section on the roles and impacts of religions that covers apocalyptic dreams, cults, religious archetypes, Islamic fundamentalism, and religious fanaticism.

Volume IV—Programs and Practices in Response and Prevention—provides a mix of preventative ideas and methods for youth and communities, as well as therapeutic aspects for those in trouble. For example, it includes articles on ethnopolitical warfare, family traumatic stress and refugee children; children's responses to traumatic events; aggression in adolescents; peace building; cooperative learning communities; antiviolence programming in school settings; and raising inclusively caring children. Granted, not all of these programs can be applied to a global set of venues, but they may offer much to those interested in developing their own variations on the theme.

What is my goal with this project? As noted earlier, I hope it provides readers with a mix of opinion and perspectives from which further thought and dialogue may occur. As you read these volumes, I would like you to keep in mind that through the work you do, no matter who you are, you can have an impact upon others that affects not only the individuals you encounter today, but potentially generations thereafter.

Part I:
Global Perspectives

1

A Community Psychology Perspective on Terrorism: Lessons from South Africa

Craig Higson-Smith

South Africa's violent history of colonization and apartheid rule is well known, but relatively little analysis of the significant role that terrorism has played in that history has been published in mainstream literature. (A great deal of material about terrorism in South Africa was generated under the apartheid government, but with a strong political bias.) The fact that little scholarly work exists is both puzzling and unfortunate. It is puzzling because terrorism has been widely used as a political weapon in South Africa, and unfortunate because the history of South Africa challenges many common assumptions about both terrorism and terrorists. It also provides interesting insight into how societies and governments might most effectively respond to acts of politically motivated violence. Of course, South Africa's history of terrorism is not the only one that is largely ignored in the mainstream literature. Many countries in South and Central America, Africa, the Middle East, and Asia with a history of colonial rule have much to teach us about terrorism. The aim of this chapter is to look critically at some of the assumptions made about terrorism by some writers on the subject, and to explore briefly several social factors that might protect society from this form of violence.

TERRORISTS: WHO ARE THEY?

Governments, the media, and mainstream public discourse portray terrorism as the most horrific and immoral of acts—senseless killing aimed at the destabilization of economy, government, and law and order, and a threat to the moral framework of society. In South Africa, as in nearly every country in the world, the word *terrorist* has strong negative moral implications. The term *freedom fighter*, which might be used to describe exactly the same person as *terrorist*, carries an implication of moral courage and rectitude. In 1994, Nelson Mandela, South Africa's most famous "terrorist," became the country's first democratically elected president. Looking back over the decisions of his life in his autobiography, Mandela remarks,

> . . . I argued that the state had given us no alternative to violence. I said it was wrong and immoral to subject our people to armed attacks by the state without offering them some kind of alternative. I mentioned again that people on their own had taken up arms. Violence would begin whether we initiated it or not. Would it not be better to guide this violence ourselves, according to principles where we saved lives by attacking symbols of oppression, and not people? (Mandela, 1994, p. 322)

Shortly after Mandela's inauguration, the Truth and Reconciliation Commission began to make public a seemingly endless litany of acts of terror, perpetrated by various parties, including agents of the state. Clearly, the image of the terrorist as an irrationally fanatical individual determined to challenge the authority of the state at the cost of the lives of innocent citizens does not accommodate the reality of terrorism in South Africa.

Students of terrorism who approach the topic from a broad social, political, economic, and historical perspective are not surprised that popular discourse constructs terrorism in this manner. It is unfortunate, however, to note how many social researchers and writers approach the topic with a similarly narrow bias that deifies the individual terrorist and ignores the societal context. Despite thirty years of research having failed to produce a convincing terrorist personality type or reliable evidence of patterns of psychopathology in terrorists, researchers continue to speculate on the personality variables and individual histories that might create a terrorist. In fact, "terrorism studies" as a field of inquiry is criticized as preserving this bias through working in close collaboration with the numerous counterterrorism agencies of the Western world and making so little attempt to engage directly with terrorists themselves (Brannan et al., 2001; Crenshaw, 2000; Ruby, 2002a; Silke, 1998). In contexts such as South Africa, the possibility of doing face-to-face research with terrorists is much greater. Many people who have committed acts of terrorism are living openly in society and can reflect, albeit retrospectively, on the factors that determined their actions.

When we look for the causes of terrorism only within the individual psychologies of terrorists or particular groups, we learn very little that is useful. The same is true for debate about the effects of terrorism. Although the traumatic effects on people exposed to acts of terrorism, and on their families, must not be underestimated, if we do not look at the less obvious—but nevertheless much more weighty—effects of terrorism on society as a whole, we are in danger of misunderstanding the terrible consequences of terror in our lives. However, when we try to understand terrorism in terms of both the historic and current dynamics of a society, we find that there is a great deal more to be learned (Oliverio, 1997).

TERRORISTS IN SOUTH AFRICA

Debates about an appropriate definition of "terrorism" remain unresolved and it is difficult to differentiate such related concepts as "communal violence," "guerrilla warfare," and "repressive terror"(Ruby, 2002b). A working definition consisting of four criteria is adopted for the purpose of this discussion. Terrorism is defined as 1) a politically motivated act of violence, 2) of clandestine nature, 3) directed at non-combatants, and 4) intended to induce fear in a population.

In terms of this definition, South Africa's long history of terrorism includes acts perpetrated by the apartheid security forces against activists and black South Africans generally, by anti-apartheid activists against the state as well as alleged spies and sell-outs among fellow citizens, and by members of different anti-apartheid movements against each other. It is, however, misleading to lump together acts of violence and terrorism perpetrated by the apartheid regime and the anti-apartheid movement.

> On a purely numerical basis, the deaths or injuries inflicted by the ANC in the course of the struggle simply cannot be compared with the numbers of those killed in the defence of apartheid . . . Subtract illegitimate violence from apartheid and zero remains. Conversely, the use of force as part of the resistance to apartheid was a legitimate exercise of the right to self-determination and an expression of constitutionalism . . . (Asmal, Asmal, & Roberts, 1996, pp. 41–42)

Nevertheless, although methods and objectives may have differed, these various acts of terror did occur in relation to each other as part of the same system. They can usefully be understood as dynamics in a longer process of social change.

The apartheid government came into being in 1948 and suppressive legislation began almost immediately, including the Suppression of Communism Act of 1950, the banning of the African National Congress (ANC) and Pan African Congress (PAC) in 1960, and the proclamation of several "states of emergency," which granted far-reaching powers of arrest, detention, and interrogation to the state security forces. The ANC's decision to adopt armed struggle in 1961 came directly on the heels of the banning orders of the previous year. In this way, the stage was set for more than thirty years of political and military struggle. Coleman (1998) documents 370 assassinations between 1974 and 1994, during which time the state's aim was to reverse the "revolutionary" situation, "pacify," and demoralize the population, and to create a "political wasteland" by crushing the democratic movement. Acts of terror were an important component of this strategy. Summerfield (1992), citing the Amnesty International submission to the United Nations Commission on Human Rights (UNCHR), records that death squads terrorizing township residents killed 2,500 men, women, and children in 1991 alone.

The apartheid government applied the label "terrorist" very broadly as part of a substantial propaganda campaign and used this label to deny political prisoners the protection afforded by international agreements, most notably the 1977 addenda to the Geneva conventions of 1949. (These addenda extend the 1949 conventions to include "wars of liberation.") Liberation fighters in South Africa were never granted prisoner-of-war status and many were executed as criminals.

Perhaps the most in-depth study of terrorism in South Africa is to be found in the process, testimonies, investigations, and reports of the Truth and Reconciliation Commission. This body was mandated by the South African government to investigate and document "gross human rights abuses" that occurred in South Africa between March 1, 1960, and May 10, 1994. Although "gross human rights abuses" is defined very broadly, it certainly includes acts of terrorism as defined above. The final report of the TRC documents a wide range of terrorist actions undertaken by both the forces of state security and anti-apartheid activists in the ANC and other organizations. Also included is a summary of the experiences of those who suffered as a result of these actions, as well as an attempt to describe as broadly as possible the effects of South Africa's violent history on the state of the country today (Truth and Reconciliation Commission, 1998).

A COMMUNITY PSYCHOLOGY PERSPECTIVE ON TERRORISM

The pointlessness of pursuing a study of terrorism in South Africa along the lines of individual deviance demands that other tools are used to guide our thinking. The tools used in this chapter are some of those employed by the community psychologist.

Community psychology as a broad theoretical and research paradigm has not been applied to the study of terrorism in a systematic manner. This paradigm is founded upon several core principles about how society functions, and about how social science relates to society. Several of these principles lead to interesting perspectives on the nature of terrorism.

Understanding Society Ecologically

Some of the greatest advances in scientific knowledge have derived from scientists borrowing concepts from fields other than their own. Social scientists have very successfully borrowed the idea of ecologies from the natural sciences, and, as an extended metaphor, this concept guides our thinking about society in useful ways.

Ecologies in the natural sciences comprise multiple organisms that survive in competitive and cooperative relationships with each other. Such relationships are often organized hierarchically. Furthermore, organisms adapt and change in order to survive within the ecology. Because the organisms exist interdependently, they impact upon each other as they change and adapt. Finally, the entire ecology adapts and changes (as a function of the changes of the organisms that compose it) in order to survive changing environmental circumstances.

The complexity of unraveling all the tangled interdependencies that characterize society is somewhat daunting and has had the negative consequence that social scientists tend to focus their attention either on the extreme micro levels (including the study of individual psychology) or on the extreme macro levels (including international political and economic policies). An entire range of different levels of dynamics exist between these two extremes; they receive a much lower level of attention, and consequently we understand substantially less about them.

In order to assist in breaking down this false dichotomy within the field, a four-level model of society is proposed, the four levels being the individual person, the small group, geographically defined communities, and society as a whole. To understand a social phenomenon such as terrorism, we need to understand it at multiple interdependent levels. This is illustrated in Figure 1:

FIGURE 1. SYSTEMIC MODEL OF CIVIL VIOLENCE

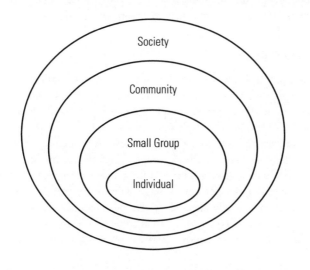

Thus, at the level of the individual we are concerned with the personal histories, beliefs, values, and psychologies of people. At the small group level, family dynamics, friendships, work colleagues, and the other most significant human relationships of our lives are of great importance. At the level of community, we are concerned with neighborhood dynamics, schooling, religious practices, sporting and other social structures, and so forth. Finally, the level of society involves the issues of international relations, economic differences, wars, and other macro-level dynamics.

These principles remind us that all the different individuals, small groups, and community structures that compose human society are interconnected in complex ways, the majority of which we do not readily perceive or understand. Any change in one part of the system will necessarily result in multiple and often unforeseen changes in many other parts of the system. This is the principle of interdependence. Furthermore, when the social environment begins to change, individuals, small groups, and community structures will also begin to change in order to ensure their continued survival. This is the principle of adaptation. Taken together, these two principles demand that social scientists think differently about causality and recognize that in the case of complex social phenomena, clear cause-and-effect relationships are actually extremely rare. Thus, discussions of terrorism that seek to uncover its "causes" or "consequences" are unlikely to yield much useful information.

An ecological perspective on society challenges us to question how the "terrorist organism" has come to exist in society, how it changes our society, how it adapts in order to survive, how it relates to all the other organisms in our society, and how responses to the "terrorist organism" change our entire social ecology in positive as well as negative ways.

A second area in which community psychology has a great deal to offer to the study of terrorism is through its emphasis on the collective histories and cultures in terms of which people define themselves. The history of human civilization is a history of different peoples encountering and adapting to each other.

History and Culture

With the rapid and ongoing development of communication and travel technology, geographic distance between people is becoming less and less of a barrier between cultures and societies. Although the developing world lags behind many countries of the Northern Hemisphere in this regard, it remains true that diverse cultures are interacting more today than they ever have before. South Africa provides a particularly multicultural background—including a broad range of ethnic, linguistic, and religious groups—for thinking about terrorism. Today, virtually nobody in the country can claim to belong solely to any particular culture. People from rural villages are deeply affected by the values and beliefs of cultures whose origins lie in Europe and North America. People whose ancestry is European but whose families have lived in South Africa for several generations find themselves feeling estranged from relatives in the North. In fact, like so much of the world, South Africa is at once a multicultural and an "a-cultural" place. In this context, understanding one's own culture often means grappling with the complex, often painful, and ultimately personal issues of identity, loyalty, and belief. The speed with which cultures are changing is such that most young people in South Africa today find their own values and beliefs at odds with those of their parents and grandparents.

And yet the processes of cultural contact and transformation, although an inevitable part of a developing world, are also the source of much of the anger and fear that fuel terrorism. Stamm and Stamm (2000) have summarized and simplified the process of cultural transformation as it has been repeatedly played out in the past, and is still reenacted today. These authors present cultural transformation as a predictable process that begins in a time of cultural stability before contact with other cultures. Following contact with other cultures, a process of cultural challenge, loss, and reorganization and revitalization ensues. Eventually this process results in a new period of cultural stability. This is depicted in Figure 2.

The eras of cultural challenge and loss—with their competing belief systems; disruption of language, culture, and society; changes in economic structure; and so on—contain the seeds for conflict. This model very usefully describes the changes that South African society has experienced since the seventeenth century, with foreign rule by a colonial power, the dismantling of indigenous social structure and government, and disruption of traditional culture and language.

By thinking about history and culture in this way, social scientists are challenged to confront the extent to which terrorism is rooted in the historical and current experiences of cultural groups with less economic and military might. This question is of central importance when considering the most effective strategies for deterring future acts of terror.

RESPONDING TO TERRORISM

Options are limited in responding to terrorism. Ginges (1997) describes the strategy of refusing to negotiate with terrorists while simultaneously increasing police powers and violent retaliation as the "denial strategy." This strategy typically involves sweeping punishment of all individuals and groups thought to be supportive of terrorist structures. Byman (1998) refers to this approach as "conventional" counterterrorism, but points out that there is a second alternative: the "ingroup policing strategy." This latter strategy proceeds by attempting to fracture the identity of terrorist groups by introducing new and rival identities. Moderates within the group may be encouraged through incentives to punish radical activity within their own community. Both of these strategies have been used within the South African context, as is discussed in the following sections.

FIGURE 2.

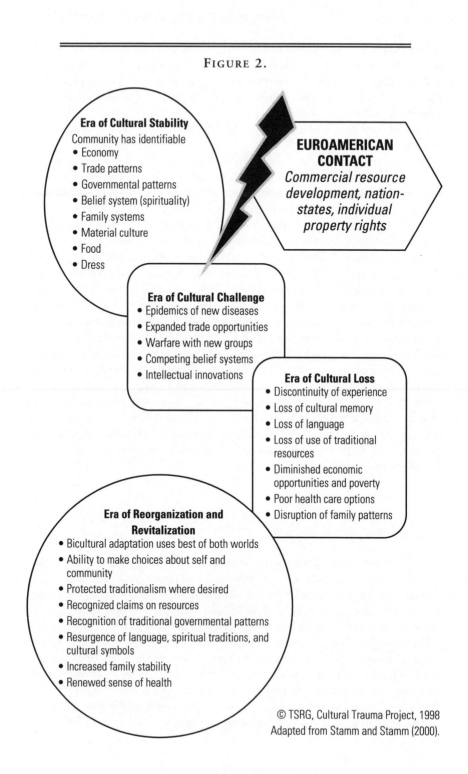

Era of Cultural Stability
Community has identifiable
- Economy
- Trade patterns
- Governmental patterns
- Belief system (spirituality)
- Family systems
- Material culture
- Food
- Dress

EUROAMERICAN CONTACT
Commercial resource development, nation-states, individual property rights

Era of Cultural Challenge
- Epidemics of new diseases
- Expanded trade opportunities
- Warfare with new groups
- Competing belief systems
- Intellectual innovations

Era of Cultural Loss
- Discontinuity of experience
- Loss of cultural memory
- Loss of language
- Loss of use of traditional resources
- Diminished economic opportunities and poverty
- Poor health care options
- Disruption of family patterns

Era of Reorganization and Revitalization
- Bicultural adaptation uses best of both worlds
- Ability to make choices about self and community
- Protected traditionalism where desired
- Recognized claims on resources
- Recognition of traditional governmental patterns
- Resurgence of language, spiritual traditions, and cultural symbols
- Increased family stability
- Renewed sense of health

THE "DENIAL STRATEGY" IN SOUTH AFRICA

The majority of terrorist acts in South Africa's history occurred within the context of a war of liberation. Both the apartheid forces and the liberation armies were prepared to use terrorist tactics to retain or seize power. Nevertheless, it is worth asking what societal factors facilitated the use of terrorist techniques. Two fundamental enabling factors for terrorism in South Africa were the extent to which society had become militarized and the high levels of racism and prejudice prevalent in most communities. This is in large part due to the fact that for most of the past five decades the apartheid government responded to acts of terrorism through refusal to negotiate and increased use of force against any individuals and groups suspected of supporting terrorist groups.

Militarization, racism, and prejudice permeate every part of South African society, from the broadest societal levels to the private attitudes, choices, and actions of individuals. In this way, all of the levels of thinking outlined in the ecological model of society are important. A community psychology approach to terrorism is best initiated at the level of society, since it is in large part a function of societal dynamics. Nevertheless, dynamics in communities, small groups, and families, as well as in individual psychology and behavior, also play an important role in the development of a detailed understanding of terrorist acts. To this end, it is important that the analysis is extended from the societal level to increasingly more-detailed analysis as appropriate.

Militarization of South African Society

The militarization of South Africa took place at the broadest level of society and was by no means a new phenomenon. Dutch and British colonial rule was always supported by military force, and this practice was continued and expanded under the apartheid government. In terms of the model of Stamm and Stamm (2000), the eras of cultural challenge and loss in South Africa were characterized by high levels of conflict and militarization of society.

By the early 1980s, South Africa's defense budget accounted for approximately 20 percent of government spending, a figure that increased still further in later years (Archer, 1989). The more militarized a society, the more difficult it is to distinguish military from nonmilitary structures, and the less likely it is that civil society will succeed in controlling military and paramilitary action. Covert operations are more easily justified in a militarized society and the likelihood of state terrorism is increased.

An important component of the militarization of South African society was conscription. Until the early 1990s, military service was compulsory for white South African men upon completion of their schooling. For most conscripts, military service comprised two years of basic training followed by regular military camps for the best part of their adult lives. Military conscripts composed roughly half the full-time forces of the South African Defense Force (SADF). Most conscripts viewed national service as a rite of passage and as a moral duty to defend their country and religion. At the special hearing of the TRC for conscripts it was convincingly argued that at the age of 17 or 18, these young men had neither the tools nor the information required to challenge the dominant ideology of the country (TRC, 1998, Volume 4, Chapter 8).

And yet the militarization of South African society did not happen only through conscription of men into the military. It also occurred at the level of the community through such institutions as schools. In 1989, 300,000 white school children participated in school cadet programs. Evans (1989) lists some topics in cadet training, which include the structure of the SADF, civilian defense, and the nature of the "threat" against South Africa. Training was received in military procedure as well as various skills of warfare including concealment and camouflage, firearm training, and tracking. Evans continues by citing the cadet training manual for boys in the first year of high school (around the age of thirteen), which states that boys must learn the characteristics of terrorists, whom they should report to their cadet officer, because the enemy "aims to overthrow the present government and create a black majority government" (Evans, 1989, p. 286).

Militarization of schoolchildren and young adults was also a feature of life for black South Africans. Schoolchildren played a leading role in the Soweto Uprising of 1976, and for the next fifteen years young people continued to leave the country to join the ANC in exile, many of them to receive training in guerrilla warfare and return to the country as liberation fighters/terrorists.

The militarization of schools meant that when virtually all South African boys and many girls left school they had already been groomed to take their place within the military machinery of the apartheid forces or the liberation movements. In this way, the shaping of terrorists in South Africa began in childhood and the process of militarization was carried down into family structures in which young men and women left home to participate in the war between the apartheid government and the liberation movement. In so doing they either made their parents proud or shamed their parents in the eyes of the extended family and surrounding community. Soldiers who were fathers spent years immersed in military affairs and away from their growing children. And, finally, this dynamic filtered down to the individual level, with entire generations of men identifying themselves as soldiers— some of whom, years later, still suffer the psychological consequences of traumatic exposure in the line of duty.

It is worth noting that conscription, the overall militarization of society, patrolling of communities, and ideological control through schools and other community structures did not succeed in reducing the level of terrorist activity in the country. This form of counterterrorism runs the risk of punishing the innocent along with the guilty and may succeed only in creating hostility against the government and increasing the population's awareness of the terrorists' cause. The conflict is therefore heightened and the entire culture and ecology of society changes and adapts to that of a community at war.

Racism and Prejudice

Racism is one of the more salient features of South African society. At the level of society, apartheid was constructed around group differences, with the white minority group controlling a disproportionately large share of political and economic power. But as threat between groups increases, the very nature of those groups starts to change—a community level effect. Such changes are closely linked to terrorism. Bar-Tal and Labin (2001) found that following terrorist attacks, adolescent Israelis' stereotypic perceptions and attitudes changed for the negative toward Palestinians (with whom the attacks are associated), toward Arabs in general, and even toward Jordanians (with whom Israel was at peace). As threat between groups increases, group boundaries become less and less permeable. In exactly the same way, ethnic and cultural differences within South Africa were exaggerated and exacerbated and levels of racism and prejudice rose accordingly.

At the same time, the style of leadership of such groups changes. Mandel (2002) looks at the way leaders serve to increase the impermeability of groups and to legitimize violence through propaganda of the "good versus evil" variety. The apartheid government warned all South Africans of the evils of Soviet-inspired communist rule, labeled *Die Rooi Gevaar* (literally, the Red Peril). The apartheid government was presented to South Africans as the protector of Christianity, Christian values, and freedom. In this way, violence against anti-apartheid activists was encouraged and justified. Leaders and the media play an important role in presenting or challenging stereotypical thinking.

At the individual level, increased threat has been linked to increased authoritarianism, which in turn is predictive of acts of violence including hate crimes against members of other groups, particularly social minorities (Unger, 2002). Freyd (2002) points out that the most common human response to situations of danger is the "fight or flight" response. She points out that when a person is afraid, rage is one way of feeling safer and in control. Thus, in a society characterized by a culture of racism and prejudice it is not surprising that acts of terrorism occur. However, Freyd (2002) also points out an alternative response, namely that of "tend and befriend," by which people under threat support each other. If people can be encouraged to respond in the "tend or befriend" manner rather than in the "fight or flight" manner, a real possibility exists of reducing the level of terrorist activity within a society.

THE "INGROUP POLICING STRATEGY" IN SOUTH AFRICA

One form of violence that is seldom spoken about in relation to South Africa is the civil conflict that lasted for nearly twenty years between the followers of the ANC and the Inkatha Freedom Party (IFP). Although this conflict has its roots in

KwaZulu-Natal (a province on the country's eastern seaboard), it spilled over into high levels of civil violence in communities around Johannesburg as well. The origins of this conflict are directly linked to the apartheid government's use of the "ingroup policing strategy" to control the South African population.

One of the first acts of the apartheid government was to create separate residential areas for people of different ethnic backgrounds, South Africa's "homelands." With the homelands came the long and brutal period of South Africa's history during which people's homes and communities were destroyed and they were taken by force to other parts of the country. Land and property appropriated in this way was in most cases sold to white farmers or white-controlled industry, and the land allocated to black South Africans was for the most part extremely poor agricultural land, far removed from the cities and industrial centers of the country. Many black South Africans were forced to live and work at great distances from their families and were closely regulated while outside their homeland. The indigenous people of South Africa had become aliens in their own land.

One such homeland, created for the Zulu people, was KwaZulu. KwaZulu was governed by the KwaZulu Administration under Chief Gatsha Buthelezi, a well-known Zulu leader and significant person in the anti-apartheid movement. As a result of his participation within government structures, he was perceived to have become more politically moderate and this placed him at odds with the ANC leadership.

In response to the ANC's announcement that it was embarking on a course of armed struggle, Buthelezi released the following statement to international journalists:

> We cannot afford voluntarily to precipitate a holocaust in this country. We are not afraid to die for our freedom, but we cannot assist the racist regime to make an unarmed people cannon fodder. (Interview with *Time* journalists, cited in Jeffery, 1997, p. 24)

In addition to his rejection of the decision to turn to armed struggle, Buthelezi also resisted the ANC's call for international sanctions. While this is understandable given the rural poverty of the KwaZulu homeland, many people felt that he was collaborating with the apartheid regime. Buthelezi, together with some Zulu leaders, began to mobilize support on the strength of Zulu ethnicity and the Inkatha Freedom Movement was formed. The seeds of a most crippling conflict had been sown, and the eventual harvest would be civil war in KwaZulu-Natal. The most comprehensive account of hostilities between supporters of the ANC and the IFP is contained in Jeffery (1997).

In 1980, students in the predominantly ANC community of KwaMashu north of Durban staged a protest march. A month later, students in Pietermaritzburg started a school boycott. Buthelezi campaigned actively against these protests, stating that the students were being manipulated by enemies of Inkatha and the Zulu people. Inkatha supporters and police attacked boycotting schoolchildren in KwaMashu and confiscated "Free Mandela" posters. This action earned Inkatha supporters the nickname "vigilantes" among ANC supporters. The student action did not end, however, and was repeatedly and forcibly opposed by Buthelezi, Inkatha, and the KwaZulu Police (KP). Irregular violent battles continued in the communities around Durban.

ANC members were cast as communists bent on the destruction of civilized society, and were blamed for all the evils of the world including the conflict and poverty in Africa. Although the split between Inkatha and the ANC was a dynamic at the level of broader society, the ensuing civil war was played out at the community level. Unavoidably, families were divided and destroyed in the fighting and many individuals were killed or severely handicapped by injuries and suffered emotionally as the result of their violent exposure. This is graphically illustrated by a young man's memories of his childhood, contained in the following quotation:

> My father used to talk about *inkatha*. He used to call them "vigilante".
> He really hated *inkatha* . . . When people from Ethiopia were on TV
> [during the famine and starvation in that country] . . . my mother
> used to say, "Just look, if we are also under communists we are also
> going to be like this". (Interview with ANC activist in KwaZulu-
> Natal, aged 18)

The different opinions ascribed to his mother and father describe the political confusion of their generation. While the apartheid regime and Inkatha were portraying the ANC as puppets in a Soviet-inspired strategy to control Africa, the ANC was portraying Inkatha as puppets of the apartheid government. The above reflection neatly summarizes the battle lines of the civil war that would overwhelm this young man's teenage years and result in him taking a life and surviving a bullet wound before his eighteenth birthday.

With the liberation movement irreconcilably divided by these events and ideological differences, the people of KwaZulu-Natal were forced during these early years to choose between the United Democratic Front (which had arisen to continue the work of the banned ANC) and the Inkatha Freedom Movement (later to become the Inkatha Freedom Party that contested the election of 1994). By aligning themselves explicitly with one or other political movement, people were guaranteed a degree of protection for themselves, their families, and their property. Whole communities were declared "no-go zones" for opposition groups and anyone living in those communities who did not publicly express allegiance to the appropriate movement was driven from his or her home by violence and intimidation. In this way, virtually the entire province of KwaZulu-Natal was divided into ANC and IFP areas.

As the situation worsened, leaders within the ANC and IFP camps established and trained local paramilitary structures. Drawn largely from the ranks of adolescent males in the community, these structures were named Self Defence Units (SDUs) on the side of the ANC and Self Protection Units (SPUs) on the side of the IFP. In 1990, as the conflict continued to escalate, the word "war" was used for the first time.

> Headlines trumpeted the news in huge bold print: "Natal on the boil";
> "Thousands in impi attack"; "'War' in Maritzburg!" . . . Among the
> public at large, and even in the editorial columns of certain newspapers,
> the prevailing reaction was one of bewilderment. (Kentridge, 1990)

Although the conflict is still not entirely over today, levels of violence have vastly diminished. To date, the conflict in KwaZulu-Natal has claimed approximately fifteen thousand lives. A further twenty-five thousand people have been seriously injured and handicapped. As many as five hundred thousand have been displaced from their homes and communities (Higson-Smith, 2002; Jeffery, 1997). As Byman (1998) points out, the "ingroup policing strategy" has some disadvantages. As KwaZulu-Natal so clearly illustrates, this strategy carried to its logical conclusions can result in a civil war, thousands of deaths, and economic ruin for an entire region.

SOUTH AFRICAN SOCIETY TODAY

South Africa has been struggling for several years with elevated levels of violent crime, including domestic and sexual violence, hate crimes, armed robbery, and gang violence. Despite various special state interventions, the statistics do not seem to be improving. One major consequence of this high level of violent crime is that society's regulatory structures become overwhelmed. Police, courts, and prisons find it more and more difficult to fulfill their mandate, namely that of protecting the citizens of the country. Although a less-regulated environment might not explain the motives behind terrorism, it is most likely to facilitate terrorist activities. This is because such activities are by nature illegal and covert and depend upon secrecy for success. At the same time, acts of terrorism consume enormous investigative and judicial resources, placing the police and courts under even greater pressure.

Further links between violent crime and terrorism have been drawn by other authors. For example, Dishman (2001) links terrorist structures with organized crime syndicates and argues that in some cases terrorist action is financed through criminal activity, and that some terrorist groups may be wholly transformed into criminal organizations. Certainly there are some parallels in the South African situation, where some liberation fighters considered armed robbery and theft to be viable strategies to fund their struggle activities.

Personal Consequences of Living with Violence and Fear

One of the consequences of living in such a violent society is that individuals become inured to acts of violence around them. To many people in the developed world, South African society is characterized first and foremost by violent crime. To many South Africans this seems unjustified, at least in part due to the extent to which local people have become desensitized to violence. The following local case is offered by way of illustration. On February 9, 2002, an off-duty security guard whose girlfriend had broken up with him ran amok in a small South African town. He shot and killed ten people, wounded seven others, and then committed suicide. Despite the extreme violence of this incident, it was only considered important enough for a short article on page five of a major national newspaper (*The Star*, 2002). The fact that extreme violence is tolerated in this manner has serious implications for the long-term future of South African society. It also reveals much about the context that has created the terrorist acts, and the ways such acts have impact in turn upon society.

Growing up in South Africa at the end of the twentieth century entailed high levels of exposure to violence and terror, either directly or indirectly. Many people in South Africa today have survived experiences of violence within the family; criminal violence; state violence such as forced removals, detentions, and torture; and, most recently, civil conflict. Henderson (1998, p. 186) speaks of this experience as "a complex layering of broken bonds and the accumulation of betrayals of trust." She explores these ideas further by citing the work of Reynolds (1995) who argues that all families in South Africa "bear the residues of state policies and actions" and remarks that "there has been for most South Africans this century no minimal stability for children in families, [or] for families in relation to place . . ."

The effect of such ongoing violent exposure on people and families is highly detrimental. Chikane (1986) introduced the concept of continuous traumatic stress disorder as an alternative to the more Western construct of post-traumatic stress disorder (PTSD), which to some extent assumes isolated traumatic incidents against a social context of relative safety. Herman (1992) speaks of complex traumatic stress disorder, a term that encapsulates some of the difficult realities of township dwellers in situations of political violence in South Africa where individuals are exposed to repeated, multiple, and prolonged trauma. Straker and Moosa (1994) advanced this work further by exploring how continuous traumatic stress differs from PTSD and the implications of those differences for treatment.

These various formulations of the effects of traumatic stressors on people tend to focus on the ways that violent exposure incapacitates people. Another way of looking at ongoing violent exposure is to ask how people have managed to survive both emotionally and socially under such circumstances. The negative-resilience model examines ongoing traumatic exposure from this perspective (Friedman & Higson-Smith, 2002; Friedman, Friedman, van der Kolk, McFarlane, & Higson-Smith, 2000; Kopel & Friedman, 1999). This model argues that because, under conditions of ongoing threat and violence, a person does not have sufficient emotional resources and time to process his or her traumatic experiences, that person survives by becoming negatively resilient. Negative resilience is presented as a complex of psychological numbing, avoidance, and dissociation.

The negative-resilience model has other important implications for people who grow up and live in violent contexts. First, being negatively resilient places people at greater risk of more debilitating psychological problems, including PTSD. Second, people who are negatively resilient may need to bolster their emotional numbing and dissociation through the abuse of alcohol and other substances. Finally, people who are negatively resilient are less likely to be able to empathize with other human beings. Empathy is an important inhibiting factor for acts of violence.

It is well known that a high proportion of perpetrators of violent crime have themselves been victims of violence. Negative resilience provides one mechanism by which years of direct and indirect violent exposure can create people who are prepared to commit acts of extreme violence to achieve their goals. From this point of view, terrorism is a predictable product of a violent society. The very responses to terrorism, whether through direct security force action against individuals, families, and communities, or through the indirect means of control, carry the potential to create new terrorists.

Although negative resilience is itself a phenomenon at the individual level of analysis, its roots are in the high level of violent exposure in society. Such high exposure is related to a wide range of family, community, and societal dynamics. At the same time, the effects of many individuals within a society being negatively resilient are felt at the other levels too. The implications on child development of negatively resilient parents are enormous, and the implications of having a community policed by negatively resilient men and women are very serious.

LESSONS FROM SOUTH AFRICA'S HISTORY

Many bombings and other events in the last three years in South Africa show quite clearly that terrorism is still a problem. Of course, acts of terrorism against an oppressive minority regime should not be judged in the same way as acts aimed at a democratically elected government. And yet such events continue and have been variously linked to ethnic, political, or religious minority groups. However, South Africa has a potential advantage in dealing with this problem because many of its most senior politicians were themselves terrorists not so long ago. Hopefully this means that the present government will think more carefully about responding to terrorism than its predecessors did.

As has been illustrated above, the two strategic responses explored by Byman (1998), namely denial and ingroup policing, had little effect on terrorist action, but damaged the social fabric of society. It is not an exaggeration to say that more damage has been done to South African communities by various responses to terrorism than by acts of terrorism themselves. It is likely that further use of such strategies will be similarly unsuccessful in the future, and for exactly the same reasons. Ginges (1997) offers a further and perhaps more useful response to terrorism, in the form of the Reintegrative Punishment Strategy employed in Italy in the 1980s. The Italian government agreed to negotiate with and grant leniency to terrorists on the condition that they denounce terrorism and show a willingness to reenter society. This strategy depends for success on the terrorist believing that real change through negotiation is possible, and this may be the greatest stumbling block for this strategy.

However, there are other kinds of longer-term intervention that governments, including the South African government, should consider in their fight against terrorism. First and foremost is the need to demilitarize society as much as possible and to reduce levels of exposure to violence suffered by the population. In a society that rejects violence, the task of the terrorist is made much more difficult. Far from calling attention to his or her cause, the terrorist in a society that rejects violence is more likely to draw condemnation upon the cause. However, in a society where people have become blunted to the horror of violence, and where the use of force is perceived as an effective problem-solving technique, the climate is right for terrorism to prosper.

Second, racism and other forms of prejudice are dangerous in the extent to which they legitimize violence, including acts of terrorism. Energetic programs of cultural integration, especially with younger generations, are important if stereotypical thinking and attitudes are to be challenged. One of the great challenges in the developing world is the integration of multiple cultures, languages, and ethnic groups. The final stage of Stamm and Stamm's (1998) model of cultural transformation, presented as the era of reorganization and revitalization, describes an integrated society in which human diversity is respected and enjoyed.

Third, the development of a society in which speech and the media are unrestricted is fundamental. Where it is possible to challenge publicly stereotypical thinking and irresponsible leadership, it is possible to undermine the propaganda that legitimizes acts of terror.

In the eight years since the apartheid government lost power in South Africa, the country has made important steps forward on all three of these issues. Young people are no longer conscripted into the military, civil conflict is lower than it has ever been, and many schools are integrated, as are universities and colleges, businesses, residential communities, and all other institutions of the state. Finally, the country has an outspoken political opposition, a constitution that guarantees freedom of speech, and active and critical media.

Proportionally little work on terrorism focuses on the developing world. This is unfortunate because the social contexts are different, as are the most appropriate strategies for response. This paper attempts to present a look at terrorism in a developing-world context, and to demonstrate that—as in most areas of endeavor—prevention is more likely to be effective than cure.

REFERENCES

Archer, S. (1989). Defense expenditure and arms procurement in South Africa. In J. Cock & L. Nathan (Eds.), *War and society: The militarization of South Africa.* Cape Town, South Africa: David Philip.

Asmal, K., Asmal, L., & Roberts, R. S. (1996). *Reconciliation through truth: A reckoning of apartheid's criminal governance.* Cape Town, South Africa: David Philip.

Bar-Tal, D., & Labin, D. (2001). The effect of a major event on stereotyping: Terrorist attacks in Israel and Israeli adolescents' perceptions of Palestinians, Jordanians and Arabs. *European Journal of Social Psychology, 31*, 265–280.

Brannan, D. W., Esler, P. F., & Ander Strindberg, N. T. (2001). Talking to "terrorists": Towards an independent analytical framework for the study of violent substate activism. *Studies in Conflict and Terrorism, 24*, 3–24.

Byman, D. (1998). The logic of ethnic terrorism. *Studies in Conflict and Terrorism, 21*, 149–169.

Chikane, F. (1986). The effects of the unrest on township children. In S. Burman & P. Reynolds (Eds.), *Growing up in a divided society.* Evanston, IL: Northwestern University Press.

Coleman, M. (1998). *A crime against humanity: Analyzing the repression of the apartheid state.* Johannesburg, South Africa: Human Rights Committee.

Crenshaw, M. (2000). The psychology of terrorism: An agenda for the 21st century. *Political Psychology, 21*, 405–420.

Dishman, C. (2001). Terrorism, crime and transformation. *Studies in Conflict and Terrorism, 24*, 43–58.

Evans, G. (1989). Classrooms of war: The militarization of white South African schooling. In J. Cock & L. Nathan (Eds.), *War and society: The militarization of South Africa.* Cape Town, South Africa: David Philip.

Freyd, J. J. (2002). In the wake of a terrorist attack, hatred may mask fear. *Analyses of Social Issues and Public Policy, 2*, 5–8.

Friedman, M., & Higson-Smith, R. C. (2002). Building psychological resilience: Learning for the South African police service. In D. Paton, J. M. Violanti, & L. M Smith, (Eds.), *Promoting capabilities to manage posttraumatic stress: Perspectives on resilience.* Springfield, IL: Charles C. Thomas.

Friedman, M., Friedman, M. J., van der Kolk, B., McFarlane, A., & Higson-Smith, R. C. (2000). Resilience in the face of exposure to trauma. Symposium presented at the 16th Annual Conference of the International Society for Traumatic Stress Studies, San Antonio, TX.

Ginges, J. (1997). Deterring the terrorist: A psychological evaluation of different strategies for deterring terrorism. *Terrorism and Political Violence, 9*, 170–185.

Herman, J. (1992). Complex PTSD: A syndrome in survivors of prolonged and repeated trauma. *Journal of Traumatic Stress, 5*, 377–420.

Henderson, P. (1998). Tracing fragility in families: Children's reflections on mobility in new Crossroads, Cape Town. In *In view of school: Preparation for and adjustment to school under rapidly changing social conditions.* Johannesburg, South Africa: Goethe Institute.

Higson-Smith, R. C. (2002). *Supporting survivors of violence: A casebook from South Africa.* Oxford: Oxfam Great Britain.

Jeffery, A. J. (1997). *The Natal story: Sixteen years of conflict.* Cape Town, South Africa: South African Institute of Race Relations.

Kentridge, M. (1990). *An unofficial war: Inside the conflict in Pietermaritzburg.* Cape Town, South Africa: David Philip.

Kopel, H., & Friedman, M. (1999). Effects of exposure to violence in South African police. In J. M. Violanti & D. Paton (Eds.), *Police trauma: Psychological aftermath of civilian combat.* Springfield, IL: Charles Thomas.

Mandel, D. R. (2002). Evil and the instigation of collective violence. *Analyses of Social Issues and Public Policy, 2*, 101–108.

Mandela, N. (1994). *Long walk to freedom: The autobiography of Nelson Mandela.* London: Abacus.

Oliverio, A. (1997). The state of injustice: The politics of terrorism and the production of order. *International Journal of Comparative Sociology, 38*, 48–53.

Reynolds, P. (1995). Not known because not looked for: Ethnographers listening to the young in Southern Africa. *Ethnos, 60*, 193–221.

Ruby, C. L. (2002a). Are terrorists mentally deranged? *Analyses of Social Issues and Public Policy, 2*, 15–26.

Ruby, C. L. (2002b). The definition of terrorism. *Analyses of Social Issues and Public Policy, 2*, 9–14.

Silke, A. (1998). Cheshire-cat logic: The recurring theme of terrorist abnormality in psychological research. *Psychology, Crime and Law, 4*, 51–69.

Stamm, B., & Stamm, H. (1998). Project for community revitalization and healing of cultural trauma in indigenous peoples. Symposium presented at the Annual Congress of the International Society for Traumatic Stress Studies, Washington, DC.

Stamm, B., & Stamm, H. (2000). Theory, research and practice: Healing of cultural trauma in indigenous communities. Symposium presented at the 16th Annual Congress of the International Society for Traumatic Stress Studies, San Antonio.

Straker, J., & Moosa, F. (1994). Interacting with trauma survivors in contexts of continuing trauma. *Journal of Traumatic Stress, 7*, 1–9.

Summerfield, D. (1992). South Africa, Mozambique: Impact of death squads. *Lancet, 339*, 669–670.

The Star (2002, February 11). "Madman" slays 10 in killing spree.

Truth and Reconciliation Commission (1998). *Final report of the Truth and Reconciliation Commission, Volumes 1–5.* Retrieved from http://www.polity.org.za/govdocs/commissions/1998/trc/index.htm.

Unger, R. K. (2002). Them and us: Hidden ideologies—differences in degree or kind? *Analyses of Social Issues and Public Policy, 2*, 43–52.

SUPPLEMENTARY BIBLIOGRAPHY

Gerstenfeld, P. B. (2002). A time to hate: Situational antecedents of intergroup bias. *Analyses of Social Issues and Public Policy, 2*, 61–67.

Gidron, Y., Gal, R., & Zahavi, S. (1999). Bus commuters' coping strategies and anxiety from terrorism: An example of the Israeli experience. *Journal of Traumatic Stress, 12*, 185–192.

Higson-Smith, R. C. (1995). Dealing with social violence at community Level: Experiences of the KwaZulu-Natal programme for survivors of violence. Presented at the Annual Congress of the Association of Children and Adolescent Psychiatry and Allied Professions, Durban, South Africa.

Higson-Smith, R. C. (1998). The cost of violence to development. Presented at the Conference on Political Violence in the KwaZulu-Natal Midlands, 1984–1994, University of Natal, Pietermaritzburg, South Africa.

Jensen, C. J. (2002). Beyond the tea leaves: Futures research and terrorism. *American Behavioral Scientist, 44*, 914–936.

Lanning, K. (2002). Reflections on September 11: Lessons from four psychological perspectives. *Analyses of Social Issues and Public Policy, 2*, 27–34.

Louis, W. R., & Taylor, D. M. (2002). Understanding the September 11 terrorist attack on America: The role of intergroup theories of normative influence. *Analyses of Social Issues and Public Policy, 2*, 87–100.

Miller, K. E. (1996). The effects of state terrorism and exile on indigenous Guatemalan refugee children: A mental health assessment and an analysis of children's narratives. *Child Development, 67*, 89–106.

Olson, B. D. (2002). Applied social and community interventions for crisis in times of national and international conflict. *Analyses of Social Issues and Public Policy, 2*, 119–129.

Perkins, E. J. (1997). An international agenda for change. *American Behavioral Scientist, 40*, 354–359.

Phillips, M. (1989). The nuts and bolts of military power: The structure of the SADF. In J. Cock & L. Nathan (Eds.), *War and society: The militarization of South Africa.* Cape Town, South Africa: David Philip.

Scheper-Hughes, N. (1998). Undoing social suffering and the politics of remorse in the new South Africa. *Social Justice, 25*, 114–132.

Slone, M. (2000). Responses to media coverage of terrorism. *Journal of Conflict Resolution, 44*, 508–522.

Staten, C. L. (1999). The evolution and devolution of terrorism: The coming challenge for emergency and national security forces. *Journal of Counter-Terrorism and Security International, 5*, 8–11.

Tolan, P., Keys, C., Chertok, F., & Jason, L. (1990). *Researching community psychology: Issues of theory and methods.* Washington, DC: American Psychological Association.

Weitzman, E. A., & Kew, D. (2002). Responding to September 11: A conflict resolution scholar/practitioner's perspective. *Analyses of Social Issues and Public Policy, 2*, 109–117.

Yanay, N. (2002). Understanding collective hatred. *Analyses of Social Issues and Public Policy, 2*, 53–60.

2

Social-Psychological Considerations in the Emergence and Growth of Terrorism

Olufemi A. Lawal

INTRODUCTION

Terrorism, in its various forms, has suddenly become a significant threat to the contemporary world order. It is plausible to base an assessment of the scale of the devastating consequences of the recent terrorist attacks on the United States on how freely and secretly they were probably planned and carried out. However, such an assessment will not suffice in explaining the real dynamics that arguably are involved in the growth and development of terrorism in general. International efforts at eradicating terrorism now abound. But recourse to a proper understanding of how terrorism grows, and of the factors that facilitate such growth, is imperative. Without this, many of the efforts may prove grossly inadequate in achieving the crucial goal of eradicating terrorism, especially in the long run.

This chapter defines terrorism as a deviant, aggressive, and collective behavior embarked on by individuals with the sole motive of inflicting injury and harm on other, targeted individuals. Individuals embarking on this behavior can be referred to as *terrorists*, and those at whom the behavior is aimed can be referred to as *targets*. Terrorists seek to inflict harm or injury on their targets, which may be physical (for example, destruction of lives and property) or psychological (stimulation of fear, anxiety, anger, confusion, grief, and a sense of tragedy). Terrorism is thus a form of deviant behavior.

Terrorists usually act as groups or in groups that have common interests and goals. They also act as individuals when overwhelmingly backed and inspired by their groups. Terrorism, therefore, always qualifies as a collective behavior. Terrorist acts can also be carried out overtly or covertly and violently or nonviolently. Whichever of these methods is used, terrorist behavior can be understood as a form of aggressive behavior.

While terrorism can be seen as an unfortunate attitude embedded in the ways of life of some peoples and societies, it is highly prohibitive and unpatriotic in others. We can agree that an individual can display any attitude for a variety of reasons and under various circumstances. But the same cannot hold for a whole society or a sizable part of a nation if odd and rare attitudes have become a norm among its people. A society is the setting where people with different attitudes live. For any attitude to saturate a society, such must have become a culture, transmissible through the society's socialization processes. Social learning, as the essence of socialization, is the medium of cultural transmission in all societies. Therefore socialization, through social learning, is to be seen here as bearing on the growth dynamics of terrorism in cultures, subcultures, or countercultures where terrorism thrives.

HOW A TERRORIST ATTITUDE MAY DEVELOP IN INDIVIDUALS

There are various ways of looking at the incipience and/or etiology of terrorism. But one good way is to consider a "potential terrorist" as developing from certain *cognitions*, progressing through unusual *affects*, and growing into wanting to exhibit strange *behaviors* toward targeted individuals. As a tripartite human attribute, attitude includes these three components.

A good definition of attitude refers to it as a psychological tendency to evaluate a particular entity with some degree of favor or disfavor (Eagly & Chaiken, 1993; Jonas, Eagly, & Stroebe, 1994; Zanna & Rempel, 1988). In this view, the entity toward which an attitude can be held, which can thus be discriminated and evaluated, is an *attitude object* (for example, people, social policies, and ideologies). The view also defines the three major components of attitude mentioned above. The first, cognitions, are thoughts or beliefs that are held about an attitude object. The second, affects, are the feelings, moods, and emotions that are experienced in relation to an attitude object. The third, behaviors, are overt actions toward an attitude object and include intentions to behave that may not be expressed in actions.

Cognitions of the Potential Terrorist

Although many acts of terrorism have taken place in different parts of the world, their origins may be located in a common denominator, the "cognitions of the terrorist(s) involved." These are beliefs and thoughts—which may be real or delusive, realistic or unrealistic—that are held by the potential terrorist about his or her attitude objects or targets. Such thoughts and beliefs revolve mostly around power and religious differences, whereby the potential terrorist may perceive his or her attitude objects (that is, targets) as being more powerful than himself or herself. Such thoughts and beliefs may be grossly unwarranted, especially when they stem from perceptions of situations that the potential terrorist cannot help.

For example, potential terrorists, most of whom live in developing countries, may perceive some developed countries and their nationals as being more powerful technologically, economically, and militarily at the terrorists' expense. Often, the terrorists cannot distinguish between their (perceived) targets' enormous strength and the targets' religious persuasions. This becomes more difficult for the potential terrorists, whose religious persuasions are usually different from their targets'. It may be instructive here to reason that the potential terrorist knows very well that such a situation cannot be helped and this knowledge seems to be the reinforcing element behind his or her thoughts and beliefs. He or she may eventually become obsessed with these thoughts and beliefs and thereby begin to feel compelled to continue to entertain them. This bizarre state will not only render the potential terrorist more deluded, it will also pave the way for associated affects to set in.

Affects of the Potential Terrorist

As already implied, there is an essential reinforcement behind the potential terrorist's thoughts and beliefs. It is the fact that he or she knows quite well that there is nothing he or she can do to change his or her (perceived) situation relative to the targets'. Hence, the potential terrorist cannot be helped to get the targets out of his or her thoughts. Consequently, the potential terrorist may begin to feel inferior relative to these targets while his or her self-esteem generally dwindles at the same time. Since the potential terrorist preoccupies himself or herself with thoughts and beliefs about the targets, what he or she thinks or believes about the targets may soon become a barometer for measuring his or her life satisfaction and/or quality of life (Mumuoja, 1989). If "inferiority complex" and low self-esteem are sustained in the potential terrorist, they may develop into worse states of affects.

Understandably, the only condition for reversing or remedying such a state (inferiority complex and low self-esteem) is to equate the potential terrorist with his or her targets regarding political, economic, military, and probably "religious" powers. But this is absolutely unrealizable. And, coupled with the popular notion that the need for self-esteem is usually very strong, the potential terrorist may become more frustrated and, eventually, depressed.

Since the potential terrorist is expected to become further depressed, he or she may begin to move into higher levels of affects. These may include feelings of extreme worthlessness and a significant loss of the "life instinct" (the inborn drive to want to live and have one's situation matter). He or she may begin to feel that he or she has nothing to live for. But since the potential terrorist is frustrated at the same time, aggression may also set in. This may occur because frustration gives rise to aggression as proposed by Dollard, Doob, Miller, Mowrer, and Sears (1939).

Behaviors of the Potential Terrorist

The unrealistic thoughts, beliefs, emotions, moods, and feelings of the previous stages would already have worked in concert to prepare the individual to become a full-fledged terrorist. And, at this critical psychological stage, one of the few options that he or she would find desirable is to join exclusive groups of like-minded people. He or she may also advocate the importance of membership in such groups.

After consorting with members of such groups, who would share similar cognitions and affects, the feelings of frustration may yield a double consequence in the potential terrorist. First, the feelings may become so intense as to reinforce his or her belief in "having nothing to live for" (i.e., a suicidal tendency). Second, combined with this belief, the feelings may also lead to the potential terrorist's becoming extremely aggressive toward his or her targets. Consequently, the potential terrorist may be ready both to die and to injure or destroy his or her targets, whom he or she constantly blames for his or her predicament. Apart from having moved to the behavior stage of attitude at this juncture, the former *potential* terrorist has now become a *full-fledged* terrorist. And much of what he or she would now engage in is action or overt behavior, including plots, spying, threats, outright attacks, and so forth.

Since behavior is the hallmark here, old members of terrorist groups may work relentlessly on the psyches of new members, getting them optimally motivated and reinforced for desired behaviors. The old members also ensure that the new members are properly indoctrinated in the "crux" of the job, that is, deciding to participate in an attack even when the terrorist must die in order for the attack to be successful.

SOCIOCULTURAL FACTORS: SOCIALIZATION PROCESSES IN TERRORISM

Terrorism appeals to some people so much that they seek to affiliate and identify with terrorist groups and to adopt the major features of terrorist culture. Are terrorists born or do they learn terrorism from their social environments? Is nature in interaction with nurture to produce terrorists? Whatever the answers, the point is that terrorism and terrorist activities are significantly concentrated in certain parts of the world. Most of their victims or targets, however, are found in other, different parts of the world.

Prevailing Cultures in Societies

The literature provides enough support for the characterization of any country or society by four dimensions of culture (Hofstede, 1980). *Power distance* is a dimension defined as the extent to which a society accepts unequal distribution of power. *Uncertainty avoidance* is defined as the extent to which a society feels threatened by uncertainty and ambiguity. *Individualism versus collectivism* is another dimension, defined as the extent of social coupling and group identity expected of and experienced by individuals in a society. The last dimension, *masculinity versus femininity*, is defined as the extent to which dominant values in society emphasize assertiveness and material acquisition.

High power distance societies are said to be those whose peoples accept as natural the fact that power and rewards are inequitably distributed in society. Peoples in low power distance societies hold values to the contrary: Access to power and rewards ought to be everyone's right. Individualistic societies are described as those in which individuals are expected to take care of their self-interest. But individuals in collectivist societies are said to be characterized by tight social frameworks and strong ingroup identity. In such societies, the ingroup takes care of the individual in exchange for loyalty. Furthermore, collectivists are expected either to make no distinction between collective and personal goals or to simply subordinate their own goals to the collective goals.

Power Distance and Collectivism as Correlates of Terrorism

The features described of high power distance and collectivist cultures appear to favor the growth of terrorism in the group or societal context. Since power distance is very high, the leaders of terrorist groups and movements have to be seen as "gods" who must not be challenged. Further, as collectivists, terrorists also see themselves as owing their allegiance and loyalty to their groups. As far as they are concerned, their group identity is far more important than themselves or their private lives. It can thus be seen why it may not be difficult for terrorist movements to recruit and maintain terrorists.

It may also explain why and how it may be easy for terrorist leaders to brainwash and indoctrinate their subjects into undertaking all assignments regardless of their consequences. Since these people (terrorists) live in the society, they already have the necessary orientation or tendencies. They (terrorists) would have been socialized into these through their society's relevant agents of socialization.

Essentially, if high power distance and collectivist cultures predominate for long in societies, they will become embedded in the minds of the majority of the people. Little wonder then that culture is sometimes referred to as the "collective programming" of all minds within the cultural environment. These people's minds might have already been programmed with the belief that power has been naturally concentrated in the hands of a leader (in this case, the leader of a terrorist movement). This may imply that when such a leader assigns any member a duty, the member is bound to recognize the supremacy of that leader. And the only way to demonstrate this is to accept the assigned duty with "fear and trembling," and without questioning or objecting. Besides, accepting in such a manner is seen as a responsibility and proof of loyalty to the group or to the society. It also helps the members to maintain their sense of belonging to the group or their group identities, which they all value.

Learning Terrorism: Beliefs and Intention to Model as Motivators

As discussed in the foregoing section, the potential terrorist becomes a terrorist at the point when he is joining the terrorist group. This is when he or she can be assumed to have become psychologically capable of carrying out terrorist attacks. Because of the power distance norm and the collectivistic ways of life in terrorist camps, members inside or outside these camps should likely be easily trainable. This can be so because their focus and dreams have become that of modeling themselves after their leaders and after older members. These may include members who may have died while carrying out attacks, or who conducted attacks that were successfully and accurately carried out on targets.

An important aspect of terrorists' socialization processes is the belief that the gains of dying while destroying their targets are inestimable for them after death. In socializing their subjects into believing this, terrorist leaders may easily capitalize on the already mature suicidal and aggressive tendencies in their subjects. With their orientation toward their leaders, after whom they also model themselves, terrorists will not find it difficult to believe this kind of "fantasy." This is probably why there are many terrorists ready to volunteer to undertake suicide attacks. Although this aspect of their beliefs has a religious undertone, terrorist leaders often use it to galvanize their subjects into action.

In the same spirit of blind compliance with high power distance and collectivism, absolute group loyalty may be demonstrated even by terrorists abroad. These are terrorists who carry out attacks on behalf of their groups and against their groups' targets. Such attacks are usually executed according to specific plans and instructions even if doing so entails having to die in the process. All these precepts and ideas are learned, taught, and shared over many years.

It may be instructive here to underscore the seemingly strong relationships between terrorism, high power distance, and collectivism. The socialization processes involved in the transmission of the culture of terrorism is society-biased. That is, the said relationships are limited in their applicability to different societies. Terrorism is indeed limited to some societies, and none of those societies can yet be said to be an exception to the rules of power distance and collectivism.

Culture-Dependent Attributes of Terrorists

Three main factors can be identified as responsible for the "dogmatism" and helplessness of the terrorists and of their societies. These are lack of sense of independence, lack of assertiveness, and low self-esteem. Due to their collectivist orientation, terrorists may not be at all capable of doing anything independently. Individuals would not believe in their personal abilities. They have a group-oriented approach to everything that may erode most senses of the self, especially self-efficacy. This is an advantage for the ongoing war against terrorism, since terrorists abroad cannot possibly operate successfully unless they continue to enjoy the constant, overwhelming support of their groups.

Lack of assertiveness also has to do with collectivism. Members of groups are not expected to assert their personal opinions or objections, especially if these are at variance with their group's positions and/or interests. These experiences may not, however, affect the self-esteem of the terrorist adversely, all the more since they likely are related to the norms in such settings. Low self-esteem may, however, have set in for an individual terrorist during the attitudinal stage of his or her becoming a terrorist. In the end, high power distance will reinforce the influence of collectivism.

In the literature on self-expression, every individual in any culture is said to possess at least two selves: an independent self and an interdependent self (Gudykunst et al., 1996; Markus & Kitayama, 1991; Singelis, 1994). The independent self is said to involve cognitions concerning individual personality traits, which are seen as residing in the person and as being independent from social context and situational constraints. On the other hand, the interdependent self is said to involve cognitions concerning characteristics that are inherently more indicative of how one relates to others. A very recent study investigated culture-dependent assimilation and differentiation of the self (Aaker & Schmitt, 2001). In that study, individuals with a dominant independent self stated attitudes that were consistent with a self-expression process that highlights the self as differentiated from others. Those with a dominant interdependent self stated attitudes that were consistent with a self-expression process centered on the self as similar to others. Interestingly, the individuals with a dominant independent self were sampled from a Western society in North America while those with a dominant interdependent self were sampled from a non-Western society in East Asia.

These two distinct forms of self-expression are said to emanate from antecedent variables such as culture (Lonner & Adamopoulos, 1997). Since culture is what is important or transmitted in socialization, it has so much to do with an individual's sense of self, personality, and, ultimately, behavior. For example, Americans are said to encourage their children to be unique and self-determining (Bellah, Madsen, Sullivan, Swidler, & Tipton, 1985). In contrast, the Chinese are said to describe a good child as one who is group-oriented and cooperative (Wu, 1996). To attain this, the Chinese are said to encourage their children to pursue collective goals and to elaborate on their own inadequacies relative to other children, so as to assimilate with (as distinct from being independent of) other children (Yu, 1996).

Terrorism may not have emerged in many non-Western societies, but it is clear that the few societies that can best be described as the *capital* of terrorism are not only non-Western societies, they are also developing societies. It is also clear, as has already been mentioned in this chapter, that the targets of these terrorist societies are some of the Western, developed societies. Power distance is low and individualism is high in Western, developed societies, which are not known to engage in terrorism. This probably explains why people in these societies are free and independent and have no constraints in expressing their private selves. However, in many non-Western and developing societies, few of which are known to have engaged in terrorism before, power distance and collectivism are rather high. This probably explains why people in these societies are not expected to value their personal opinions and goals, let alone to express them. Some literature provides evidence in support of this. For example, Kanungo and Jaeger (1990) specifically characterized developing countries as being relatively high on power distance and relatively low in individualism (i.e., relatively high on collectivism). More specifically, African culture has been described as being collectivist (e.g., Hofstede, 1980; Kanungo & Mendonca, 1994; Triandis, 1989).

TYPES AND STAGES OF TERRORISM

Two types or stages of terrorism are identified in this chapter. These are *local or internal terrorism* and *international terrorism*. Local or internal terrorism is essentially about intrasocietal terrorist attacks. International terrorism is about attacks on peoples who do not have the same nationalities, beliefs, religions, cultures, and so forth, as the terrorists attacking them. The victims of international terrorism are usually found outside the domains, societies, and countries of the terrorists.

Developing societies, especially in Africa, are tensed with chaos and wars, most of which erupt from struggles for power and ethnic/tribal differences. Ingroup members become local or internal terrorists and enjoy inflicting pain and injuries on outgroup members. These are common features in the "rebellions" or guerrilla warfare that has ravaged Africa for ages. Since similar acts of terrorism are also found in other developing cultures outside Africa, these may well be due to the fact that power distance and collectivism are both high across those cultures. Besides, local or internal terrorists may become more and more hardened with the constant struggles and warfare and may be best referred to as international terrorists in the making. If and when they become international terrorists, they may leave their troubled domains to terrorize people in other countries.

One characteristic that apparently distinguishes between internal and international terrorists is that an internal terrorist does not seem to be ready to die. In most communal and local terrorist attacks that have been taking place in Africa, specifically in Nigeria, terrorists have not gone to the extent of being prepared to die to destroy their targets. Suicide bombing, for example, has not occurred in Nigeria.

What this dimension reveals is that terrorism is a cowardly act and that terrorists are cowards. Terrorist leaders, however, have a very strong weapon in their ability to brainwash or indoctrinate their followers into wanting to kill themselves in order to kill others. Essentially, the "suicide factor" is the distinguishing factor between internal and international terrorists. While the internal terrorists wish all their targets dead, they themselves are not ready to die. In contrast, the international terrorist is fully motivated to kill himself or herself so as to kill or be able to kill perceived enemies.

The overall solution this chapter recommends is twofold. The first is to explore ways in which the people of the developing world could be resocialized toward becoming independent and assertive. The second is to explore ways to interrupt the socialization processes of terrorist group, especially the training/indoctrination of suicide attackers.

REFERENCES

Aaker, J., & Schmitt, B. (2001). Culture-dependent assimilation and differentiation of the self: Preferences for consumption symbols in the United States and China. *Journal of Cross-Cultural Psychology, 32,* 561–576.

Bellah, R. N., Madsen, R., Sullivan, W. M., Swidler, A., & Tipton, S. M. (1985). *Habits of the heart: Individualism and commitment in American life.* New York: Harper & Row.

Dollard, J., Doob, L. W., Miller, N. E., Mowrer, O. H., & Sears, R. R. (1939). *Frustration and aggression.* New Haven, CT: Yale University Press.

Eagly, A. H., & Chaiken, S. (1993). *The psychology of attitudes.* Fort Worth, TX: Harcourt Brace Jovanovich.

Gudykunst, W. B., Matsumoto, Y., Ting-Toomey, S., Nishida, T., Kim, K. S., & Heyman, S. (1996). The influence of cultural individualism-collectivism, self construals, and values on communications styles across cultures. *Human Communication Research, 22,* 510–543.

Hofstede, G. (1980). *Culture's consequences: International differences in work-related values.* Beverly Hills, CA: Sage Publications.

Jonas, K., Eagly, A. H., & Stroebe, W. (1994). Attitudes and persuasion. In A. M. Colman (Ed.), *Companion encyclopedia of psychology* (Vol. 2). New York: Routledge.

Kanungo, R. N., and Jaeger, A. M. (1990). Introduction: The need for indigenous management in developing countries. In A. M. Jaeger & R. N. Kanungo (Eds.), *Management in developing countries.* London: Routledge.

Kanungo, R. N., & Mendonca, M. (1994). *Work motivation: Models for developing countries.* New Delhi: Sage Publications.

Lonner, W. J., & Adamopoulos, J. (1997). Culture as an antecedent to behaviour. In J. W. Berry, Y. H. Poortinger, & J. Pandey (Eds.), *The handbook of cross-cultural psychology* (pp. 45–81). Boston: Allyn and Bacon.

Markus, H. R., & Kitayama, S. (1991). The cultural construction of self and emotion: Implications for social behaviour. In S. Kitayama & H. R. Markus (Eds.), *Emotion and culture: Empirical studies of mutual influence* (pp. 89–132). Washington, DC: American Psychological Association.

Mumuoja, B. (1989). Inferiority complex. *The Behavioural Scientist, 3,* 24–25.

Singelis, T. M. (1994). The measurement of independent and interdependent self construals. *Personality and Social Psychology Bulletin, 20,* 580–591.

Triandis, H. C. (1989). The self and behaviour in differing cultural contexts. *Psychological Review, 96,* 506–552.

Wu, C. (1996). Chinese childhood socialization. In M. Bond (Ed.), *The handbook of Chinese psychology* (pp. 143–154). Hong Kong: Oxford University Press.

Yu, A. (1996). Ultimate life concerns, self and Chinese achievement motivation. In M. Bond (Ed.), *The handbook of Chinese psychology* (pp. 227–246). Hong Kong: Oxford University Press.

Zanna, M. P., & Rempel, J. K. (1988). Attitudes: A new look at an old concept. In D. Bar-Tal & A. W. Kruglanski (Eds.), *The social psychology of knowledge* (pp. 315–334). Cambridge: Cambridge University Press.

3

Countering International Terrorism: Perspectives from International Psychology

John M. Davis

> I believe in the power of love in interpersonal relations, but love directed toward the missile or the distant anonymous human being pushing the button would be useless. The alternative, therefore, once diplomacy and other steps short of violence fail to destroy or end the evil, is either submission to it or a reluctant use of force and violence to destroy it.
>
> Max M. Kampelman (1991, p. 377)

The focus of this chapter is on understanding and predicting the development of international terrorist activities through the perspective of international psychology. This chapter is written with full awareness that much information that would be helpful and relevant in countering terrorism is not accessible to the scholar. Both the terrorist organizations and the intelligence organizations responsible for countering terrorism depend heavily on secrecy for their effectiveness. So the scholar has to work without access to much important information. A further difficulty is that the scholarly work of developed societies, because it is public, is accessible to both the intelligence organizations and the terrorist organizations. In addition, in an open society, as opposed to a police state, the terrorist has access to targets and many resources that can be turned to destructive use. Because of these obstacles, the task of the researcher seems like a balancing act. This is the challenge that faces us today. It is not a new problem, even though the world in general has become aware of terrorism only within the last year and terrorism is now a byword in the daily news. I believe that, in spite of the challenges, research into terrorist activity can substantially ameliorate this pressing problem.

THE DANGER OF INTERNATIONAL TERRORISM

How serious is the threat of international terrorism? Experts disagree. In a recent article on the future of terrorism, Johnson (2001) concluded that terrorism is on the decline. He based this conclusion on the small number of Americans who have died as a result of terrorism compared with the much larger numbers of deaths due to other causes.

Segal (1993) also downplayed the threat of international terrorism and characterized it as low-level warfare. He observed, "It is the terror in terrorism that almost makes it modern day political theatre on our television screens. But despite the 'good copy' the hijackings, shootings, and bombings provide, there is little evidence that all the sound and fury actually has forced great political change" (p. 119). He further commented that terrorists "usually resort to terror because they are too weak and the opposing state too strong to be challenged in more conventional guerilla warfare or via the ballot box. Thus, an upswing of terrorism is often a sign of stability rather than imminent collapse" (p. 119).

On the other hand, Laqueur (1999) pointed to a rising danger of terrorism. He attributed this increasing danger to the increasing availability of weapons of mass destruction combined with increasing numbers of fanatics (the latter he attributes to the prevalence of science fiction, religious cults, conspiracy theories, and apocalyptic beliefs, as well as areas of state-sponsored terrorism in geographic areas experiencing conflict). Narcotics and organized crime also contribute.

These works addressing the issue of whether terrorism is a decreasing or an increasing danger were all written prior to the attacks on September 11, 2001. The attacks on the World Trade Center in New York City and on the Pentagon in Washington, D.C., have changed the perspective, not only of Americans, but also of all people in developed countries. Earlier discussions centered on the small number of deaths in comparison to death caused by other factors. However, a simple "body count" to measure the seriousness of the damage from terrorism is far too narrow a criterion. I will argue that terrorism is a substantial problem for both developed and developing countries, and that the potential damage wreaked by terrorism is far broader and the danger much greater than some of the above authors have perceived. The costs of terrorism include not only the number of people killed and wounded but also the effects of fear on people's behaviors, thoughts, feelings—indeed, on their entire lifestyle. In addition, there are very serious economic costs. Bombing and destruction cause devastation of physical infrastructure, as well as Internet and other nonphysical disruption. Perhaps most important are the costs involving diminished freedom in society. Hostage taking, plane hijacking, assassination, killing of political or military personnel, and murder of civilians are becoming frequent occurrences and each restricts our freedom and/or costs lives.

The fact that terrorism is on the rise globally and is an increasing threat to all civilized countries means that now is the time for psychologists to pay more attention to it and to improve public understanding of the problem and its possible solutions. This chapter discusses the lessons that can be learned from social, cross-cultural, and international psychology for countering international terrorism. It includes issues of language and communication, as well as social identity and social influence. It embraces issues of majority/minority influence processes and group processes. In addition, the chapter draws on international psychology's knowledge of intercultural communication, including aggression and violence and interpersonal attraction/dislike. Finally, this chapter includes practical proposals derived from research and theory for reducing and countering the threat of international terrorism.

PROBLEMS OF DEFINING INTERNATIONAL TERRORISM

The definition of terrorism poses numerous challenges and has been discussed by many authors (Cooper, 2001; Hoffman, 1998; Laqueur, 1987; Pillar, 2001). There is much disagreement and there are many differing viewpoints. I will refer to several definitions and discuss the merits of each.

The earliest definition is that given by Laqueur (1987). He traced the term *terrorism* to the Jacobin period (late eighteenth century) when it had a positive connotation. The definition of terrorism in the 1798 supplement of the *Dictionnaire de l'Académie Francaise* stated simply: "système, régime de la terreur." Laqueur also provided historical examples of terrorist movements from a variety of cultures, including European, Middle Eastern, Christian, Indian, Chinese, and North American.

Pillar (2001) also addressed the difficulty raised by attempts to define the term and noted, in particular, the problem of indiscriminate use and application of the word *terrorism*. His discussion included a summary of the failure in the United Nations General Assembly to reach an internationally accepted definition. In his discussion of terrorism and U.S. foreign policy, he used primarily the definition quoted below from the U.S. Code and explicated the various elements of the definition. Pillar argued that the most salient aspect of terrorism is that it is a method rather than a set of causes or adversaries. Thus, in Pillar's words, "terrorism is a problem of what people (or groups or states) *do,* rather than who they are or what they are trying to achieve" (p. 18).

Reich (1998) carried this argument a step further. He stated that terms such as *hatred, revulsion,* and *revenge* best represent the feelings and motivations of many terrorists, and that precisely these words should be used in discussing the subject rather than milder terms, such as *anger* or *frustration,* that psychologists may be more comfortable with. Of necessity, the conditions that psychologists have been able to study scientifically in the laboratory are merely pale reflections of the more extreme emotions and behaviors involved in terrorism. Nevertheless, even the milder conditions that are ethically possible for laboratory study can inform theory and policy, and this section of Reich's chapter is especially useful in this regard. It is ripe with reasonable and heuristic suggestions for connections between the questions raised by terrorist activity and possible answers from psychological research. He suggested ways to conduct research on aggression, group dynamics, interpersonal relations, and social influence.

Simmons and Mitch (1985) are among the few empirical researchers who have reported work along the lines that Reich advocated. Their study examined the consequences of applying the label *terrorism* to an act of public aggression. They varied the descriptions of violent events along several dimensions and identified the characteristics that most influence the labeling of an event as a terrorist act.

Hoffman (1998) devoted an entire chapter to defining terrorism, and his final definition is the most useful one. He traced the term from its definition in the *Oxford English Dictionary*, through its use during the French Revolution, and discussed other European uses as well. He addressed some of the reasons why terrorism is so difficult to define and pointed out that even different departments and agencies of the U.S. government (for example, the U.S. Department of State, the Federal Bureau of Investigation, and the U.S. Department of Defense) use different definitions for terrorism. He further noted that terrorism is often erroneously considered to be synonymous with guerrilla warfare or violent criminal behavior. He emphasized, however, that it is important to distinguish it from these other terms. In conclusion, he organized twenty-two definitional elements of terrorism (such as violence, force, threat, coercion, and publicity) into a table that could be helpful to psychologists seeking to develop an operational definition. He concluded that the most viable and commonly used definition is the one contained in Title 22 of the United States Code, Section 2656f(d): "Premeditated politically-motivated violence perpetrated against noncombatant targets by subnational groups or clandestine agents, usually intended to influence an audience" (p. 38).

As stated above, the term *terrorism* has been extensively defined and explored. For the subject of this chapter, all that remains is to broaden the definition to include an international application. This is easily done. According to the U.S. Department of State Report *Patterns of Global Terrorism 2000*, the term *international terrorism* means "terrorism involving citizens or the territory of more than one country" (p. vi).

PROBLEMS FACED BY THE SCHOLAR IN RESEARCHING TERRORISM

In addition to the major challenges surrounding the research of terrorism, a number of more specific areas of concern have been described. Crenshaw (2000) identified and briefly commented on persistent problems faced by researchers of political terrorism. While she did not focus specifically on international terrorism, the problems she identified are still relevant. They involve definitions, collecting empirical data, building theory, and avoiding the attribution of pathology to terrorists. She argued that psychological explanations of terrorism must take multiple levels of analysis into account, linking the individual to the group and to society. She also argued that future research should look not only at the causes of terrorism, but also at the termination of terrorist campaigns, at government decision making, and at policy effectiveness. She discussed the possible use of psychological research on terrorism and the divide between the scholar and the policy maker or between the academic and the government. She cited George (1993) as an example of work that seeks to "bridge the gap" between academics and policy makers in the field of foreign affairs and agreed with George's suggestion that the task of academics is to diagnose problems rather than prescribe solutions. Crenshaw (2000) also interestingly commented that, as terrorism becomes less linked with communism and left-wing ideologies and as it increasingly also includes right-wing ideologies, scholars, at least in the United States, appear more willing to contribute their research and knowledge to the issue of terrorism. For a thorough discussion of the predominantly liberal bias of American psychologists, see Redding (2001).

Perhaps the most thorough and detailed discussion of the challenges faced by any scholar seeking to use a systematic and scientific approach to analyze and understand the phenomenon of terrorism is provided by Groebel (1989). Groebel pointed out that most of the data necessary for understanding international terrorism are either not available at all, or are available only in part. Moreover, the data that *can* be collected are often of uncertain reliability and validity. Groebel also provided a very useful framework (to be discussed in more detail later) for organizing and analyzing the data that are available.

INTERNATIONAL PSYCHOLOGY AND ITS PERSPECTIVES

International Psychology Defined

Holtzman (2000, 2001) has provided useful descriptions and discussions of international psychology. He defined the term as "various forms of organized psychology at the international level, including societies, congresses, journals, and other kinds of scientific and professional exchanges" (Holtzman, 2001, p. 781). He added that it can also refer to "the social psychology of international relations, or the comparative study of psychological processes across different nations and cultures, as in cross-cultural psychology" (Holtzman, 2001, p. 781).

The Development of Psychological Science Around the World

Rosenzweig (1999) reported the preliminary results of a survey of the national psychological associations of thirty-four countries, conducted by the International Union of Psychological Science. The survey reported (among other things) the state of development and the level of resources available for psychological science. It also provided a useful summary both of the resources and of the growth and development of psychology in various nations of the world. Rosenzweig's findings showed that psychology is growing rapidly throughout the world, both in terms of the number of students and also in terms of the number of scientific researchers in the field. In addition, his report showed increasing pressure for the scientific work to demonstrate practical value within the cultures of the various nations.

Major Organizations of International Psychology

The growth of international psychology is reflected in the existence of four major organizations of international psychology that are described by Davis (2000b). The four organizations are the International Association of Applied Psychology (IAAP), the International Council of Psychologists (ICP), the International Association for Cross-Cultural Psychology (IACCP), and the International Union of Psychological Science (IUPsyS). Each of these organizations holds international conventions or congresses on a regular basis and issues a variety of publications. The membership of the first three associations is comprised of individual psychologists, while membership of the fourth consists of the national associations of psychology in various countries around the world. These four organizations have extensive networks of committees and task forces. They also support extensive communication among themselves, both formal and informal, and they cooperate on many projects. "Together the four associations represent psychologist members from more than 100 countries ranging from Albania to Zimbabwe" (Davis, 2000b, p. 37).

The International Association of Applied Psychology (IAAP)

IAAP was founded in 1920 in Geneva, Switzerland, and for many years held international conventions at irregular intervals in various countries of Europe. The first non-European meeting of IAAP was held in Montreal in 1974. Since 1974, congresses have been held at regular four-year intervals and have included non-European venues: Jerusalem in 1986; Kyoto in 1990; San Francisco in 1998; Singapore in 2002. IAAP publishes the journal *Applied Psychology: An International Review* (Davis, 2000b; Merenda, 1995).

International Council of Psychologists (ICP)

ICP is an outgrowth of the National Council of Women Psychologists, founded in 1941 in the United States. For its first two decades, the membership of this organization consisted either exclusively or primarily of women. Until 1970, when it met in Tel Aviv, its meetings were held annually only in the United States. Its next non-U.S. meeting was held in 1976 in Paris. Currently, ICP schedules a meeting in a country outside the United States in alternate years (Davis, 2000a, 2000b; Merenda, 1995).

International Association for Cross-Cultural Psychology (IACCP)

The IACCP was founded in 1972 in Hong Kong. It has held its meetings mostly outside the United States. The first U.S.-held meeting was in Bellingham, Washington, in 1998. IACCP publishes the *Journal of Cross-Cultural Psychology*, which focuses on mainstream cross-cultural research and is available in most university libraries (Davis, 2000b).

International Union of Psychological Science (IUPsyS)

IUPsyS was founded in 1951 in Stockholm. It has grown out of a series of international congresses of psychology that began in 1889 in Paris. These congresses convened at approximately four-year intervals in various cities of Europe through 1951, when IUPsyS was formed. At that time, the national associations of twenty countries became its charter members. By the time IUPsyS met in Stockholm in the year 2000 there were sixty-four national members. IUPsyS publishes the *International Journal of Psychology* (Davis, 2000b; Merenda, 1995; Rosenzweig, Holtzman, Sabourin, & Bélanger, 2000).

In summary, each of these four groups has contributed to the development of education and scientific knowledge in the various countries represented by their members. They have also made contributions toward increased understanding of human psychology. Much of the research presented at the meetings of these organizations has focused on comparisons across cultures. On both personal and professional levels, they have promoted international communication and understanding. Finally, through the contributions summarized above, they represent an important potential resource for countering the problems that foster international terrorism.

Perspectives from International Psychology

The reason the four organizations can be so effective is that they deal with different but complementary perspectives. IAAP maintains a primary focus on advancing the application of scientific knowledge internationally in the various fields of applied psychology. The work of IAAP is organized into thirteen divisions. Of particular importance to understanding and countering international terrorism are the divisions of psychology and law, political psychology, and psychology and national development (Davis, 2000b; Merenda, 1995; Pawlik & d'Ydewalle, 1996).

Promoting psychologist-to-psychologist networks around the world is the main focus of ICP. With the development of these networks, ICP aims to promote international understanding, cooperation across national boundaries, and goodwill among people of different cultures (Davis, 2000a, 2000b; Merenda, 1995; Pawlik & d'Ydewalle, 1996).

IACCP facilitates and conducts cross-cultural experimental research around the world (Davis, 2000b; Pawlik & d'Ydewalle, 1996).

Connecting national psychologies and building scientific infrastructure worldwide is the ambitious aim of IUPsyS. An important function is the encouragement and support of educational and scientific resources in underdeveloped countries. IUPsyS is also the most encompassing organization of international psychology. Because it works with national psychological associations of member countries rather than with individual psychologists, it is able to influence hundreds of thousands of individual psychologists worldwide (Davis, 2000b; Merenda, 1995; Pawlik & d'Ydewalle, 1996).

These four major international organizations coordinate many of their initiatives through a network of liaisons, joint projects, and coordinated calendars for their various congresses, conventions, and meetings. Each of these organizations also has liaisons with many smaller, more specialized associations in psychology.

CAUSES OF TERRORISM: APPLICABLE PSYCHOLOGICAL THEORY AND RESEARCH

Psychological Causes of International Terrorism

Personality of Terrorists

Traditional cross-sectional descriptions of personality are of little value for understanding terrorism unless these descriptions can be unified with the findings and theories of experimental psychology. As Eysenck (1997) has noted, descriptive and correlational approaches lack information about the causal nexus of behavior. More useful are longitudinal studies of hostile, aggressive, antisocial patterns of behavior such as those reviewed by Caprara (1996) and Rutter (1997). Even longitudinal approaches to the study of the aggressive personality may be less useful than the recognition that schemas of "enemy, evil, revenge, hate" probably predict aggressive behavior best. What is the most reliable cause of aggression? Attack is, or threat, or the perception of threat.

Brown (1944) recognized that it was not just the personality of Hitler but the psychologically threatened condition of the entire German society that explained German behavior during World War II. Brown wrote:

> Ever since 1933 I have listened to all of Hitler's broadcast speeches, as well as those of Goering, Goebbels, and other leading Nazi, and—especially since the outbreak of war—to the German broadcasts for German listeners, because they throw important light on the special psychological problem of German mentality. It is the duty of anyone who is trained in psychology to study these revelations as fully as possible, with a view to the future. The problem is really a medico-psychological one. Germany is a sick nation, and we need to understand how she has reached the state in which she now is if we are to form a reliable opinion as to the best way of treating her later on. If we treat her in the wrong way later on it will be more that an international calamity, it will be a world crime. (pp. 49–50)

Thus, Brown stated quite clearly that psychologists have a duty to study such threats.

A particularly useful resource on the motivation and personality of the individual who becomes a terrorist is the book edited by Reich (1998), *Origins of Terrorism: Psychologies, Ideologies, Theologies, States of Mind.* Particularly useful are the two lead chapters by Crenshaw (1998) and Post (1998). Crenshaw analyzed the actions and motivations of terrorists with the assumption that they are the result of logical thinking and strategic choice in pursuit of a rational goal. Post examined the actions and motives of terrorists with the assumption that they are, instead, driven by psychological forces. Other valuable chapters are those by Bandura (1998), Kellen (1998), Kramer (1998), and Rapoport (1998). Bandura argued that psychological processes of moral disengagement are involved in terrorist behavior and thought. Kellen provided a detailed analysis of terrorism in West Germany. Kramer examined the moral logic of Hezbollah, and Rapoport examined the religious terrorism of Islam.

Aggression and Human Nature

While many areas of psychological research are useful to an understanding of psychological terrorism, research and theory on human aggression bear the most obvious and directly relevant relationship. For that reason, I will review the work on aggression first.

The psychological literature contains numerous definitions of aggression. Most of these are similar to that offered by Baron and Richardson (1994). They defined aggression as "any form of behavior directed toward the goal of harming or injuring another living being who is motivated to avoid such treatment" (p. 5).

Psychologists have searched for at least a century for answers to the question of the extent to which human aggression is due to innate factors and the extent to which it is due to the influence of the social environment. Early psychologists favored a biological view. For example, James (1936, 1987) considered human violence to be a powerful instinct that was a natural result of the struggle for survival. Another early psychologist, McDougall (1908), also considered aggression to be a basic human instinct. Freud (1963) concurred; he considered aggression to be a basic component of human motivation and anger to be activated by objects of hate. This biological view was further strengthened by the discoveries of brain mechanisms involved in aggressive behavior (Cannon, 1925).

The research supporting the view that human aggression has biological aspects continues to this day. However, most psychologists—and social psychologists in particular—now see the causes of human aggression as complex: biological processes contribute to aggression in combination with aversive stimuli from the environment. Stimuli arising from conflict with others is seen as a particularly potent cause. Much of the work in social psychology has focused on the cultural/environmental conditions and the psychological processes combining all these factors—that is, those involving frustration, poor impulse control, the cultural and individual construal of negative emotions, and social and group norms that support violence. Thus, the view of today's social psychologists is that the causes of aggression are much more complex than previously thought. They include the individual's genetic endowment, past learning and experience, and also the individual's assessment of aspects of the situation that punish (inhibit) or reward (promote) aggression.

Geen (1998) has organized the current social psychological research on aggression and antisocial behavior into five psychological processes. These processes are instigation (usually in the context of interpersonal conflict and involving cognitive processes), social and learning history of the individual (which determines the likelihood that aggressive behavior will be enacted in situations of conflict), skills in processing interpersonal information and tendencies to attribute hostile intent to others, social and cultural variables (norms, beliefs, expectations) regarding the appropriateness of aggression in conflict situations, and personality variables that moderate aggressive behavior patterns.

These five processes can be best understood by incorporating them into the framework of social learning theory, which also provides a structure for understanding the influences that contribute to the development of enduring patterns of individual aggression. Social learning theory emphasizes the role of observation and imitation in the acquisition of responses and behavior patterns and it emphasizes reinforcement and punishment as the primary influences on the performance and maintenance of these behaviors. The normal child in many societies has frequent opportunities to observe many aggressive behaviors. These opportunities occur in real-life situations at school, in the community, and at home, as well as in the fantasy world provided by the media. Thus, from a very early age humans learn, at least in rudimentary form, how to enact many aggressive behaviors. Fortunately, the vast majority of children and adults never perform the aggressive acts that have been demonstrated to them countless times. Most children and adults never shoot a gun at another person, or stab another with a knife or other sharp object, or seek to harm another with explosives, even though these aggressive acts have been modeled over and over in the media. A few individuals, however, because of real or imagined patterns of reinforcement for past aggressive behavior, do carry out aggressive acts. Thus, social learning theory makes an important distinction between the learning of aggression (acquired through observation) and the performance of aggression (influenced by reinforcement and punishment).

These principles have been well supported. Research has shown that most people learn how to perform many aggressive acts but only a few perceive that the reinforcement contingencies make it worth their effort to perform these acts. For example, Bandura (1986) reviewed studies that showed the influence of aggressive models on learning and also showed the effects of expected rewards and punishments on aggressive performance. Thus an individual who has used aggression many times to achieve valuable goals expects that future aggression will be similarly rewarded. The validity of this analysis has been supported by the research of Perry, Perry, and Rasmussen (1986) and by Boldizar, Perry, and Perry (1989). Furthermore, social learning theory also proposes that all individuals develop and refine mental frameworks (scripts/schemas) that serve as internal standards to guide their behaviors. In addition, people learn and refine mental representations of social norms regarding which actions are appropriate responses to interpersonal conflicts. Thus, as Huesmann (1988) has shown, individuals who persistently show aggressive behavior are those who have used aggression successfully in the past, have participated in many aggressive situations, and continue to add to and perpetuate their aggressive behavior patterns.

While much psychological research on aggression contains the implicit assumption that all aggressive behavior is undesirable and should be controlled or eliminated, a few researchers regard aggression as a normal part of much social interaction rather than as a deviant element. Such researchers include Da Gloria (1984), Da Gloria and DeRidder (1977), Felson and Tedeschi (1993), Mummendey and Mummendey (1983), and Tedeschi and Nesler (1993). All have investigated social groups, subcultures, and cultures in which aggression and violence are considered appropriate and desirable as a means of reaching a goal. Obvious examples come from sports and law enforcement. However, even in these situations where high levels of aggression are considered appropriate and desirable, powerful rules or social norms generally exist. When these rules and social norms are violated (for example, police brutality), the aggressive behavior is generally perceived as reprehensible.

The Melding of Aggression and Political Ideology

Just as norms regarding appropriate and inappropriate aggression have developed to regulate many types of interpersonal aggression, norms have also developed to regulate types of intergroup aggression. Cultures and social groups have various norms regarding the appropriate use of aggression in inter-group conflict and hostility. When a member of one group transgresses against a member of another group, the victim or aggrieved individual or group engages in a process of attribution regarding the cause. Was it an accident or an intentionally hostile act indicating evil traits and malicious intent? Whether overt aggression will follow is influenced by several factors, including the nature of the original transgression, the outcome of the attribution process, and the degree of preexisting negative attitudes toward the out-group (DeRidder, Schruijer, & Tripathi, 1992; Schruijer, 1992).

Many lessons learned from research on aggression can be applied to aspects of terrorism. A number of cross-cultural studies have examined factors related to levels of violence and aggression embedded in the social norms of various cultures and subcultures. Archer and Gartner (1984) compiled statistics from 110 nations for the period from 1960 to 1970 to create a comparative crime data file. These data indicate that nations typically exhibit levels of postwar violence that have increased relative to prewar levels.

Attack or perceived threat of attack is perhaps the most reliable cause of aggression (Buss, 1961). Terrorist aggression is probably no exception. Social psychological research on aggression has shown that attack, threat, and even perceived threat serve as the most reliable instigators of aggression. Moreover, when individuals respond to an attack of another person by harming the attacker, they do not label their own behavior as aggression but rather as justified behavior (Harvey & Enzle, 1978). In an interesting historical example, Brown (1944) recounted how Hitler brought the various parts of the German nation under his control by convincing them they were under attack. Even music and drama played a part: Wagner made the ancient epic of *Das Nibelungenlied* into a vehicle for rousing German national feeling and making the theme of terrible vengeance widely known and emotionally acceptable. The epic provided the theme that became the preoccupation of the Nazis and was expressed in Hitler's use of concentration camps, his development of secret cells (Gestapo), and his policy of "meeting terror with ten-fold terror" (Brown, 1944, p. 55). The theme was also apparent in Goebbels's use of propaganda containing the stark message that the German people were fighting for their lives and must fight or be annihilated.

The situation of Germany under Hitler is not unique, and cultures of violence wherever they are found provide the conditions that can breed terrorism. Individuals trapped in those cultures are especially susceptible to the allure of violence and they come to see it as the only solution. For example, Brown (1944) described Hitler's "idealism" as the individual sacrificing for the group. Brown went on to assert that the "will to power" was aligned in primitive societies with the struggle for existence and the survival of the fittest, but in later times was aligned with cooperation rather than competition. Closely related to cultures of violence are cultures of war. Brown referred to Nietzsche's glorification of war and the justification of violence as a solution; Nietzsche had argued that war is a great good and had glorified it in *Also Sprach Zarathustra.*

For political violence to occur, a theoretical justification must legitimize the destructive activities (Groebel, 1989). Insight into the ideology of terrorist movements can be gained from a study of the literature of the German revolutionaries of the 1960s and 1970s. Kellen (1998) and Markovits (2001) have discussed the ideologies from this period that provided foundations for revolutionary and terrorist thinking and actions. The revolutionaries of the 1960s believed that the Western powers (mostly the United States) were inherently evil. They pointed out that, after World War II, the Western powers had propped up the very individuals who were prominent Nazi figures under Hitler. The revolutionaries argued that many of the judges in Germany and many of the political leaders supported by the Marshall Plan had previously been Nazis and supporters of Hitler during the war. Therefore, both the establishment in Germany and its Western supporters were corrupt. Arguments of a similar nature have become familiar in the ideologies of many terrorist movements and they bear a striking similarity to those used today. Although they will have somewhat different ideological bases, there will be a number of similarities to the German ideologies and conceptualizations. For example, in current revolutionary arguments from the Middle East, very similar arguments are being made to justify the terrorists' actions. Terrorists point to the government of Saudi Arabia, and argue that it is corrupt and would be unable to remain in power except for the support of the Western governments. They also argue that Israel unjustly occupies land and oppresses the Palestinians and can continue to do so only because of Western (primarily U.S.) support.

Group Dynamics and International Terrorism

The study of group dynamics in psychology makes it clear that groups exert strong and subtle powers on the behaviors, thoughts, and emotions of individual group members. At the most basic level, groups provide categories of in-group versus out-group, us versus them, friend versus foe. Group pressure can exert a powerful influence on one's behavior and decision making, and even on one's perception of reality. A series of classic studies by Asch (1951, 1955) showed that people would erroneously perceive a simple visual diagram when subjected to subtle group pressure. A substantial minority of those individuals even denied that they had been influenced by the group and that their objectively incorrect answers were wrong. Bond and Smith (1996) have provided a more recent review of the cross-cultural results of the type of group conformity research pioneered by Asch.

Interpersonal Attraction and International Terrorism

The work on attraction, both at the individual level and at the group level, provides a useful framework for understanding many of the psychological dimensions of international terrorism. The attraction of individuals to groups; the dynamics within the groups; and the establishment of dislike, repulsion, and hate toward individuals and groups perceived as the enemy can all be better understood through the lens of interpersonal attraction research and theory. This theory also provides a useful framework for understanding the determinants as well as the consequences of attraction and repulsion, love and hate, and perceptions of friend and enemy. Moreover, while primarily concerned with elucidating the determinants of the positive and negative sentiments that individuals hold toward other individuals (Berscheid, 1985, 1998; Byrne, 1971; Davis & Lamberth, 1974; Gonzales, Davis, Loney, LuKens, & Junghans, 1983), this framework is useful at multiple levels. For example, it has been expanded to include the attraction and repulsion that individuals feel toward various groups (Davis, 1984).

Familiarity is an important determinant of attraction (Berscheid, 1985, 1998; Byrne, 1971). It is widely recognized that, in contrast to familiar people who are perceived as safe and friendly, unfamiliar people are often perceived as potentially dangerous. As demonstrated by Hartley (1946), people report dislike for and negative evaluations of national groups that are completely unfamiliar. When familiarity with a stimulus is varied through repeated exposure, attraction to that stimulus increases as a function of the number of exposures (Zajonc, 1968). This "mere exposure" effect has been found under a variety of conditions. For reviews, see Bornstein (1989) and Harrison (1977).

Another important determinant of attraction is reciprocity. Individuals are attracted to others who like them or evaluate them positively, and they dislike others who dislike them or evaluate them negatively. Attraction theorists conceptualize expressions of liking and esteem from another person as a powerful reward that is likely to be reciprocated; moreover, expressions of dislike or disapproval from another person is a powerful punishment that is also almost certain to be reciprocated. Positive evaluations and expressions of liking and/or respect from another person result in the expectation that that person is a potential source of help and support. To an even greater degree, negative evaluations and expressions of dislike from another lead to the expectation that that person is a potential source of threat and harm (Berscheid, 1985, 1998; Byrne, 1971).

Similarity of attitudes, values, and beliefs comprises another powerful determinant of interpersonal attraction. Lamberth, Gouaux, and Davis (1972) demonstrated that similar attitude statements possess the rewarding properties of traditional reinforcers in an operant conditioning experiment. Thus, individuals who express similar attitudes provide pleasant experiences and are likely to be approached and perceived in positive ways. Byrne and Nelson (1965) combined data from a number of similarity-attraction experiments in order to examine the functional relationship between attitude similarity and attraction. The relationship can be expressed by the function $y = 5.44x + 6.62$. In other words, the level of attraction (y) that one individual reports for another person increases in a linear pattern as the proportion of similar attitudes (x) increases. In an experiment using this formula to make predictions of interpersonal attraction, Gonzales et al. (1983) found that people recognize the general effects of attitude similarity and dissimilarity on attraction but consistently underestimate the magnitude of these effects. Particularly noteworthy was the degree to which they underestimated how much a stranger would dislike them in the case of dissimilar attitudes. Disagreement in the form of dissimilar attitude statements also induces negative arousal that can adversely influence learning (Davis & Lamberth, 1974).

While most of the research on interpersonal attraction has focused on the determinants of one individual's attraction to another individual, Davis (1984) extended this approach in order to examine an individual's attraction to a group. He found that individuals are attracted to some groups and repelled by others as a function of similarity of attitudes, beliefs, and values. The factors that determine an individual's attraction to one group and avoidance of another are important precursors to understanding the gradual process by which individuals become attracted to, and in some cases members of, terrorist groups.

COUNTERING INTERNATIONAL TERRORISM

The preceding sections provide a theoretical and empirical foundation for understanding the psychology of terrorism and the importance of international psychology. I believe there are four principal ways in which international psychology can effectively contribute to the long-term effort to counter international terrorism. These are as follows: training more psychologists worldwide, sharing information worldwide, further utilizing the resources of the major international organizations in psychology, and educating the general public.

Train More Psychologists Worldwide

An important gap in psychological knowledge relevant to international terrorism is the lack of information, understanding, and skill in dealing with individuals of diverse cultures. While physicians, economists, and certain other professionals can apply their expertise internationally with fair success because they are dealing with circumscribed domains, the psychologist must be capable of accurately defining and investigating the multiple determinants of human behavior—a much more varied domain. Because so many determinants are embedded in language and in the cultural meanings and symbols that motivate and shape behaviors of individuals, thorough familiarity with and deep understanding of the relevant culture are essential. For many important cultures, such familiarity and understanding are lacking in the psychological literature.

In many cultures there is not an adequate body of professionals who are both culturally familiar and trained in psychology. In many other cultures there are individuals with both intimate knowledge of the culture and training in psychology, but the barriers of language and of publication processes prevent their contributions from being widely disseminated. For example, the work of an Italian psychologist who publishes only in Italian will be unavailable to most of the community of international psychology. Similarly, within the community of English-speaking psychologists, no one is available to provide a thorough understanding of Afghanistan or the Sudan or Lebanon or even the Palestinian West Bank of Israel.

Increase Psychological Research and Information-Sharing Worldwide

In addition to the need for training professional psychologists, there is a need for sharing information. Currently few psychological databases regarding terrorism are available in English, the language of the majority of present-day psychologists. Perhaps the most comprehensive database is one compiled by the German Ministry of the Interior that is available only in German (BMI, 1981–1984). Groebel (1989) provided a cogent summary in English of the findings from these data. These data are a valuable resource on terrorism and should be translated into other languages for wider accessibility.

Language differences are the greatest barrier to worldwide sharing of information. The need for translation is a pressing one in today's world. However, a number of practical obstacles must be acknowledged. There are 191 nation-states in the world today and most are ethnically and linguistically heterogeneous. There are an estimated 2,000 to 5,000 distinct ethnic-linguistic groups (National Intelligence Council, 2000). Perhaps a viable solution to the problem of translation would be to begin translation efforts with the world's ten foremost languages: Mandarin, English, Spanish, Arabic, Bengali, Hindi, Portuguese, Russian, Japanese, German (list-ed in order of number of native speakers). Approximately 900 million individuals speak Mandarin as their native language; only 100 million speak German. While only 380 million people speak English as their mother tongue, approximately 1.6 billion people (almost one-third of the world's population) use English in some form on a daily basis. Thus, the world's published material is primarily available in English, and the U.S. media export English-language culture worldwide. Over 80 percent of Internet communication is in English, although an estimated 44 percent of Internet users have another first language (Fishman, 1998–1999). Thus, English is clearly the dominant repository for scientific data at present; nevertheless, increased translation to and from the other major world languages is needed.

Further Utilize the International Organizations of Psychology

Currently, one of the chief contributions of the international organizations of psychology is translation. For example, IUPsyS has sponsored the development and publication of several trilingual dictionaries of psychological terms. Such translation will continue to be an important part of the work of the international associations of psychology.

An additional important contribution that international psychological organizations are uniquely prepared to offer is capacity building for national psychological organizations that lag behind. Capacity building involves aiding and facilitating the development of education and training for psychologists, the establishment of psychological laboratories and clinics, the promotion of support for research funding, and the development of other essential infrastructure (Adair, 1995). A number of reference works in international psychology describe the status of psychological education and training, opportunities for scientific research, and the professional recognition of psychologists in various countries throughout the world (Gilgen & Gilgen, 1987; Ross, Alexander, & Basowitz, 1966; Sexton & Hogan, 1992; Sexton & Misiak, 1976).

In their programs for capacity building, the international associations in psychology periodically assess and report the level of development of national psychologies. In countries where psychology is nonexistent or not well developed, there is a high probability that other elements of modern infrastructure are poorly developed as well and that conditions are therefore ripe for fostering terrorism. Afghanistan can be taken as an example. In a guide to international opportunities for advanced training and research in psychology, Ross, Alexander, and Basowitz (1966) included a chapter on psychology in Afghanistan (Ajmal, 1966). That chapter was authored by a psychologist from Pakistan and reported only a single university, Kabul University, which had no department of psychology. Only a few courses in psychology were offered and these by the faculty of education to prepare students for administrative positions. Three subsequent similar reference works over the next three decades (Gilgen & Gilgen, 1987; Sexton & Hogan, 1992; Sexton & Misiak, 1976) had nothing to report on psychology in Afghanistan. For a personal and informative account of the plight of Afghan refugees fleeing the Soviet-Afghan war, see Dadfar (1994).

In addition to their roles in assessing development and providing translation services, the international psychology associations are also uniquely positioned to promote cross-cultural communication and international understanding. IUPsyS, for example, accomplishes this role by publishing articles in both English and French in the *International Journal of Psychology*. In a typical article, the psychological ethics codes of twenty-four countries were compared (Leach & Harbin, 1997). Also, IUPsyS, in cooperation with IAAP and IACCP, sponsors the biennial Advanced Research Training Seminars (ARTS) to train young psychologists from developing countries in research skills. All four of the major international associations in psychology promote cross-cultural and cross-national research and cooperation. These initiatives range from small-scale, cross-cultural projects involving researchers and participants from two nations to large-scale projects involving dozens and sometimes scores of researchers, as many countries, and tens of thousands of participants.

Educate the Public

The above measures, while undoubtedly helpful, will be of little value without the support of the average citizens of many nations. Terrorists are adept at infiltrating open societies and are careful to disguise their intentions. Thus, the danger they pose can be countered only with the vigilance of alert citizens. These citizens must have accurate and reliable information about terrorism and also must have avenues for action when the need arises. Thus, the role of psychology in educating the general public becomes of prime importance in combating international terrorism. With increased alertness, initiative, and vigilance, ordinary people can find ways to maintain the privacy and other norms of an open society while still countering the dangers of terrorism. President George W. Bush's urgings that citizens be vigilant acknowledges the important role that average citizens must play in order to address the problem of terrorism. The alert flight attendants who in December 2001 detected a passenger with explosives in his shoes before he could destroy the plane and its passengers are a good example of citizen vigilance.

The situation in Germany under Hitler provides useful lessons. After World War I, Germany was devastated and the German people demoralized. Hitler put people to work and, in the early years, gave many hope and increased self-esteem. Tragically, this change was accomplished by the production of war materials and at the expense of "scapegoats"—Jews, Gypsies, and other groups. When individuals suffer chronic threats to their self-concept, as did the Germans after defeat in World War I, they may seek to restore self-esteem by comparing themselves with and derogating other individuals. For a discussion of downward social comparison, see Osborne (1996). What can be learned? Wherever there are pockets of people who are suffering, there is potential for violence and terrorism. Much of the problem can be addressed by providing hope and opportunities for productive work. Of course, the hope must be realistic and the work must fit the skills of the people and be focused on positive values. Here education and educated people play a central role. The Afghan professionals living in Western countries and now returning to

Afghanistan to help rebuild their country and bring it into the twenty-first century provide an excellent example.

Other broad and useful suggestions for countering the threat of international terrorism by ameliorating the cultural conditions that foster terrorism are reported by Reeves (1999). He recommended that "intelligence agencies must start working to separate hardcore terrorists from members of their gang and from their recruiting pool" (p. 264). He stated that, to accomplish this goal, legitimate grievances of the terrorists must be taken seriously and responded to constructively whenever possible. Moreover, there must be "a concerted international effort to create greater harmony between the West and the East" (p. 265). These things will not happen without broad support from the citizens of both Western and Eastern societies.

In particular, university personnel have an important role to play in this international effort to create greater harmony. In fact, universities must lead in the effort to pay attention to (rather than ignore) both the dangers and the suffering inherent in expressions of anger and hate. In Western countries, revolutionary groups may at times be found living and working at or near universities. University environments offer opportunities for easy and anonymous communication via the Internet. In addition, they offer resources for obtaining extensive information on many subjects that the terrorist may wish to learn about, access to inexpensive living arrangements, ostensible reasons for being in a country, access to libraries, and relative anonymity. Also, university and college campuses are locations where widely diverse ideologies are discussed and advocated. Such diversity of opinion is not only accepted but encouraged on campuses, and advocates of extreme ideologies often find a receptive audience there.

On university campuses one is also likely to find speakers and events that offer opportunities to express a variety of ideas. While some of these speakers and events may generate responses of antagonism or hate, it is in the best interests of citizens and governments in both Western and Eastern countries to support and encourage the expression of diverse opinions and ideologies. This atmosphere can be especially useful at universities in countries where terrorism may be brewing. It will encourage greater latitude of ideas, but may also serve to allow for unobtrusive measurement of the level of antagonism or hate and to identify individuals who are attracted to terrorist ideologies. Such persons are most likely to be in a cultural and social climate where many people agree with them and where they feel safe. This preference for being with others who share similar attitudes, beliefs, and values suggests the possibility of using a variety of unobtrusive techniques to detect the presence of individuals drawn to terrorist ideologies. One such technique for detecting the presence of individuals hostile to a particular ideology involves placing symbols of that ideology in public places and measuring the degree to which they are defaced or removed. For example, printed flyers or posters that announce speakers on Western-oriented topics could be placed on walls or bulletin boards around universities and other public places. The extent to which these posters and flyers are defaced or removed will indicate the extent to which they have aroused hostility. In locations where substantial defacement or removal of the symbols occurs, they can be replaced and the area put under more careful surveillance in order to observe and identify the responsible individuals. While such unobtrusive measures may be limited in their usefulness, they nevertheless provide simple and inexpensive methods for monitoring the level of hostility to particular ideas and groups. Webb, Campbell, Schwartz, and Sechrest (1966) have provided a wealth of guidance and further ideas for developing and using unobtrusive measures in a variety of contexts.

While citizens, psychologists, and various government agencies can each play their part, it is only by working together at the community, state, national, and international levels that we will successfully counter the danger of international terrorism. Netanyahu (2001) recently presented a series of recommendations for fighting international terrorism. He has served as a soldier in an elite anti-terrorist unit of the Israeli army and also as prime minister of Israel. He was invited to address the U.S. Congress nine days after the September 11 terrorist attacks. His recommendations are presented below:

1. Impose sanctions on suppliers of nuclear technology to terrorist states (p. 132).
2. Impose diplomatic, economic, and military sanctions on the terrorist states themselves (p. 134).
3. Neutralize terrorist enclaves (p. 136).
4. Freeze financial assets in the West of terrorist regimes and organizations (p. 137).
5. Share intelligence (p. 138).
6. Revise legislation to enable greater surveillance and action against organizations inciting to violence, subject to periodic renewal (p. 139).
7. Actively pursue terrorists (p. 143).
8. Do not release jailed terrorists (p. 144).
9. Train special forces to fight terrorism (p. 144).
10. Educate the public (p. 146).

While Netanyahu presented these recommendations to a broad audience and while in most instances such actions remain the purview of governments, he has nevertheless provided a useful array of actions that address the problem of international terrorism. The recommendation that is most relevant to psychologists of any nation is the final one, that of educating the public. That recommendation is echoed by the goals of this chapter: to point out the value of applying the scientific knowledge and resources of international psychology to the effort to counter international terrorism, and to educate society in general about these matters.

REFERENCES

Adair, J. G. (1995). The research environment in developing countries: Contributions to the national development of the discipline. *International Journal of Psychology, 30*, 643–662.

Ajmal, M. (1966). Afghanistan. In S. Ross, I. E. Alexander, & H. Basowitz (Eds.), *International opportunities for advanced training and research in psychology* (pp. 4–5). Washington, DC: American Psychological Association.

Archer, D., & Gartner, R. (1984). *Violence and crime in cross-national perspective.* New Haven, CT: Yale University Press.

Asch, S. E. (1951). Effects of group pressure upon the modification and distortion of judgement. In H. Guetzkow (Ed.), *Groups, leadership, and men.* Pittsburgh, PA: Carnegie.

Asch, S. E. (1955). Opinions and social pressure. *Scientific American, 193*, 31–35.

Bandura, A. (1986). *Social foundations of thought and action: A social cognitive theory.* Englewood Cliffs, NJ: Prentice-Hall.

Bandura, A. (1998). Mechanisms of moral disengagement. In W. Reich (Ed.), *Origins of terrorism: Psychologies, ideologies, theologies, states of mind* (pp. 161–191). Washington, DC: Woodrow Wilson Center Press.

Baron, R. A., & Richardson, D. (1994). *Human aggression.* New York: Plenum.

Berscheid, E. (1985). Interpersonal attraction. In G. Lindzey & E. Aronson (Eds.), *Handbook of social psychology* (3rd ed., pp. 413–484). New York: Random House.

Berscheid, E. (1998). Attraction and close relationships. In D. T. Gilbert, S. T. Fiske, & G. Lindzey (Eds.), *Handbook of social psychology* (4th ed., pp. 193–281). Boston: McGraw-Hill.

BMI (Bundesministerium des Innern) (Ed.) (1981–1984). *Analysen zum Terrorismus* (Vol. 1–4/2). Opladen, Germany: Westdeutscher Verlag.

Boldizar, J. P., Perry, D. G., & Perry, L. (1989). Outcome, values and aggression. *Child Development, 60*, 571–579.

Bond, R., & Smith, P. B. (1996). Culture and conformity: A meta-analysis of studies using Asch's line judgement task. *Psychological Bulletin, 119*, 111–137.

Bornstein, R. F. (1989). Exposure and affect: Overview and meta-analysis of research, 1968–1987. *Psychological Bulletin, 106*, 265–289.

Brown, W. (1944). The psychology of modern Germany. *British Journal of Psychology, 34*, 43–59.

Buss, A. H. (1961). *The psychology of aggression.* New York: Wiley.

Byrne, D. (1971). *The attraction paradigm.* New York: Academic Press.

Byrne, D., & Nelson, D. (1965). Attraction as a linear function of proportion of positive reinforcements. *Journal of Personality and Social Psychology, 1*, 659–663.

Cannon, W. B. (1925). *Bodily changes in pain, fear, hunger, and rage.* New York: Appleton-Century-Crofts.

Caprara, G. V. (1996). Structures and processes in personality psychology. *European Psychologist, 1*, 14–26.

Cooper, H. H. A. (2001). Terrorism: The problem of definition revisited. *American Behavioral Scientist, 44*, 881–893.

Crenshaw, M. (1998). The logic of terrorism: Terrorist behavior as a product of strategic choice. In W. Reich (Ed.), *Origins of terrorism: Psychologies, ideologies, theologies, states of mind* (pp. 7–24). Washington, DC: Woodrow Wilson Center Press.

Crenshaw, M. (2000). The psychology of terrorism: An agenda for the 21st century. *Political Psychology, 21*, 405–420.

Da Gloria, J. (1984). Frustration, aggression, and the sense of justice. In A. Mummendey (Ed.), *Social psychology of aggression: From individual behavior to social interaction* (pp. 127–141). New York: Springer.

Da Gloria, J., & DeRidder, R. (1977). Aggression in dyadic interaction. *European Journal of Social Psychology, 7*, 189–219.

Dadfar, A. (1994). The Afghans: Bearing the scars of a forgotten war. In A. J. Marsella, T. Bornemann, S. Ekblad, & J. Orley (Eds.), *Amidst peril and pain: The mental health and well-being of the world's refugees* (pp. 125–139). Washington, DC: American Psychological Association.

Davis, J. M. (1984). Attraction to a group as a function of attitude similarity and geographic distance. *Social Behavior and Personality, 12*, 1–6.

Davis, J. M. (2000a). International Council of Psychologists. In A. E. Kazdin (Ed.), *Encyclopedia of psychology* (Vol. 4, pp. 341–343). Washington, DC/New York: American Psychological Association/Oxford University Press.

Davis, J. M. (2000b, Spring). Four international organizations in psychology: An overview. *Eye on Psi Chi, 33*–37.

Davis, J. M., & Lamberth, J. (1974). Affective arousal and energization properties of positive and negative stimuli. *Journal of Experimental Psychology, 103*, 196–200.

DeRidder, R., Schruijer, S. G. L., & Tripathi, R. C. (1992). Norm violation as a precipitating factor of negative intergroup relations. In R. DeRidder & R. C. Tripathi (Eds.), *Norm violation and intergroup relations* (pp. 3–37). Oxford, England: Oxford University Press.

Eysenck, H. J. (1997). Personality and experimental psychology: The unification of psychology and the possibility of a paradigm. *Journal of Personality and Social Psychology, 73*, 1224–1237.

Felson, R. B., & Tedeschi, J. T. (Eds.) (1993). *Aggression and violence: Social interactionist perspectives* (pp. 13–45). Washington, DC: American Psychological Association.

Fishman, J. A. (1998–1999). The new linguistic order. *Foreign Policy, 113*, 26–40.

Freud, S. (1963). Instincts and their vicissitudes. In P. Rieff (Ed.), *Freud: General psychological theory* (pp. 83–103). New York: Collier. (Originally published 1915)

Geen, R. G. (1998). Aggression and antisocial behavior. In D. T. Gilbert, S. T. Fiske, & G. Lindzey (Eds.), *The handbook of social psychology*, (4th ed., Vol. 4, pp. 317–356). Boston: McGraw-Hill.

George, A. (1993). *Bridging the gap: Theory and practice of foreign policy*. Washington, DC: U.S. Institute of Peace.

Gilgen, A. R., & Gilgen, C. K. (Eds.) (1987). *International handbook of psychology*. New York: Greenwood Press.

Gonzales, M., Davis, J. M., Loney, G., LuKens, C., & Junghans, C. (1983). Interactional approach to interpersonal attraction. *Journal of Personality and Social Psychology, 44*, 1192–1197.

Groebel, J. (1989). The problems and challenges of research on terrorism. In J. Groebel & J. H. Goldstein (Eds.), *Terrorism: Psychological perspectives* (pp. 15–38). Seville, Spain: Publicaciones de la Universidad de Sevilla.

Harrison, A. A. (1977). Mere exposure. *Advances in Experimental Social Psychology, 10*, 39–83.

Hartley, E. L. (1946). *Problems in prejudice.* New York: King's Crown Press.

Harvey, M. D., & Enzle, M. E. (1978). Effects of retaliation latency and provocation level on judged blameworthiness for retaliatory aggression. *Personality and Social Psychology Bulletin, 4,* 579–582.

Hoffman, B. (1998). *Inside terrorism.* New York: Columbia University Press.

Holtzman, W. H. (2000). International psychology. In A. E. Kazdin (Ed.), *Encyclopedia of psychology* (Vol. 4, pp. 343–345). Washington, DC: American Psychological Association/Oxford University Press.

Holtzman, W. H. (2001). International psychology. In W. E. Craighead & C. D. Nemeroff (Eds.), *The Corsini encyclopedia of psychology and behavioral science* (3rd ed., Vol. 2, pp. 781–783). New York: John Wiley & Sons.

Huesmann, L. R. (1988). An information processing model for the development of aggression. *Aggressive Behavior, 14,* 13–24.

James, W. (1936). *The varieties of religious experience.* New York: Modern Library. (Originally published 1902)

James, W. (1987). The moral equivalent of war. In *William James: Writings, 1902–1910* (pp. 1281–1293). New York: Library of America. (Originally published 1910)

Johnson, L. C. (2001). The future of terrorism. *American Behavioral Scientist, 44,* 894–913.

Kampelman, M. M. (1991). *Entering new worlds: The memoirs of a private man in public life.* New York: HarperCollins.

Kellen, K. (1998). Ideology and rebellion: Terrorism in West Germany. In W. Reich (Ed.), *Origins of terrorism: Psychologies, ideologies, theologies, states of mind* (pp. 43–58). Washington, DC: Woodrow Wilson Center Press.

Kramer, M. (1998). The moral logic of Hizballah. In W. Reich (Ed.), *Origins of terrorism: Psychologies, ideologies, theologies, states of mind* (pp. 131–157). Washington, DC: Woodrow Wilson Center Press.

Lamberth, J., Gouaux, C., & Davis, J. (1972). Agreeing attitudinal statements as positive reinforcers in instrumental conditioning. *Psychonomic Science, 29,* 247–249.

Laqueur, W. (1987). *The age of terrorism.* Boston: Little, Brown and Company.

Laqueur, W. (1999). *The new terrorism: Fanaticism and the arms of mass destruction.* New York: Oxford University Press.

Leach, M. M., & Harbin, J. J. (1997). Psychological ethics codes: A comparison of twenty-four countries. *International Journal of Psychology, 32,* 181–192.

Markovits, A. S. (2001). The minister and the terrorist. *Foreign Affairs, 80,* 132–146.

McDougall, W. (1908). *An introduction to social psychology.* London: Methuen.

Merenda, P. F. (1995). International movements in psychology: The major international associations of psychology. *World Psychology, 1,* 27–48.

Mummendey, A., & Mummendey, H. D. (1983). Aggressive behavior of soccer players as social interaction. In J. H. Goldstein (Ed.), *Sports violence* (pp. 111–128). New York: Springer.

National Intelligence Council (2000). *Global trends 2015: A dialogue about the future with nongovernment experts.* Retrieved November 4, 2001, from http://www.cia.gov/cia/publications/globaltrends2015/index.html

Netanyahu, B. (2001). *Fighting terrorism: How democracies can defeat the international terrorist network.* New York: Farrar, Straus and Giroux.

Osborne, R. E. (1996). *Self: An eclectic approach.* Boston: Allyn and Bacon.

Pawlik, K., & d'Ydewalle, G. (1996). Psychology and the global commons: Perspectives of international psychology. *American Psychologist, 51*, 488–495.

Perry, D. G., Perry, L. C., & Rasmussen, P. (1986). Cognitive social mediators of aggression. *Child Development, 57*, 700–711.

Pillar, P. R. (2001). *Terrorism and U.S. foreign policy*. Washington, DC: Brookings Institution Press.

Post, J. M. (1998). Terrorist psycho-logic: Terrorist behavior as a product of psychological forces. In W. Reich (Ed.), *Origins of terrorism: Psychologies, ideologies, theologies, states of mind* (pp. 25–40). Washington, DC: Woodrow Wilson Center Press.

Rapoport, D. C. (1998). Sacred terror: A contemporary example from Islam. In W. Reich (Ed.), *Origins of terrorism: Psychologies, ideologies, theologies, states of mind* (pp. 102–130). Washington, DC: Woodrow Wilson Center Press.

Redding, R. E. (2001). Sociopolitical diversity in psychology: The case for pluralism. *American Psychologist, 56*, 205–215.

Reeves, S. (1999). *The new jackals: Ramzi Yousef, Osama bin Laden and the future of terrorism*. Boston: Northeastern University Press.

Reich, W. (1998). Understanding terrorist behavior: The limits and opportunities of psychological inquiry. In W. Reich (Ed.), *Origins of terrorism: Psychologies, ideologies, theologies, states of mind* (pp. 261–279). Washington, DC: Woodrow Wilson Center Press.

Rosenzweig, M. R. (1999). Continuity and change in the development of psychology around the world. *American Psychologist, 54*, 252–259.

Rosenzweig, M. R., Holtzman, W. H., Sabourin, M., & Bélanger, D. (2000). *History of the International Union of Psychological Science (IUPsyS)*. Philadelphia: Taylor and Francis.

Ross, S., Alexander, I. E., & Basowitz, H. (Eds.) (1966). *International opportunities for advanced training and research in psychology*. Washington, DC: American Psychological Association.

Rutter, M. J. (1997). Nature-nurture integration: The example of antisocial behavior. *American Psychologist, 52*, 390–398.

Schruijer, S. G. L. (1992). On what happens when Dutchmen and Turks violate each other's norms: A perfect match of mutual expectations? In R. DeRidder & R. C. Tripathi, (Eds.), *Norm violation and intergroup relations* (pp. 51–69). Oxford, England: Oxford University Press.

Segal, G. (1993). *The world affairs companion: The essential one-volume guide to global issues*. New York: Simon & Schuster.

Sexton, V. S., & Hogan, J. D. (Eds.) (1992). *International psychology: Views from around the world*. Lincoln: University of Nebraska Press.

Sexton, V. S., & Misiak, H. (Eds.) (1976). *Psychology around the world*. Monterey, CA: Brooks/Cole.

Simmons, C. H., & Mitch, J. R. (1985). Labeling public aggression: When is it terrorism? *The Journal of Social Psychology, 125*, 245–251.

Tedeschi, J. T., & Nesler, M. S. (1993). Grievances: Development and reactions. In R. B. Felsen & J. T. Tedeschi (Eds.), *Aggression and violence: Social interactionist perspectives* (pp. 13–45). Washington, DC: American Psychological Association.

U.S. Department of State (2001). *Patterns of global terrorism 2000* (U.S. Department of State Publication 10822). Washington, DC.

Webb, E. J., Campbell, D. T., Schwartz, R. D., & Sechrest, L. (1966). *Unobtrusive measures: Nonreactive research in the social sciences*. Chicago: Rand McNally College Publishing Company.

Zajonc, R. B. (1968). Attitudinal effects of mere exposure. *Journal of Personality and Social Psychology Monograph Supplement, 9,* 1–27.

NOTE

A grant from Psi Chi, the National Honor Society in Psychology, provided support for some of the research cited in this chapter. I thank Carol J. Davis and Randall E. Osborne for helpful comments on earlier versions of this chapter and Brigitte Vittrup for help in locating some of the references.

4

Terrorism, Social Injustice, and Peace Building

Michael Wessells

The September 11, 2001, attacks and their aftermath are without precedent in U.S. history and have transformed public consciousness, policy discourse, and international action regarding security. In response to the attacks, the United States elevated terrorism to the top security concern and has sought to combat terrorism using a broad spectrum approach that integrates military, financial, intelligence, and law-and-order elements. Public discourse has emphasized military responses, and discussions of peace have either been muted or made to seem irrelevant to the current situation.

From a psychological perspective, a key question is how effective the U.S. approach is likely to be in preventing terrorism. The central thesis of this essay is that the approach is inherently limited because it fails to address the causes of terrorism, which, left unattended, are likely to boost anti-U.S. sentiments and produce new generations of terrorists. It argues that issues of peace building and terrorism prevention are intimately connected and that policy discussions about terrorism need to be enlarged accordingly. The essay begins with a sketch of the psychological atmosphere of the post-attack environment and analyzes why the situation lends itself to predominantly military, punitive responses. Although such responses are valuable, they are too reactive and limited to provide comprehensive terrorism prevention. The essay attempts to show that the present approach fails to address the sources of terrorism, particularly issues of social justice. It suggests that a peace-building focus is needed to complement the current approach and to construct a comprehensive, psychologically informed strategy of terrorism prevention.

A WOUNDED NATION RESPONDS

Prior to the attacks, terrorism had been an important item on the national security agenda, yet it was one among many. Although it garnered some public concern, most Americans had never experienced terrorism directly, and most felt relatively secure inside U.S. borders. Terrorism seemed a distant threat that lacked immediacy, salience, and emotive power. The September 11 attacks exploded the bubble of felt security, left Americans feeling vulnerable at home, and brought into play powerful national and international responses that would forever change Americans' views of safety and security. The attacks brought home in a highly personal manner the fact that Americans are vulnerable even as they go to work on a sunny, fall day and that activities such as taking commercial flights, previously regarded as relatively safe, could be dangerous. Boundaries evaporated, as many wondered by noon, September 11, where the next attacks would occur and who would be the next victims. The fact that the threats came from within led citizens to fear an imminent attack in many locations. In the region where the author lives, gun sales reached record highs on September 11, as many people armed themselves for the siege. The sense of vulnerability was piqued by the attack on the Pentagon itself, which drove a stake through the heart of the tacit assumption that fortress America is invulnerable. After all, the United States is overwhelmingly the world military superpower and exceeds by far the military capabilities of the five next strongest military powers worldwide. Most Americans had assumed that the Pentagon was secure. When it turned out to be quite vulnerable, the lid came off the box of citizen fears. Many different targets, even the White House, seemed at risk.

The attacks were stunning in their scale, their brutality, and the cleverness and coordination with which they were executed. What affected Americans most, however, was the fact that the attacks slaughtered masses of innocents and were perceived as completely unprovoked. Widely, Americans viewed these as horrific, evil deeds that wholly lacked justification, and they felt profoundly wronged and wounded. Consistent with theories of emotional and instrumental aggression (Berkowitz, 1993), it was natural for many Americans to want to strike back, to make the attackers pay, and send a message that attacks would not be allowed to stand with impunity. Policymakers immediately launched a strong push for military response both to punish the attackers and to weaken them and prevent additional attacks. President Bush's immediate declaration of war against terrorism set the tone. Within a week of the attacks, Americans expressed strong support for military action against the presumed perpetrators, assuming at that point that they could be identified. In the weeks following, a mixture of investigation, political rhetoric, and media portrayals targeted the prime suspects as Osama bin Laden, the al-Qaeda network, and the Taliban government of Afghanistan that had given them sanctuary. The hunt was on.

In many respects, the question had never been whether the United States would use military force but how. In fact, the president's choice of a label—"war on terrorism"—prescribed military action, which remains the sine qua non of war. This choice of words was not incidental but part of a deliberate strategy of legitimating military action, mobilizing patriotism, marshaling support for striking back, building collective support amid great pain and suffering, and increasing public will to sacrifice. Bush's strident rhetoric painted a black-and-white picture of the world, announcing to all that "you're either for us or against us." If this drop in cognitive complexity is predictable in times of increasing conflict (Tetlock, 1985), it fit with the view that current world forces pit Good versus Evil, with the United States being the protectors of the Good. This theme was prominent in Bush's State of the Union Address January 29, 2002, in which he deplored countries that harbor terrorists or oppose the United States, calling them an "axis of evil."

Bush's angry, stereotypical rhetoric has reflected the public mood rather well, and his words have not been idle threats. By November 2001, it had become clear the United States would fight the war on terrorism with elite troops, precision-guided munitions, ferocious bombing by B-52s, targeted military attacks against Taliban forces and suspected al-Qaeda hideouts, and use of indiscriminate killers such as daisy cutters and cluster bombs. Bush fought the war in partnership with Great Britain and with support from Central Asian powers such as Russia, India, and Pakistan. U.S. air assaults enabled rapid military conquests by the Tajik- and Uzbek-dominated Northern Alliance, which had long fought against the Pashtun-dominated Taliban. By December 2001, the Taliban had fled Kabul and lost control of most of Afghanistan. While a few cave hideouts remained to be targeted and some Taliban sought to hold out near Kandahar, it was clear the Taliban had suffered a crushing defeat.

Beyond military means, Bush's war on terrorism has entailed building international coalitions against terrorism, vigorous intelligence work, criminal investigations and arrest of suspected terrorists worldwide, and freezing the financial assets of terrorist groups. Within the United States, it has also entailed tightening security of borders and airports, increased vigilance for possible terrorist activity, and, via the USA Patriot Act and Homeland Security legislation, significant liberalization of the means of identifying, tracking, arresting, and prosecuting suspected terrorists. As Bush has stated repeatedly, the war on terrorism must be fought with many different means, not with weapons alone, and it requires a sustained, multilateral effort. Overall, then, Bush's approach is best described as one that combines military, financial, intelligence, and law-and-order elements and that reflects military, political, and economic realities.

Despite its successes and popularity within the United States, the Bush administration's approach has encountered multiple problems. Among these are the failure to capture or kill Osama bin Laden and his highest lieutenants; the unintentional bombing and killing of non-Taliban, Afghan civilians; the failure to capture large numbers of Taliban troops, many of whom deserted, cut their beards, and tried to blend into the civilian society; continuing skirmishes with Taliban troops or their supporters; alleged beatings of prisoners and violations of their rights as stipulated by the Geneva Conventions regarding treatment of prisoners; the possibility that military attacks will harden extremist positions and invite new recruits; the compromising of hard-won liberties within the United States as a result of the new security legislation; the uncritical lumping together of different states into a monolithic "axis of evil" that can be targeted by attacks; and the acceptance of military tribunals that are more characteristic of totalitarian regimes than of democratic states (Dworkin, 2002). These and related problems evoked a steady chorus of stinging criticism from European quarters, including some supposed "coalition" members.

It is not within the scope of the present paper to analyze in depth these and related problems. Rather, it examines whether the approach is comprehensive and well suited to the prevention of terrorism. This question invites analysis of both the psychology of Bush's approach and important psychological sources of terrorism that Bush's approach does not address. This is not to reduce the complex, multidisciplinary issues of terrorism to psychological ones but to use psychological analysis as a means of showing the limits and the reactive nature of Bush's approach.

THE PSYCHOLOGY OF BUSH'S APPROACH

Looking behind Bush's strategy, five features of his war on terrorism are prominent. First, although it is laudably a long-term approach, it is highly reactive in that it is animated by powerful fears and designed to address the most immediate security threats. In view of the strength of public fears, no U.S. president in the post-September 11 context could have survived long without responding rapidly and on a massive scale. With terrorism so salient in the public consciousness, nothing less than a concerted, urgent focus on terrorism would have sufficed. Second, the combination of pain and perceived victimization and injustice created a powerful, immediate push for retribution. Bush, like most Americans, believed the attackers deserved to be killed or punished for their heinous actions, and that failure to strike back would only be interpreted as a sign of weakness that would invite further attacks.

Third, Bush used a potent psychology of enemy imaging (Silverstein, 1989; White, 1984) to support these perceptions of the justice and necessity of U.S. strikes against the presumed attackers and their supporters. Bush's Us–Them thinking and framing of the issues as Good versus Evil helped to set the stage for war. In particular, Bush dehumanized the attackers, portrayed them as implacable enemies who could be dealt with only through force, and created a sense of moral exclusion (Opotow, 1990) that made it easier psychologically to kill the Other while absolving oneself of moral pangs. This analysis recognizes the reality of the enmity toward the United States of Osama bin Laden and the al-Qaeda network. Enemy images, however, go beyond the reality of the threats, play upon and expand fears, create simplistic, self-serving portrayals of the ingroup and the outgroup, and "justify" human rights abuses. In the current context, Bush's demonic imagery has provided a potent tool for mass mobilization and for activating uncritical patriotism. Ironically, as shown later, such enemy imagery is one of the fundamental psychological mechanisms that motivates terrorism and lifts moral restraints against committing horrific acts of violence (Bandura, 1990).

Fourth, Bush's approach is steeped in national pride. Beyond seeking justice, it is a big-stick approach that sends a message that attacks on the United States will be met with severe punishment. It is also coupled with triumphalist rhetoric likely to cement the perception of U.S. arrogance and bullying so prevalent in the Arab world. While pride can help to build solidarity and reflects the fact that Americans have much to be proud of, excessive pride can be blinding (Frank, 1986) and enables excessive reliance on military force as the instrument of choice in handling terrorism. Psychologically, one of the main ways to restore damaged pride following an attack is to unleash a massive attack on one's assailants.

Fifth, Bush's approach reflects black-and-white thinking that carves the world into a titanic struggle between Good and Evil and creates a relatively simple picture of terrorists as bad, aggressive people who must be contained and destroyed. Although Bush has been careful to make some crucial distinctions, notably (and laudably) that the United States is not at war with Islam, a lack of subtlety and nuance is conspicuous in his thinking and rhetoric. For example, Bush's war treats terrorism as a monolithic category when, in fact, there are many different kinds of terrorism that involve different motives, actors, and kinds of organizations (Laqueur, 1987). It is inappropriate to lump terrorist activities conducted as part of a liberation struggle such as the anti-apartheid struggle in South Africa together with those conducted by neo-fascist groups.

Further, a key feature of the war on terrorism has been the paucity of critical scrutiny about what terrorism is. The U.S. State Department (1999) definition of terrorism limits the term to "politically motivated violence perpetrated against noncombatant targets by subnational groups or clandestine agents . . ." Unfortunately, this definition rules out state terrorism, a concept that the United States has avoided in no small part because it wants to deny responsibility for its own wrongdoings (cf. Pilisuk & Wong, Volume 2 of this work). Moreover, there has been little reflection about the moral loading of the label "terrorist." It is denigrating to call a group "terrorist," while other, euphemistic labels such as "freedom fighters" are laudatory and obscure the political violence and terrorism beneath the labels. Among the many subnational groups worldwide that engage in politically motivated violence against noncombatants, on what basis does the United States define some groups but not others as "terrorist"? Too often, the answer is "when their goals and interests do not coincide with those of the United States." Such a self-serving approach is as ill advised as it is intellectually contestable.

Bush's labeling and approach have also enabled uncritical acceptance of pathology models of terrorism. The demonic portrayal of Osama bin Laden as an evil mastermind embodies the "madman" account of terrorism that holds that only pathological, twisted minds could perpetrate such heinous actions as slaughtering masses of innocent people. Despite the public appeal of this view, psychological research has provided scant support for pathology and personality models of terrorism (Cairns, 1996; Crenshaw, 1992, 2000; Rubenstein, 1990; Ruby, 2002). There has been a conspicuous lack of dialogue about a host of other factors—social injustices, historical grievances, radicalized social identities, and extremist ideologies, among others—that fuel terrorism. This lack of dialogue reflects in part constricted, black-

and-white thinking, but it is also part of a politically motivated strategy Bush uses to influence public opinion. If the perpetrators were not madmen or fanatics whose views could be dismissed by rational, peace-loving people, one might have to admit or at least explore the possibility that they had some legitimate complaints against the United States or that their hatred of the United States was at least understandable even if their actions were thoroughly repugnant and contemptible.

To prevent terrorism, one must first understand it. In this spirit, the next section shows that social injustices have played an important role in inflaming hatreds of the United States. Although social injustice such as political oppression is widespread in Arab and Islamic societies, the emphasis in this essay is on the injustices, real and perceived, that help to create the sense of "just cause" that many feel in the struggle against the United States and other Western powers and that helped to motivate or enable the September 11 attacks.

SOCIAL INJUSTICE

Social injustice takes many different forms and consists of a mixture of objective and subjective elements. Objectively, it includes human rights violations, direct victimization, political and social oppression, and structural violence through preventable failure to meet basic human needs as a result of conditions such as poverty (Galtung, 1996; Gurr, 1993). Subjectively, it includes perceived transgressions, inferences about who the transgressors are, attributions of hostile intent, perceptions of entitlement, perceived (relative) deprivation and devaluation at the hands of the Other, perceptions of unequal treatment, changes in the scope of justice, and perceived fairness of process and outcome in the handling of conflict, among others (Christie, Wagner, & Winter, 2001; Deutsch, 1985, 2000; Messick, 1993; Mikula, 1993; Rubin, Pruitt, & Kim, 1994). Although these objective and subjective elements are completely interwoven, the analysis below emphasizes the subjective since views of political conflict and terrorism are socially constructed and perceptions of objective injustices are often as influential as the objective conditions themselves. Ultimately, perceptions define one's subjective reality and shape behavior.

This section outlines some of the primary perceived grievances and injustices but makes no attempt to present different sides or to identify where the author agrees or disagrees with the perceptions described. Rather, the attempt is to understand Arab and Islamic perceptions that ignite anger and hatred, political violence, and terrorism. Arab and Islamic perceptions are treated together since they are interrelated and mutually influential, yet the author recognizes the significant differences in perspective within the Arab world and between Arab peoples and the Islamic peoples of Central and South Asia.

Arab and Islamic peoples perceive many injustices in regard to U.S. behavior and motives, but none are more salient than the mistreatment of the Palestinians. On a per capita basis, Israel has received more U.S. economic and military aid than any other nation. Israel's special relationship with the United States has enabled it to become the top military, economic, and political power in the Middle East, capable of defeating any combination of Arab attackers. U.S. support for Israel, guided by interests such as protecting access to oil, strengthening democracy, and, previously, containing the spread of communism, has come with relatively few strings attached. In particular, no U.S. administration has made aid contingent upon the cessation of Israeli violations of Palestinians' human rights and international law. The United States has allowed the brutal Israeli occupation, which violates numerous aspects of international law (Gerner, 1994; Khouri, 1985). Under the occupation, large numbers of Palestinian youth have been arrested and detained, and many have been beaten or tortured. Many have witnessed deaths and violence, experienced losses of family members or friends, and seen presumed peace processes such as the Oslo Accords fail to deliver the expected independent Palestinian state, to which Palestinians feel entitled. Through direct victimization, the infliction of daily humiliations, and institutionalized inequities regarding necessities such as water, education, and health care, the occupation has provided a fertile bed for growing new generations of angry, disaffected youth increasingly inclined to use violence as an instrument of achieving liberation.

Nor has the United States taken a strong position against Israeli settlements in the West Bank of the Occupied Territories, which are highly inflammatory and typically are accompanied by land seizures, evictions, and local repression. The United States has not expressed strong opposition to the (at time of writing) more recent Israeli practices of assassinating suspected terrorists, sending tanks into Palestinian neighborhoods, and keeping Yasir Arafat under house arrest. In addition to feeling displaced and dispossessed, Palestinians feel abandoned and perceive few positive alternatives for achieving their objectives. Amid their hopelessness and despair, frustration and rage run strong, and this encourages young Palestinians to turn increasingly to terrorism. Although there is nothing intrinsic in Arab or Islamic culture that incites terrorism, the Palestinian situation makes terrorism seem intelligible, even justified to many.

Many Arabs believe that the United States applies a double standard in dealing with Arabs and Israelis. For example, the United States deplores human rights violations committed by Arab regimes but looks the other way in regard to Israeli violations. Why, many Arabs ask, did the United States respond so stridently to Saddam Hussein's violations of international law but has never held Israel accountable for its violations of international law? In addition, many regard it as hypocritical that the United States criticizes the human rights record of many Arab regimes when, during the Cold War, the United States backed highly repressive regimes in Indonesia, the Philippines, Angola, South Africa, Guatemala, El Salvador, and Nicaragua, among others (Blum, 1995).

Arab and Islamic peoples also see profound injustices associated with U.S. interventions. When the United States attacked Iraq in 1991, it bombed electrical facilities, knocking out water purification devices and causing a sharp rise in diarrheal diseases and sharply increased rates of infant and child mortality. By amplifying poverty and already severe shortages of basic necessities, U.S. sanctions against Iraq are believed to have resulted in the deaths of more than five hundred thousand civilians. This situation, together with the deplorable conditions in many Palestinian refugee camps, has encouraged the view prevalent in the Arab world that, for the United States, Arab lives have little value.

Further, U.S. intervention is often viewed as an instrument of imperialism. During the Gulf War, the United States increased sharply its military presence in countries such as Saudi Arabia, and it has not demilitarized to prewar levels. Although bin Laden has shamelessly exploited this and related U.S. military deployments in the region, such activities have enabled perceptions of U.S. imperialism even among moderate Arabs. Perceptions of imperialism are viewed as having economic roots, as evident in the United States' relationship with Saudi Arabia. Even the Afghanistan chapter of the "war on terrorism" is seen as part of a wider pattern of economic imperialism. It is no secret that the U.S. government needs oil, wants badly to harvest Central Asia's abundance of oil and gas resources, and seeks to build oil and gas pipelines from Turkmenistan into Pakistan, through Afghanistan (Rashid, 2000). U.S. activities in the region are perceived by Arab and Islamic peoples as the contemporary extension of "The Great Game" (Rashid, 2000). In this context, even humanitarian aid is suspect since it is viewed as a carrier of exploitative, economic interests and actors. These perceptions play into wider perceptions of the United States as arrogant, bullyish, and inclined to act unilaterally and with little sensitivity to the needs, values, and situation of other countries. The United States is seen as meddling in or controlling the affairs of others when it wishes, and using its military and economic strength to impose its will on others.

The current intervention in Afghanistan also has enormous potential for fueling perceptions of injustice. No doubt Taliban supporters and other radicals in areas such as Kandahar and Pakistan perceive the U.S. attacks as unjustified and as a reflection of the U.S. brand of evil. More moderate Afghans, most of whom are pleased to see the Taliban expelled from power, may also have negative perceptions. The large-scale use of cluster bombs, which leave unexploded bomblets (approximately 5 percent of those dropped) that tend to detonate when picked up by children or moved amid rubble, strengthens perceptions that the United States has too little concern about killing civilians. Attack and killing of civilians has been reported repeatedly and on a widespread basis (Traynor, 2002).

Accidental bombings and killings of civilians who had been suspected of being Taliban leaders or fighters but who turned out to be neither have sparked much anger. It is always difficult to substantiate allegations of such events—the perceptions surrounding these events can be as important as the events themselves. To date, the U.S. government has been reluctant to admit mistakes, much less to apologize or to offer reparations. These actions inflame anger and strengthen negative attributions about the behavior of the U.S. government. In addition, Afghans remember well that U.S. aid supported the *mujahideen* in the anti-Soviet struggle but that once the Soviets had withdrawn, the United States left the area with a sea of weaponry and in a power vacuum, both of which invited the next vicious round of armed conflict. Such behavior invites perceptions that the U.S. government has little genuine concern for the well-being of Afghans.

Objective social injustice is also prevalent in the Arab and Islamic world, where large populations live in preventable, chronic poverty and basic needs for food and health care go unmet. Afghanistan itself is a stunning case in point. A recent joint assessment conducted by the Asian Development Bank, the United Nations Development Programme, and the World Bank (2002) reported that the life expectancy of Afghans is only forty-four years; approximately 25 percent of children die under the age of five years; drought, land mines, and war have created widespread hunger and food insecurity; and only 12 percent of the population has adequate sanitation. That people are subject to radicalization and political manipulation in such circumstances is hardly surprising. Similarly, in Palestinian refugee camps in Jordan, for example, people live in abject poverty, in extreme crowding, and without adequate sanitation. For young people who grow up under such conditions and with the humiliations and hopelessness of their situation, violence may seem to be the only option for achieving their objectives. Both cases fit the old saw that hunger breeds desperation.

With the increased globalization of the economy and communications, however, objective conditions stimulate subjective elements such as a felt sense of relative deprivation. Many Arab and Muslim peoples are acutely aware of the global wealth gap and the fact that over one billion people live in absolute poverty, while people in the United States enjoy what is by global standards enormous prosperity. More than 1.2 billion people, 44 percent of whom live in South Asia, live on less that $1 a day (World Bank, 2001). Further, in the richest twenty countries in the world, the average income is thirty-seven times that in the poorest twenty countries (World Bank, 2001). Sensing the injustice of the gap between their own poverty and U.S. wealth, they wonder how people can live in relative opulence while watching the rest of the world struggle in poverty and doing too little to provide relief and development assistance. This gap feeds perceptions of Americans as greedy, materialistic, and exploitative. For some people, it apparently also invited actual strikes against the perceived sources of wealth and financial control, symbolized in the twin towers of the World Trade Center.

The links between social injustice and terrorism are complex, and simplistic, mechanistic accounts should be avoided. For one thing, there are different kinds of social injustice, and each may have distinctive effects. Direct victimization such as personal attack or torture, for example, may evoke responses of rage and anger that correlate highly with intent to use violence to address one's grievances. In contrast, living in chronic poverty may have relatively weak correlation with the tendency to engage in terrorist activity. In fact, most people who live in chronic poverty do not engage in terrorism. Engagement in terrorism stems from a mixture of social conditions, activities by terrorist groups, and personal orientations, including cognitive construals of one's role, situation, and responsibilities (Bandura, 1990). Nevertheless, social injustices create conditions ripe for the rise of and support for terrorist groups, and they give terrorist leaders such as bin Laden a strong hand to play. The risks of terrorism become even greater when social injustices combine with radical ideology and social identities.

SOCIAL IDENTITY

Social identity confers a sense of meaning and place in the world. It designates both who one is and who one is not, defines one's perceived roots, increases one's sense of self-worth, and creates a sense of belongingness with others who share common values, heritage, and practices. When social identities are threatened or identity groups feel oppressed, attacked, or wounded, the risks of radicalization and violence increase sharply (Volkan, 1997). The upheavals of modernity, power realignments, and globalization have created profound threats to social identity among Islamic peoples. The implications become visible only when viewed in historic perspective.

In Islamic societies, religion is the very basis of social identity and the foundation of communal organization, personal practice, and legitimate authority (Lewis, 1995). Unlike Western societies, which have largely secular worldviews and values or that separate state from organized religion, many Islamic societies view religion as the organizing principle of government as well as of society and personal life. Material acquisition and hedonism have little place in Islam, which stresses right conduct over belief. It is in practices such as praying five times daily, fasting during Ramadan, abstinence, and other positive obligations that one lives in accord with the Koran and worships Allah. Through daily practices, Muslims derive a sense of meaning, connection, and salvation. Islam, like other great religions of the world, encourages peaceful coexistence with members of other religions. In the most literal sense, the term *jihad* means "striving in the path of God" (Lewis, 1995, p. 233). Whereas some interpreters of the Koran have emphasized the importance of internal struggle and purity, others have said or implied that external struggle is justified once the internal struggle has been completed (Lewis, 1995; Rapoport, 1990). These competing views and gray areas are highly incongruent with the simplistic referral by the Western media to *jihad* as "holy war" in the most literal sense. As evidenced in the Christian Crusades, any great religion can be appropriated politically as a justification or instrument of war.

Although Islam once dominated much of the world and for nearly a millennium brought high achievements in such areas as science, mathematics, and medicine, Islamic domination declined over centuries through conflict with the West, failures to keep up with Western technology, and internal political and economic practices, among others (Lewis, 1995). If this decline threatened Islamic pride and views of Islam as the natural world leader, even greater threat came from internal challenges to Islam. Stated bluntly, contact with the West brought increased secularization and threatened to undermine the purity of the faith. In the late eighteenth and early nineteenth centuries, this challenge evoked the rise of a radical order of Islam, the Wahhabis. Puritanical and militant, they sought to unite Muslims in the struggle against European invaders, and they had conquered much of the Arabian peninsula by the end of the eighteenth century. Their radicalism eventually failed to spread, but it nonetheless set a pattern wherein challenges to Islam would be met by radicalism, militancy, and local religious leadership in the fight against Western influence (Lewis, 1995).

Western ascendancy and hegemony, coupled with the rise of transnational corporations and the spread of Western culture by movies, television, computers, and other media, have provided enormous threats to Islamic identities. Western goods, images, and music have powerful, seductive appeal to young people. But Western culture, ideas, and goods are equally regarded as threatening and heathen by Islamic authorities, popular leaders, and many parents. Externally, the threat is one of economic imperialism, which creates dependency while relegating one's own culture and practices to secondary status. This dependency enables political and military domination by the West. Internally, the threat is that Western values will be internalized, traditional authority structures weakened, and Islam and Islamic societies will erode from within, as if fulfilling the post-Enlightenment prophecy that religion will die. Strong adherents to Islamic faith feel this as a deep, personal threat and see the loss of power and religious purity as having profound spiritual, moral, social, political, and cultural implications.

This context and set of perceived threats provide ripe conditions for the rise of militarized, radicalized social identities steeped in religious extremism and apocalyptic ideologies (Juergensmeyer, 2000). Although Osama bin Laden is not a legitimate Islamic leader or scholar, he sculpted a cosmic view of the Good values and forces of Islam fighting against the Evil values and forces of the West in general and the United States in particular. Bin Laden's attraction to many in the Islamic world stems in part from the social injustices discussed above and from an abiding sense that the world has gone wrong and that a new way is required to move forward. It plays upon the personal and collective disempowerment, despair, and threat felt by many Islamic peoples in the face of U.S. domination. Radical Islamic leaders such as Ayatollah Khomeini and self-proclaimed Islamic leaders such as bin Laden manipulate and exploit this felt sense of lost power, declining prestige, and threat to social identity. What they lack in ability to make durable improvements in people's lives they compensate for in fiery rhetoric that restores the moral authority of Islam, recovers eroding identity, promises eternal salvation, and calls for sacrifice in meeting the challenges of the U.S. infidel.

Bin Laden's spiritual appeal encourages terrorism in multiple respects. It gives moral sanction to acts that would otherwise be regarded as horrific and immoral. Equally important, it provides divine support for terrorist activities, assuring the attackers that they are martyrs and will reap divine rewards. There is no reason to fear death, for one's sacrifice one will receive eternal rewards in the afterlife. Saturated with divine sanction, the conflict transcends worldly politics and ordinary concepts of right and wrong. Extraordinary measures and actions are necessary, and Allah will reward those who make the ultimate sacrifice. Spiritual purity will be restored and Islamic identity, order, and life will be strengthened. In this manner, radicalized, apocalyptic ideology encourages and justifies the most heinous acts of terrorism. It wraps acts of violence in a blanket of holiness and promises deliverance for the perpetrators.

If this ideology seems an enormously large pill to swallow, one needs to remember to whom it appeals—those who feel downtrodden, disempowered, frustrated, and hopeless. Regrettably, the combined pressures of identity threat and life under conditions of extreme poverty and social injustice render this view not only plausible but attractive to many. The Taliban leadership knew this and exploited it through a highly refined, if objectionable, system of political socialization. The Taliban transformed an already ailing educational system into a system of *madrasahs* that presumably provided religious instruction but in fact taught hatred of the United States alongside the Koran, which does not prescribe hatred. The *madrasahs* provided a stream of new recruits for the Taliban war against the Northern Alliance (Rashid, 2000), and they are widely regarded as a likely source of terrorists. The Taliban, many of whom were themselves products of the *madrasah* system, used the *madrasahs* to brainwash a generation of impoverished Afghans. Using harsh punishments, they kept tight control over communications, the media, what was read, and what was taught. They succeeded in robbing a generation of education, banning all girls and women from the formal education system, and preparing young people to believe their propaganda and highly distorted view of the West.

A tragic irony is that the United States had supported the *madrasahs* as part of its support for the *mujahideen* against the former Soviet Union. The United States had also provided large amounts of weaponry, including Stinger missiles that enabled uneducated Afghan warriors to shoot down sophisticated Soviet aircraft. Youth indoctrination and widespread militarization are potent ingredients in the recipe for political violence (Machel, 2001; Wessells, 2002), which often shades into terrorism. Comprehensive approaches to terrorism prevention must take this into account.

PEACE BUILDING AND TERRORISM PREVENTION

The preceding analysis suggests that reactive, highly militaristic approaches such as Bush's are unlikely to succeed in preventing terrorism. The fundamental problem of Bush's approach is that it applies military means to problems that that require use of other means. Bush's approach assumes that terrorism will be prevented if 1) terrorist leaders and networks are damaged or destroyed through military and financial action, penetration and subterfuge, and related actions; 2) terrorist plans are detected and thwarted through superior intelligence and tough law enforcement; and 3) terrorists are pursued relentlessly and punished severely, thereby avoiding impunity and deterring prospective terrorist acts. Although this approach may be useful in punishing and limiting terrorism, it does not constitute comprehensive prevention since it fails to address the sources of terrorism.

To provide comprehensive prevention, one must complement military and other approaches outlined above with careful efforts to reduce the lure of terrorism and "drain the swamp" by limiting the flow of people into terrorist circles and activities. These efforts entail peace building that is as systemic as are the causes of terrorism and the conditions that enable it to flourish. At the macrosocial level, peace building entails the reduction of inequities and oppressive policies and institutional arrangements; the protection of human rights; the containment and weakening of extremist ideologies; the reduction of militarism, racism, and sexism; the satisfaction of basic human needs; and the creation of social systems that enable political empowerment and participation, support intergroup tolerance and cooperation, and encourage nonviolent management and resolution. At the microsocial level, peace building entails the reduction of stereotypes and dehumanized enemy images; encouragement of caring, empathy, and tolerance; development of positive values, cognitive flexibility, intercultural understanding, and constraints on killing and mistreatment of members of outgroups; and support for life skills that enable meaningful participation within one's cultural and social system and that meet basic needs without recourse to violence.

Within this broad, peace-building framework, one can identify numerous urgent priorities that ought to be part of comprehensive prevention efforts. First, the top priority is the reduction of the social injustices that enable or motivate terrorism. To begin with, the United States must end its policy of supporting repressive regimes. Often, this has been done out of short-term interests. In the long run, however, such support undermines U.S. credibility, generates animosity toward the United States, and reduces the authenticity of legitimate U.S. complaints toward and actions against those who commit heinous rights violations. An important lesson from U.S. foreign policy over the past several decades is that decisions guided by immediate security concerns and short-term gains often turn out to have long-term, adverse consequences that considerably outweigh the short-term gains. If support for oppressive regimes has seemed a necessary evil in the past, it is time to recalculate the costs and benefits in light of what we know now and to rethink the policy of supporting regimes that violate human rights on a massive scale. In practical terms, this means supporting Israel's right to exist and to defend itself while also holding it accountable for massive rights violations, just as the United States holds the Palestinians accountable for their massive rights violations. Ending the double standard and applying common benchmarks to both Arab and non-Arab states is part of building social justice.

A second, related priority is to do much more to meet basic human needs, reducing chronic, preventable poverty and structural violence. Amid widespread hunger and desperation, people will remain susceptible to political manipulation by demagogues and terrorists such as bin Laden. If Asians and other peoples suffer horrible living conditions and very short life spans in full view of U.S. opulence, the situation will be ripe for hostility toward the United States. Already, many people wonder why the United States gives so little in proportion to what it is capable of giving. In this respect, there is enormous need of additional support for humanitarian relief and long-term development in countries where people face very difficult living conditions. Both relief and development approaches should emphasize empowerment, inclusive local participation, and strengthening of civic groups, all of which help to stabilize communities and to prevent political violence and its ally, terrorism.

Third, the United States must end its practice of being the world's number one weapons supplier (Hartung, 1994). The hazards of that practice should be clear from cases such as the U.S. supply of weapons to Iraq in the 1980s during its war against Iran. The short-term policy of arming opponents of Ayatollah Khomeini's radical, anti-U.S. regime backfired badly, as Iraq's enhanced military power enabled Saddam Hussein's invasion of Kuwait, his crushing of internal dissent by Kurdish people, and ultimately, his arrogant defiance of the United States. Too often, U.S. military support has propped up dictators who eventually turned against the United States. Further, weapons trading and supply supports militarization, which in turn provides fertile soil for political violence and terrorism. The flooding of Afghanistan with weaponry helped to militarize the country, enabled ethnic fighting, and contributed to the instability that eventually made many people happy when the Taliban came to power and established strict law and order (Rashid, 2000). In developing countries, where defense budgets may constitute as much as 40 percent of the gross domestic product, militarization drains very scarce economic resources away from health, sanitation, food security, and education. The resulting hardships and failures to meet basic needs help to perpetuate violence and instability, in which armed opposition groups, terrorists, and militias flourish.

Education, a basic right of all children as guaranteed under the United Nations Convention on the Rights of the Child and a primary source of social capital, is the fourth priority. Ignorance heightens receptivity to demonic images of the United States and enables brainwashing of the kind that occurred in the radicalized *madrasahs* run by the Taliban in Afghanistan and Pakistan. As noted previously, the failure to educate people leaves young people, a society's most precious resource, without positive life options, means of earning a living, or hope. Together with a sense of victimization, hopelessness and despair encourage participation in terrorism and other forms of political violence. The Taliban exclusion of girls and women from public education constituted a massive violation of human rights and extended a system that institutionalized inequity and injustice.

To help prevent terrorism, education should go beyond traditional subjects such as language, mathematics, and science, all of which are highly valuable. Traditional methodologies oriented toward memorization and teacher authority need to be enriched or replaced by pedagogies that empower students and build skills and habits of critical thinking. Peace education is needed to increase tolerance and interethnic understanding, to counteract demonized images of the Other, to teach skills of nonviolent conflict resolution, and to strengthen a local culture of peace and human rights. Nonformal, public education is a vital component of a comprehensive approach. Radio and other public media should be used to convey effective, accurate messages about the United States, the value of nonviolent approaches to handling conflict, and the importance of respecting human rights and the value of human life. These steps will require the construction of policies conducive to open communications and flows of information.

The fifth priority is to encourage inclusive political participation and democratization. To support democratization is not to impose Western-style democracy but to empower people for participation, to enable political pluralism and elected government, and to move beyond systems that allow totalitarian rule or control by small power elites (Montiel & Wessells, 2001). This is vital for creating open systems, replacing hopelessness with voice and empowerment, and preventing dicta-torships that harbor or breed terrorists. Although this is a difficult task in Islamic societies having long traditions of authoritative rule, one should also remember that even the regime of Ayatollah Khomeini was eventually replaced by a more moderate, participatory government and leadership. One of the keys to democrati-zation is the strengthening of norms and processes of nonviolent conflict manage-ment that enable the peaceful transfer of power. This requires encouragement of the values and skills of nonviolent handling of conflict at all levels, from the family to the societal.

Collectively, these priorities and others related to them require a significant reorientation of U.S. funding and approach to the prevention of terrorism. Although the military approach should not be scrapped, it should not be the main-stay of prevention efforts. If U.S. commitment to prevention is strong, at least as much funding and attention should be given to these peace-building priorities as to the predominantly military priorities of Bush's war on terrorism. The magnitude of these peace-building tasks suggests that the task of terrorism prevention is consider-ably greater than the United States and other nations have envisioned or undertak-en so far. It may prove to be impossible to prevent all terrorism, but both security and moral considerations in the current situation require nothing less than the con-struction of the most comprehensive approaches possible.

REFERENCES

Asian Development Bank, United Nations Development Programme, & World Bank (2002). *Afghanistan: Preliminary needs assessment for recovery and reconstruction.* Washing-ton, DC: World Bank.

Bandura, A. (1990). Mechanisms of moral disengagement. In W. Reich (Ed.), *Origins of ter-rorism: Psychologies, ideologies, theologies, states of mind* (pp. 161–191). Cambridge, Eng-land: Woodrow Wilson International Center for Scholars and Cambridge University Press.

Berkowitz, L. (1993). *Aggression.* New York: McGraw-Hill.

Blum, W. (1995). *Killing hope: U.S. military and CIA interventions since World War II.* Monroe, ME: Common Courage Press.

Cairns, E. (1996). *Children and political violence.* Cambridge, England: Blackwell.

Christie, D., Wagner, R., & Winter, D. (Eds.) (2001). *Peace, conflict, and violence: Peace psychology for the 21st century.* Upper Saddle River, NJ: Prentice Hall.

Crenshaw, M. (1992). Current research on terrorism: The academic perspective. *Studies in Conflict and Terrorism, 15*, 1–11.

Crenshaw, M. (2000). The psychology of terrorism: An agenda for the 21st century. *Politi-cal Psychology, 21*, 405–420.

Deutsch, M. (1985). *Distributive justice: A social psychological perspective.* New Haven, CT: Yale University Press.

Deutsch, M. (2000). Justice and conflict. In M. Deutsch & P. Coleman (Eds.), *The hand-book of conflict resolution* (pp. 41–64). San Francisco: Jossey-Bass.

Dworkin, R. (2002). The threat to patriotism. *New York Review of Books, 49*, 44–49.

Frank, J. (1986). The role of pride. In R. K. White (Ed.), *Psychology and the prevention of nuclear war* (pp. 220–226). New York: New York University Press.

Galtung, J. (1996). *Peace by peaceful means.* London: Sage.

Gerner, D. (1994). *One land, two peoples* (2nd ed.). Boulder, CO: Westview.

Gurr, T. R. (1993). *Minorities at risk.* Washington, DC: United States Institute of Peace.

Hartung, W. D. (1994). *And weapons for all.* New York: HarperCollins.

Juergensmeyer, M. (2000). *Terror in the mind of God: The global rise of religious violence.* Berkeley, CA: University of California Press.

Khouri, F. J. (1985). *The Arab-Israeli dilemma* (3rd ed.). Syracuse, NY: Syracuse University Press.

Laqueur, W. (1987). Reflections on terrorism. In W. Laqueur & Y. Alexander (Eds.), *The terrorism reader* (pp. 378–392). New York: Penguin.

Laqueur, W. (1999). *The new terrorism.* New York: Oxford University Press.

Lewis, B. (1995). *The Middle East.* New York: Touchstone.

Machel, G. (2001). *The impact of war on children.* Cape Town, South Africa: David Philip.

Messick, D. M. (1993). Equality as a decision heuristic. In B. A. Mellers & J. Baron (Eds.), *Psychological perspectives on justice: Theory and applications* (pp. 11–31). New York: Cambridge University Press.

Mikula, G. (1993). On the experience of injustice. In W. Stroebe & M. Hewstone (Eds.), *European review of social psychology* (Vol. 4, pp. 232–244). Chichester, England: Wiley.

Montiel, C., & Wessells, M. (2001). Democratization, psychology, and the construction of cultures of peace. *Peace and Conflict: Journal of Peace Psychology, 7,* 119–129.

Opotow, S. (1990). Moral exclusion and injustice: An introduction. *Journal of Social Issues, 46,* 1–20.

Pilisuk, M., & Wong, A. (2002). State terrorism: When the perpetrator is a government. In C. E. Stout (Ed.), *Psychology of terrorism* (Vol. 2). Westport, CT: Praeger.

Rapoport, D. (1990). Sacred terror: A contemporary example from Islam. In W. Reich (Ed.), *Origins of terrorism: Psychologies, ideologies, theologies, states of mind* (pp. 103–130). Cambridge, England: Woodrow Wilson International Center for Scholars and Cambridge University Press.

Rashid, A. (2000). *Taliban.* New Haven, CT: Yale University Press.

Rubenstein, R. E. (1990). The noncauses of terrorism. In C. W. Kegley, Jr. (Ed.), *International terrorism* (pp. 127–134). New York: St. Martin's.

Rubin, J. Z., Pruitt, D. G., & Kim, S. H. (1994). *Social conflict* (2nd ed.). New York: McGraw-Hill.

Ruby, C. L. (2002). Are terrorists mentally deranged? *Analyses of Social Issues and Public Policy, 15*–26.

Silverstein, B. (1989). Enemy images: The psychology of U.S. attitudes and cognitions regarding the Soviet Union. *American Psychologist, 44,* 903–913.

Tetlock, P. E. (1985). Integrative complexity of American and Soviet foreign policy rhetoric: A time-series analysis. *Journal of Personality and Social Psychology, 49,* 1565–1585.

Traynor, I. (2002, February 14). Afghans still dying as air strikes go on. But no one is counting. *The Guardian Weekly,* p. 1.

U.S. State Department (1999). Patterns of global terrorism: 1999. Retrieved from http://www.state.gov/www/global/terrorism/1999report/intro.html.

Volkan, V. (1997). *Bloodlines.* New York: Farrar, Straus and Giroux.

Wessells, M. (2002). Recruitment of children as soldiers in sub-Saharan Africa: An ecological analysis. In L. Mjoset & S. Van Holde (Eds.), *The comparative study of conscription in the armed forces (Comparative Social Research, Vol. 20)* (pp. 237–254). Amsterdam, Netherlands: Elsevier.

White, R. K. (1984). *Fearful warriors: A psychological profile of U.S.-Soviet relations.* New York: Free Press.

World Bank (2001). *World development report 2000/2001.* New York: Oxford University Press.

NOTE

I wish to thank Aaron Wessells for his insightful critique and suggestions regarding an earlier draft of this chapter.

Part II:
Models Focused on Youth

5

Terror and Violence Perpetrated by Children

Trevor Stokes

How does the mind of a child develop in a way that leads to terror and violence?

Why would a child shoot another child?

Why would a child fly a plane into a tall building?

There is usually a complex weave of factors that lead to such aggression toward oneself and toward others. Generally speaking, the cause lies in a combination of susceptibility to aberrant influences, development of maladaptive repertoires of behavior, and control by currently functional motivational factors (Bijou & Baer, 1978; Stokes & Baer, 1977; Stokes, Mowery, Dean, & Hoffman, 1997). Aggression by children often has a longer history than is initially apparent to a casual observer. Childhood aggression toward oneself and toward others is seen in most children—both active children and calm children. It is the development and moderation of the dysfunctional circumstances and the aberrant repertoires of behavior across childhood that we need to consider, especially now in a world in which terror and violence are a serious threat.

Terror, violence, and aggression perpetrated by children challenge communities to provide better programs of monitoring and interception of dysfunctional childhood histories and repertoires. It is imperative that there be a fair, reasonable, and effective protection against the escalation of aggression in its developmental trajectory across the lifespan.

Some models of intervention have concentrated on the profiling of aberrant histories and antisocial behavior of children and youth considered at risk for extreme actions of violence. These models identify children likely to continue in their upward trajectory of aggression and violence. They also over-identify the number of children likely to engage in subsequent, more serious violations of their community's standards of conduct and the legal standards of societies. Some programs have focused on evident repertoires of behaviors constituting aggression, while recommending community responsibility, conscientious monitoring of youth activities, and a smartly targeted level of interception of dysfunctional circumstances and repertoires.

This chapter will consider the characteristic factors related to the development of aggression and actions of terror by children.

CLOSE TO HOME

Let me begin my discussion by looking around close to home. Not so long ago, I took my son to school on a pleasant, sunny, spring day in Tampa, Florida. He wanted to listen to the Backstreet Boys, so we replaced the Jewel recording that my daughter had left in the car's CD player and let the Backstreet Boys sing for us. My son likes school—as I did—and we make a game out of guessing where we will be in the line of cars waiting to drop children off when the school gate opens. We like to be first or second; then we sit and chat. Nevertheless, work had delayed me that morning, so we were fifteen minutes later than usual and ended up fifth in line—but happily on time, just a few minutes early.

It was a special academic day: A day for schoolwide testing using standardized assessments. These tests have become popular in this age of educational accountability. My son and I sat there in the car and chatted for a few minutes about how the math problems on the test would be easy. We both smiled and I told him as he got out of the car: "Do your best and have a good day."

Standardized achievement testing was a timely topic. The evening before, my son and I had seen a related movie. A crazed former government official who had been a school principal had taken over a neighborhood elementary school, using arms and violence. It was an interesting movie for both children and adults. The violence-prone principal villain had four goals: to control the world's weather, to end school summer holidays, to prevent children from ever doing standardized tests again, and, thereby, to improve the academic performance of students to an internationally competitive level.

I need not dwell on the villain's logic, but wish instead to consider the issues of violence. In the movie, the threat to the school was averted by an observant young student who was the first to notice that something was not right. He refused to allow his concerns to be pushed aside by inept community officials and persisted in his attempts to retake the school with the assistance of fellow students. His efforts were not quite successful. It was not until he later enlisted the aid of the current principal, whom he knew and respected, and who in fact cared for his students, that the tide of the battle for control of the school was turned in a favorable direction. Finally, after united and aggressive action by the students and teachers, the villains were overthrown, the day was saved, and the children were reunited with their adoring parents, who had no idea what had been happening but were happy with the outcome at the end of the day.

So that morning, the morning after watching the movie, we drove to school listening to the mainstream music preferences of eight-year-old children. Sometimes I ask my children to leave their CDs in the car so I can listen to what they like. (I also ask children to tell me about their interests and culture—Pokémon, Rugrats, Harry Potter, Lord of the Rings, Star Wars, E.T., Spiderman, or whatever is on their minds.) It is good for me to keep up, and it helps my rapport with children if I can talk about their world in an informed manner.

As often happens, these media events made me think about the perspective of young children in modern society. The Backstreet Boys and *Recess: School's Out*, a violent and inspirational cartoon movie, were both compelling media presentations with great popularity among children. I was not sure all the themes were well understood. One song by the Backstreet Boys heralded the advantages and thrill of being bad boys. *Recess* depicted sinister violence at school and its overthrow by caring and powerful counterviolence. It was all for entertainment purposes, of course, and for a little profit. These themes are not new to us—they have played many times before in this generation, in previous generations, and will again in future generations.

All of this plays against the backdrop of the real news on television. There had been many high-profile school shootings in the past few years, most notoriously at Columbine High School near Denver, Colorado, where thirteen were killed and twenty injured in a violent attack by two students who had a well-developed plan of slaughter. There had been the September 2001 terrorist attack with hijacked planes on the World Trade Center in New York, on the Pentagon in Washington, and ending in a field in Pennsylvania, resulting in thousands of innocent fatalities and casualties. There had been the death of a child who flew a plane into the Bank of America building in Tampa, Florida. There was plenty of violent reality TV quite apart from the movie theater.

So, it was easy to sit in my car at the neighborhood schoolhouse door contemplating these violent events of life in modern society. It was easy to minimize the likelihood that anything would happen to me or my family. After all, I live about thirty miles from U.S. Armed Forces Central Command (Centcom) headquarters, the nerve center for the war in Afghanistan. I could comfort myself by remembering that the immediate effects of an atomic bomb dropped there may dissipate before reaching me. I could also remember that on that fateful morning of September 11, I was within ten miles of Centcom. Even so, I was not reluctant to leave my child at his school. I did not fear for his life. It was a good neighborhood school and a nice community. I was not reluctant to live in Tampa. It was a vibrant and pleasant community.

Nevertheless, things do happen, don't they? Usually they happen somewhere else, in a different neighborhood. Yet, sometimes they happen close to home. Not so long ago, at my daughter's high school at the end of a school day, a student wearing a full ski mask opened the door of her classroom, looked around the class, closed the door, and disappeared. Not so long ago, in a nearby high school, a student brought a gun to school. While peers were handing it around in the parking lot, it fired accidentally and a student was killed. Not so long ago, the local school system was receiving an average of more than one bomb threat a week.

What is happening in our communities? Is there a link between childhood anti-social behavior and subsequent aggression? Yes, there is. Those childhood dysfunctional circumstances and maladaptive repertoires should ring an alarm bell with global implications. It is not a time to be complacent.

The specifics of extremes of aggression and violence and terror may vary from country to country. For example, guns, knives, rocks, bottles, and planes may be available in some places and not others. There is no doubt that there is aggression in communities everywhere. What changes from place to place is the availability of weapons and the motivation to use them in acts of terror and violence. So, while the alarm is global, the call for action to manage escalating aggression needs to be at a local level.

If the level of aggression, violence, and terror can reasonably be predicted to increase further, we must examine whether we have learned how to best contain it. Can our current knowledge be applied effectively to protect our children and to protect ourselves? Surely we already know that we don't want community violence or communities that perpetuate violence. Can we apply what we do know about how to intercept and prevent the development of maladaptive aggression among our children?

As I see it, aggression is a matter of probabilities. Things do happen. We see major and minor examples of aggression at school, at home, and in our communities. Both deliberate and accidental violence affect the lives of children and families seriously. There are loud and impressive examples, such as Columbine High School in Colorado. And there are quiet examples, such as when my brother lost a finger to an ax during innocent play among youngsters.

How do we protect ourselves and our children? Can such tragedies be prevented? In school shootings, and in other acts of aggression and terror perpetrated by children, why wasn't something done earlier? Why wasn't there better supervision, better monitoring, and better interception before tragedy?

In modern society, we should be asking ourselves whether children have the means and the skills to handle the challenges of life without developing life-threatening repertoires of violence. Does a community have strategies in place to protect the innocent? Social and behavioral science has established that the probability of aggression can be reduced if sound principles of ethical behavior management are applied.

PROBABILITIES

It is a matter of probabilities. Childhood aggression and violence can and will happen naturally, even in typical development. Sometimes, that violence becomes more extreme on a continuum. I can note a few examples of aggression and violence from my own clinical observations: A child hitting and biting peers and pulling their hair. A child smashing his head through the glass in a door. A child slapping and hitting the therapist about the face during therapy. A child spitting on peers and throwing objects at them. A child yelling at and threatening peers. A child sitting on a peer, holding him down, and not letting him up. A child holding scissors to his chest, the sharp end toward himself. A child saying she wants to kill herself. A child taking an overdose of medication. A child pulling a switchblade knife on the therapist during therapy for aggression. A child saying she will bring a gun to school and shoot a peer. A child reporting that voices inside his head say kill the teacher. A child saying killing made her feel better when she was stressed.

Obviously, there are serious problems ongoing in our communities. Terror and violence are being perpetrated by children, and weapons of aggression are available in their various forms.

In homes, I routinely ask whether there is a gun in the house. Sometimes, the parent's answer is "Yes." Sometimes, the parent's answer is "Yes but my child doesn't know where it is." And sometimes, the child's answer is "Yes. My parents don't think I know where it is, but I know where it is and I know how to use it." This is a sobering repetitive occurrence. Nevertheless, any community serious about the safety, growth, and development of its children would want to know how to intercept and prevent serious actions of aggression and violence. It is a matter of importance for the protection of the children and their communities. We should get the best balancing possible of the needs and rights of children and the community against the aggressors. Please remember too, some of the aggressors don't know any better. Their communities haven't been there to help enough yet to teach a more prosocial and satisfying lifestyle.

Important questions for consideration by communities relate to the assessment of threats and procedures for functionally intercepting the most problematic repertoires of aggressive children and those around them. There are many ways to intercept aggression.

Consider another example close to home. I was on a train in Perth, Western Australia, not so long ago, on my way home after a football game. From among a loud group of rowdies supporting the other team, a man pointed a long stick, with a club flag attached, at me, taunting me about the game. I smiled and sat quietly while his young children intercepted and pushed the flagpole down toward the floor to a less menacing posture. A railway security officer also asked the jubilant ones to calm down until they were off the train. I'm sure it would have been better if my preferred team had won the game. As a disappointed fan, I was happy that this aggressive gesturing was intercepted by children and by members of the community.

TOPOGRAPHY OF TERROR AND VIOLENCE

In their United States Department of Education monograph, Dwyer, Osher, and Wagner (2000) noted that violence "refers to a broad range of troubling behaviors and emotions . . . including serious aggression, physical attacks, suicide, dangerous use of drugs, and other dangerous interpersonal behavior" (p. 6).

Why is aggression, the general concurrent activity of violence and terror, so prevalent? Surely there are reasons for its occurrence within the development of a child? In fact there is as much purpose in the acts of aggression by children as there is purpose in the acts of terror and violence by adults. For individuals, the purpose may vary, but there are general characteristics of note.

Few acts of childhood aggression and violence are without precursors, even if they appear so. For the perpetrator, aggression and violence are not typically random. The personal control, attention, or release of emotion resulting from aggression are functional for the perpetrator, but not acceptable in our current societies.

Aggression by children can have an early onset in the developmental trajectory, even as young as infancy, where aggression is often an early form of communication. It is effective because friendly caregivers may respond to aggression by trying to understand the actions and motivations of the child. Caregivers enable a change in the environment that provides what the child may need or want and thereby obviate the continuation of the aggression. Unfortunately, one natural outcome of these child communications and caring reactions of others is to encourage and reinforce communication through aggression (Stokes, Mowery, Dean, & Hoffman, 1997). Subsequently, when the frequency, intensity, and elaboration of aggression and abuse toward others and toward oneself becomes problematic, caregivers try not to let it influence outcomes and cease to reinforce it. In fact, when aggression ceases to work as effectively as in the past, children and adolescents often will escalate in their repertoires until aggression and violence is effective, as it had been in the past. In this way, the children develop an effective and generalized style of aggressive control over their environment, and that repertoire is often resistant to change and is well generalized and maintained (Stokes & Baer, 1977).

Yet, even while aggression and violence communicate and control effectively, their long-term course usually does not serve children and adolescents well in life. In the extreme, this is seen in violence by children and adolescents in their schools and their communities. There is no value in this level of aggression, and there are clear alternative repertoires for children who wish to communicate and influence their own lives with greater freedom than they may currently be allowed.

Given these often natural and unfortunate developmental outcomes, it is important that communities wanting a productive and caring lifestyle will conscientiously foster and develop skills in children that will serve them well in getting what they would like, but in a more prosocial manner consistent with the values and goals of their community.

When children have been exposed to dysfunctional circumstances and have already developed maladaptive repertoires, their susceptibility to controlling tyrannies is also great. A naturally developed maladaptive behavior repertoire can be guided readily toward terror and violence. The influences controlling these susceptible children may be an antisocial group, such as a gang, or an individual within a focused group, such as a charismatic cult leader, or some aspect of media communications, such as emotion-evoking violence on the Internet. For example, an effective tyrant can control the lives and behavior of members of a cult, at first with willing participation, using charm, interpersonal persuasion, gifts, release from stress, ideology, or religion. Later come more sinister factors—isolation, regulation, stress induction, psychological control, and terrifying aggressive force over followers who wander from a tyrant's dictates. Maladaptive conformity is the pressure leading toward fear, aggression without remorse, and passionate terrorism, as found in gangs or organizations or militias. In the well-developed cult, unethical and unrelenting leadership then engages in manipulative control, abusive power, and willingness to intimidate irresponsibly, in order to demand dedicated compliance.

Whatever the history and circumstances leading to acts of terror and violence, it is important to detect them and their precursors, and it is important to change the context and motivation for them.

PROFILING

Profiling is a matter of determining who is a likely threat, or who is likely to follow through on a threat related to aggression and violence. A general maxim is that the best predictor of future aggression is past threats or past aggression. In considering school violence, O'Toole noted that a "threat is an expression of intent to do harm or act out violently against someone or something. A threat can be spoken, written, or symbolic—for example, motioning with one's hands as though shooting at another person (O'Toole, 2000, p. 6)." As with threats of suicide, most who threaten will not conclude their threat in actual violence. Nevertheless, if there are factors that make a person fit a profile, how can we determine who are the serious threats and who are not? Either way, assessment of potential is warranted, but such assessment should be conducted with the clear understanding that there will be a high rate of false positives that are determined by profiling, which thus is inherently flawed and should be used carefully, sparingly, and with procedural safeguards that give due regard to the innocence of those profiled. An appropriately measured reaction to each threat is warranted, because most threats are not carried out.

It may appear that there are no warning signs, but that is not truly so. Repertoires of aggression and violence do not present themselves without precursors. So we may ask ourselves: What are the predictors of violence and what kind of history is related to such an extreme as mortal violence perpetrated at home, at school, and in our communities?

The FBI National Center for the Analysis of Violent Crime recommends focusing on personal behavior, family, school, and social factors when assessing threats. After reviewing multiple school shooting cases, a list of factors associated with violence was distilled (O'Toole, 2000). Other reports also have presented discussion and research regarding the developmental and environmental characteristics of aggressive and violent children (e.g., Boney-McCoy, & Finkelhor, 1995; Busch, Zagar, Hughes, Arbit, & Bussell, 1990; Cairns, Cairns, Neckerman, Gest, & Gariepy, 1988; Frick, Lahey, Loeber, Stouthamer-Loeber, Christ, & Hanson, 1992; Haapasalo & Tremblay, 1994; Herrenkohl & Russo, 2001; Kingston & Prior, 1995; Meloy, Hempel, Mohandie, Shiva, & Gray, 2001; Patterson, 1982).

What follows is my own general conceptual view of those myriad factors, primarily adapted from O'Toole (2000). I will characterize factors within three themes: individual child factors; family history factors; and school and community factors. These characteristics of behavior and environments are those for which parents, teachers, and communities should be alert when considering the behavior of children and the developmental trajectory of aggressive terror and violence

Individual Child Factors

Mental health disorders and stressful life events. Depression and other disorders of mental health are risk factors when left untreated. Depression is reflected in lethargy, loss of interest in previously enjoyable activities, hopelessness about the future, psychomotor agitation, and suicidal ideation. Dramatic changes in the child's behavior at home, school, or within the community—such as with unusual changes in academic performance or disregard for family rules—are also factors of concern. Drug and alcohol abuse is another variable adversely related to mental and behavioral health outcomes.

Poor impulse control and coping skills. Children who engage in aggression often have a low tolerance for frustration, are easily brought to an anger which is difficult to manage, and show poor coping and problem-solving skills. One indication of these is the occurrence of unpredictable and uncontrollable tantrums and behavior outbursts that are out of proportion to the events of the day.

Aggression fascinations. Fascinations refer to persistent and widespread preoccupation with acts of violence and media themes of hatred, control, power, death, and destruction. Revelation of intent is when children make clear how they intend to act. Their thoughts and feelings are not so readily hidden from observant caregivers and peers. Children are not as sophisticated as adults in protecting the privacy of their preparation or engaging in planning a deceit. Signals of impending aggression might include comments, boasts, predictions, diary entries, drawings, and other indications of aggressive and violent intent.

Inadequate empathy. The paucity of appreciation for others and their personal characteristics, behaviors, beliefs, and feelings contributes to an alienation from others and to the likelihood of aggression toward others. Also relevant here is how intolerance of personal, racial, and religious diversity is related to terror and violence.

Family History Factors

Turbulent family lifestyles. Children within dysfunctional, chaotic, and turbulent families show increased violent and rebellious behaviors. Factors such as multiple family moves, parental conflict, divorce, and the psychopathology of family members contribute here.

Violent homes. The occurrence of abuse and violence within the home as a general style and as a way of exerting control over others is also a means by which children learn that violence can serve a purpose with an outcome desired by the individual perpetrator. Children imitate the styles of coping and behavior management they see around them.

Maladaptive discipline. Styles of discipline, both positive and negative management styles, influence child development. Acceptance of child misconduct with few limits on the child's conduct is problematic and leads to more disorganized behavior and social problems. An overly stringent and controlling style is also problematic.

Inadequate supervision. Monitoring of TV or Internet time related to violence and weapons is an important factor, as is access to weapons of aggression without safety precautions and without responsible adult role models. Weapons of aggression should be considered broadly to include fists, rocks, sticks, knives, guns, bombs, etc. Weapons are everywhere. Responsible self-management should be everywhere too.

School and Community Factors

Community detachment. Personal and emotional detachment from school and community people, programs, and activities contributes to greater aggression. Friendly attachment to the school and school activities, and to other students and the teachers, is a preventative circumstance limiting further aggression.

Bullying unchallenged. Within the culture of the school, tolerance for or inequitable response to disrespectful behavior between individuals and groups, and allowing activities such as bullying to go unchallenged, are occurrences requiring system attention and change. Problems occur when the school culture is unyielding and insensitive to changing needs and differentially gives more prestige, respect, and protection to some groups of students compared with others.

Peer tolerance. When a code of silence prevails and there is little trust between students and staff at school, the probability of aggression increases. If this occurs, what is known will not be told to school personnel who can help protect the students. Involvement with maladaptive peer groups that share a fascination with violence, abusive behavior, and extreme beliefs and that encourage risk-taking behavior is also a pertinent concern.

Unmonitored media and copycat effects. Unsupervised children's access to movies, television, computers, and Internet images of violence is a risk factor. Too much and too extreme content is obviously the dimension to avoid. Copycat effects are encouraged and do occur when violent incidents receive intense media attention.

Consider recent events. Not so long ago, in a period of four months, four buildings were hit by planes, three in New York and Washington, D.C., on September 11, 2001, and one in a copycat incident in Tampa on January 5, 2002. It is hard to say why the copycat event occurred because there are only media reports (*St. Petersburg Times*, 2002; *Tampa Tribune*, 2002), and truth within families is usually more complex than a public view. Nevertheless, the 15-year-old perpetrator appears to have some characteristics of the risk profiles. There is little doubt that the child intended to fly the stolen plane low over Centcom just south of downtown Tampa—the flight path showed precise and well-executed passage at 1,000 feet and then a direct flight line to the skyscraper. There were reports that this was a dramatic suicide by a quiet child, perhaps a psychologically disordered child, of a divorced family. He had attended many different schools and lived in many different places in relatively turbulent succession. Although it appears that he acted alone, he expressed sympathy for terrorism in a suicide note and had told peers to watch for him on the Saturday news. He was on the news, all over the world.

Obviously, there are many factors that can be associated with childhood aggression and violence, and no case has all of these factors. In truth, we all know many children and circumstances that show up in these profiles. Yet, the fact is that most children whom we might identify using such profiling information do not conduct any violent actions. If we identify every child who meets any of these characteristics, we would quickly find a statistical error in over-identification. Childhood perpetrators of violence may look like this, but so do many children who do not engage in these extreme forms of aggression and violence. These are the risk factors that herald dysfunctional and unhappy lives with serious adverse potential. Many adolescents who will never commit violent acts will show some of the characteristics included in the list. There is a statistical logic operating with these profiling matters: "When the incidence of any form of violence is very low and a very large number of people have identifiable risk factors, there is no reliable way to pick out from that large group the very few who will actually commit the violent act" (O'Toole, 2000, p. 2ff).

THREAT ASSESSMENT AND INTERCEPTION

Where in the continuum of aggression and violence does a community intervene? Probably aggression at school and in communities should be met with a measured and targeted reaction that is appropriate to the individual circumstances and severity of aggression.

The FBI recommends evaluation along two dimensions: How credible and serious is the threat? Does the threatener have the resources, intent, and motivation to carry out the threat?

Specific and plausible details of plans, weapons, times, and places are taken as a more serious sign of threat. An example of a high level of threat is "At eight o'clock tomorrow morning, I intend to shoot the Principal. I have a 9-mm (gun). Believe me. I know what I am doing. I am sick and tired of the way he runs this school." (O'Toole, 2000, p. 9) This serious revelation of intent includes specific details indicating substantial thought, planning, and preparatory steps relating to aggression.

In general, the capacity and means of acting in an aggressive and violent manner are affected by a history of successful use of violent actions and motivation in current circumstances. With children, apparent random acts of aggression and violence have a trajectory. It is natural for children to be assertive to gain what they wish. Even random assertiveness may lead to reinforced aggression.

The topography of aggression may change over time and circumstances, and escalation of aggression may be seen: Knock over a peer on school ground. Take the ball that you want. Engage in highly competitive contact games without regard to the rules of safety and fair play. Be a bully. Show a knife or a gun. Engage in verbal assault. Attack with a weapon. Cause psychological harm, injury, or death.

Clearly, some aggression is more serious and requires a stronger reaction than other aggression. For any one incident, it is useful to consider how widespread and generalized the aggression is. It is useful also to consider the history and severity of a child's repertoire.

On the continuum, there are two major perspectives from which to view interception and treatment of aggression. These can be loosely considered as interception on the profile and interception on the behavior repertoire. Identification by the behavior repertoire of individuals allows therapy nomination according to the actual behavior of the children. A triage system allows graduated interception matching severity of infringement. The mechanisms of intervention, of monitoring, and of treatment follow increasingly intrusive options from assessment, monitoring, therapy, and restriction to incarceration.

A community priority and strategy should involve early detection and interception, as well as the support of families, schools, and community agencies, in a coordinated community monitoring of higher-risk youth. When children and adolescents appear to lack those skills and violate the codes of conduct for their communities, there needs to be a system of effective and collaborative community response that enables the development of prosocial skills and intercepts and disables the antisocial and violent repertoires. Any such action will require strong interagency cooperation across community agencies, including education, mental health, social services, law enforcement, and the courts.

SAFE COMMUNITIES

Obviously, most homes, schools, and communities are safe most of the time, and most children are not subjected to serious threat of harm. It is a matter of probabilities. Furthermore, when there is risk, there is ample documentation that prevention and early-intervention efforts can reduce violence and other troubling aggressions. Dwyer, Osher, and Wagner (2000) outlined characteristics of schools that are regarded as safe and responsive to all children. Those factors may be adapted to consider communitywide interception of violence. Four recommendations may be made.

Activity engagement. Well-supervised and activity-engaged children can develop and maintain prosocial (or antisocial) repertoires that can be monitored and targeted during natural activities. Often this refers to programs before and after school as well as appropriate activities and supervision during school hours.

Positive relationships. Positive relationships among students and staff should be emphasized. Students should be able to turn to receptive peers and adults for advice and guidance regarding their needs. The availability of a caring and friendly adult is also invaluable as a protective factor. Children should be treated with respect, without bias and unfair treatment, with due consideration of their age, developmental level, and understanding. Victimized children are more likely to engage in aggressive and violent activities.

Open communication. A community should make clear what are the reasonable expectations and standards of acceptable behavior, and should communicate clearly the consequences for aberrant behavior. Children should also have an avenue to openly consider issues of concern to their health and well-being, as well as to have the opportunity to discuss the best strategies for resolving conflicts, expressing anger in appropriate ways, and dealing with emotional turmoil with themselves and among peers.

Family involvement and character development. The involvement of families and communities in fair and meaningful ways can be a strong positive influence in a child's life, thereby preventing the development of antisocial repertoires. Community linkages for families are also important in the provision of valuable resources to children in supporting the development of the shared values of their communities, in honest responsibility, kindness, respect for others, good citizenship, and community involvement.

CONCLUSION

There is predictability to the factors associated with terror and violence perpetrated by children at home, at school, and in the community. The media are not the only culprit. Both the Backstreet Boys and *Recess: School's Out* attend to themes of care and support among community members, as well as to themes of assertiveness, aggressiveness, and violence. There are many factors—individual, family, school and community factors—that cause a child to become aggressive, violent, and to engage in terrorist activities.

Human services providers have a critical role to play in a community's reaction to aggression and violence. Important parts of a community's reaction to aggression and violence should be support, guidance, and psychotherapy. Terror and violence should be intercepted on their developmental trajectory. They must be intercepted because they are maladaptive to the individual and to modern society in general.

You may think you are immune to such acts. If you think that and still don't act, the peril of inaction is yours. There are risk factors related to the development of a violent lifestyle. Every society must be alert to these factors. Without support of early intervention and current interception, the probability of violence will continue to escalate. That will affect us all.

REFERENCES

Bijou, S. W., & Baer, D. M. (1978). *Behavior analysis of child development*. Englewood Cliffs, NJ: Prentice Hall.

Boney-McCoy, S., & Finkelhor, D. (1995). Psychosocial sequelae of violent victimization in a national youth sample. *Journal of Consulting and Clinical Psychology, 63*, 726–736.

Busch, K. G., Zagar, R., Hughes, J. R., Arbit, J., & Bussell, R. E. (1990). Adolescents who kill. *Journal of Clinical Psychology, 46*, 472–485.

Cairns, R. B., Cairns, B. D., Neckerman, H. J., Gest, S. D., & Gariepy, J.-L. (1988). Social networks and aggressive behavior: Peer support or peer rejection? *Developmental Psychology, 24*, 815–823.

Dwyer, K. P., Osher, D., & Wagner, C. (2000). *Early warning, timely response: A guide to safe schools*. Washington, DC: U.S. Department of Education and Department of Justice.

Frick, P. J., Lahey, B. B., Loeber, R., Stouthamer-Loeber, M., Christ, M. A. G., & Hanson, K. (1992). Familial risk factors to oppositional defiant disorder and conduct disorder: Parental psychopathology and maternal parenting. *Journal of Consulting and Clinical Psychology, 60*, 49–55.

Haapasalo, J., & Tremblay, R. E. (1994). Physically aggressive boys from ages 6 to 12: Family background, parenting behavior, and prediction of delinquency. *Journal of Consulting and Clinical Psychology, 62*, 1044–1052.

Herrenkohl, R. C., & Russo, M. J. (2001). Abusive early child rearing and early childhood aggression. *Child Maltreatment, 6*, 3–16.

Kingston, L., & Prior, M. (1995). The development of patterns of stable, transient, and school-age onset aggressive behavior in young children. *Journal of the American Academy of Child and Adolescent Psychiatry, 34*, 348–358.

Meloy, J. R., Hempel, A. G., Mohandie, K., Shiva, A. A., & Gray, B. T. (2001). Offender and offense characteristics of a nonrandom sample of adolescent mass murderers. *Journal of the American Academy of Child and Adolescent Psychiatry, 40*, 719–728.

O'Toole, M. E. (2000). *The school shooter: A threat assessment perspective*. Quantico, VA: Federal Bureau of Investigation National Center for the Analysis of Violent Crime.

Patterson, G. R. (1982). *Coercive family process*. Eugene, OR: Castalia.

St. Petersburg Times (2002, January–February). Newspaper articles from the *St. Petersburg Times*, Florida.

Stokes, T., Mowery, D., Dean, K., & Hoffman, S. J. (1997). Nurturance traps of aggression, depression, and regression affecting childhood illness. In D. M. Baer & E. M. Pinkston (Eds.), *Environmental approaches to social problems*. Boulder, CO: Westview Press.

Stokes, T. F., & Baer, D. M. (1977). An implicit technology of generalization. *Journal of Applied Behavior Analysis, 10*, 349–367.

Tampa Tribune (2002, January–February). Newspaper articles from the *Tampa Tribune*, Florida.

NOTE

Sincere thanks are offered to Debra Mowery, Amy Smith Duhig, Mechy Wright, and Wendy Postbotin of the University of South Florida, Tampa, and to Christine Healy, Adam Elliot, Keith Kerrigan, Jenny Irwin, and Katharina Schmid of the University of Ulster, Belfast, for their friendly and informed assistance in the preparation of this chapter. The opinions expressed are those of the author and not necessarily those of the University of South Florida.

6

Everyday Terrorism—The Long Shadow of Our Hidden Dragon: Shared Factors of Terrorism and Juvenile Violence

Timothy H. Warneka

"We have met the enemy and he is us."

—Pogo

It is Wednesday, September 12, 2001—the day after terrorists crash planes into Washington, D.C., New York City, and Pennsylvania. My co-facilitator Debbie and I[1] are sitting in a large room in a community mental health center near Cleveland, Ohio. We are conducting our regularly scheduled meeting with the "Waging Peace" group, a treatment group for adolescents who use violent behavior.[2] We are joined, as we are every other week, by the parent(s) of the adolescents. Today—as is typical for this group—out of seven parents, there are no fathers present.

When I went out into the lobby to pick up the group members, there was an unusual quietness in the adolescents' demeanor—much less of the typical teasing, joking, and good-natured put-downs that typify regular American adolescent interactions.

During our group "check-in," many people comment on the tragedy of the previous day. My co-facilitator Debbie, who has more than 20 years' experience working with adolescents who use violent behavior, began the discussion. Standing up, Debbie asked, "What did you experience regarding the terrorist attack?" She wrote

"Effects on Myself" on a large sheet of paper taped to the wall. "I'm sick of talking about it," sighed 16-year-old Linda,[3] the newest member of our group.

"Anger!" offered Patrick, a lanky 15-year-old who rarely volunteers answers.

"I'm afraid for my children," said Linda's mom Lisa, a petite woman whose tired face reflects years of domestic violence. "Yesterday, as soon as I heard, I went to school to pick them up. The radio said not to, but I didn't care."

"I didn't want to go to school today," quietly offered the usually jovial 17-year-old Thomas.

"Worried?" asked Debbie.

"Maybe," mumbled Thomas, casting side glances at his other group members. Several heads nodded in agreement.

And slowly the list grew. Other answers given by our group included "anger," "hurt," "pain," "sadness," "fear for my children," "fear of war," "afraid to go out," "jumpy," and "can't sleep so good."

Debbie asked another question, writing "Effects on Others" on another large sheet of paper. "And what have you heard others experiencing as a result of the attack?"

"I wouldn't want to fly if I was a pilot," laughed Jake nervously, his starter jacket wrapped protectively around him.

"Everyone was talking about it at work," mused Thomas's mother Katherine, a sad-faced single mother of four children. "Lots of people said it was like watching a disaster movie—except that it was for real."

"Linda," I asked, "how about you—what do you think?"

"I heard some people talking about that it was really our government that crashed those airplanes. People said that there were too many people living in the city, and the government wanted to kill them off," said Linda.

"Think that's true?" I asked.

"I'm not sure that it isn't." said Linda.

"When people are hurt by violence," said Debbie, "they often don't know who to trust for a long period of time after being hurt."

And the second list grew. Answers that were given included: "pain," "sadness," "fear for our children," "fear of war," "afraid to go out," "hurt," "anger," "want revenge/to get back at terrorists," "feeling like it's a dream," "don't want to go to school," "sick of talking about it," "want to talk about it more," "can't believe it's real," "it was like watching a movie," "mistrust—are we hearing the truth from the media?" and "don't want to travel—especially fly."

Debbie then asked, "What kinds of thoughts or feelings do you think the terrorists had before they attacked?" and wrote "Terrorists" on a third large sheet of paper.

"I think they hate us Americans," said Ann with a glare, peering through the hair pulled over her face and sitting back in her chair with her arms folded across her chest.

"They think we are evil," said Katherine confidently. "It's a religious difference."

"They probably thought that what they were doing was right," chimed in Thomas. "They were mad at America about something."

"Yeah, *really mad,*" echoed Randy with a touch of sarcasm.

And the third list grew. Other answers that our group gave included: "America is evil," "we are right in doing what we did," "anger," "rage," "jealous," "not feeling heard/listened to," and "hatred."

Debbie stood up and walked over to the third sheet of paper. She crossed out the word "Terrorist" and wrote "Aggressive Teen" in large print. Turning to the group, she asked, softly but clearly, "And how have you been a terrorist in your own family?"

There was silence as recognition dawned across the teens' and mothers' faces as they realized that at some levels their behaviors and thoughts were very similar to the terrorists.

And the discussion began.

THE GENESIS OF THIS CHAPTER

This chapter is written from my perspective as a clinical counselor and based on my experience of working for the past nine years with aggression in children, adolescents, and their families. Psychology is one lens through which to view aggression, and this chapter is offered in the spirit of contributing toward a multidisciplinary approach to the reduction of aggression—whether by adults who engage in terrorism or adolescents who use violence.

The genesis of this chapter lies in two personal experiences that followed September 11, 2001. The first experience was the reaction of the adolescents in my group to the exercise that was described briefly above. The teens with whom I work have been through a great deal in their short lives—violence, victimization, neglect, abuse, involvements with multiple systems that are trying to help them, often with limited resources and possibilities, and the teens' own experience that they simply don't "need" the help. Consequently, by the time they come into my group they are quite jaded. It usually takes a great deal to crack their shells. Very few exercises that I have done in all the time that I have been a therapist have had as deep an impact as the terrorist exercise described above. I could almost see the light bulb of understanding coming on over the heads of both parents and teens as we talked about violence and terrorism in that group and in the weeks that followed.

The second experience that provided one of the seeds for this present chapter was more personal. In the days following September 11, 2001, I heard many, many people talk about how the world had become a different place for them. I noticed that many people's conversations frequently began with "Since September 11th . . ." And while I was shocked and horrified, grieved and saddened by the terrorist attack on America, I also found myself noticing that *my* whole world had not changed a great deal. Initially, I was ashamed of these thoughts (we will discuss shame's relationship to aggression shortly). I began to wonder if there was something wrong with me that I wasn't seeing this "whole new world," as one of my friends described how she looked at life post-September 11. However, with the support of friends, I began to understand that my relationship with and understanding of aggression was very different from others' as a direct result of the work that I do. And I became very curious about the similarities between people who engage in terrorist behavior and the adolescents who engage in violent behavior with whom I work.

ACKNOWLEDGING AGGRESSION IN DAILY LIFE

It is my intention to explore some of the psychological similarities between terrorism and juvenile aggression in this chapter. As a mental health professional specializing in violence and aggression in children and adolescents, I have an opportunity to see the impact of aggression on a daily basis. While there is an eagerness to see people who engage in aggressive actions as "evil" people, it is the premise of this chapter that the actions of terrorists are extreme actions at one end of a continuum of aggression that is occurring every day in America. To paraphrase Krishnamurti's description of war, terrorism is a spectacular expression of everyday life. Seeds of aggression are sown and harvested by individuals and families in America on a daily basis that are not much different from terrorism in kind if not in measure.

It is important to remember that aggression is an incredibly complex phenomenon and simple answers should be suspect. In order to deal with aggression, multiple perspectives from a variety of professional specializations will be required. Indeed, the very act of examining aggression is fraught with problems (Papadopoulos, 1998). As the FBI's task force on juvenile violence (O'Toole, 1999) identified,

> [T]he roots of a violent act are multiple, intricate and intertwined. The mix of factors varies according to the individual and the circumstances. Understanding violence after it has occurred is difficult enough. Trying to assess a threat and keep it from being carried out is even more of a challenge. (p. 7)

Metaphors can often be useful in helping us to understand complex phenomena, so I will offer a metaphor that has given me insight into working with aggression. Managing our aggression is like owning a very ill-tempered dragon. We can try to hide the dragon, ignore it, and pretend that it does not belong to us—and it will run amok, burning villages and plundering castles. This is how we in the West have dealt with our dragon of aggression—mostly by ignoring its presence. Another approach is to acknowledge the presence of our dragon and try to relate to it as best we can. Ultimately, we are responsible for what we own—whether we want to be or not. We need to bring our dragon of aggression out of hiding. We need to deal with our dragon—whether we want to or not. Ignoring our dragon of aggression has brought us to the edge of world destruction, and we can no longer afford to ignore it. One way to manage our dragon of aggression is to begin to address the contextual factors of aggression.

When examining terrorism and/or juvenile aggression it is crucial to attend to contextual factors. Aggression is a choice, and people—whether adults living in Afghanistan or adolescents living in Ohio—do not choose aggression in a vacuum. However, our Western worldview is so extremely individualistic that it prevents us from examining, discussing, and possibly even changing the contextual factors that support people who choose to be aggressive. By examining our own role in the contextual factors that support everyday terrorism, we become able to change the world and resolve the problem of aggression.

While there are many contextual factors that contribute to aggression, I would like to focus on five psychological ones: 1) misunderstanding the difference between feeling anger and acting on it; 2) the paradigm of individualism; 3) shame[4]; 4) negative projections; and 5) the role of power. The negative aspects of labeling/naming serve as projective functions, so labeling will be explored under the discussion of projection. Denial also provides a way of supporting negative projections, so we will examine denial as it relates to keeping our dragon of aggression hidden.

In this chapter, we will be examining each factor in a linear, ordered manner, as that is how we conceptually understand the written word. Reality is much messier, with each factor underlying, supporting, and combining with the other factors in multiply complex ways. In this present work, I will focus on briefly exploring these five psychological factors. Space does not permit a full discussion of the ways in which each factor influences and affects the other factors.[5]

The order of discussion of these factors here is arbitrary and not meant to convey more weight to any particular factor. It is very difficult, if not impossible, to identify which factor(s) precede the other(s). And to a large extent, it is not even important to determine which factor precedes which. The importance at this point in time is simply to acknowledge that the factors exist and contribute to aggression in our world.

So let us begin with an examination of anger and aggression and some of the misunderstandings that occur around these concepts.

Misunderstanding the Difference Between Anger and Aggression

"[The Wrathful] thumped at one another in that slime with hands and feet, and they butted, and they bit as if each would tear the other limb from limb."
—Dante's *Inferno* (Alighieri, 1954)

Many people see anger and aggression as the same thing. They are *not* the same thing, and the confusion surrounding the difference between anger and aggression is a crucial point of consideration for the present discussion. The consistency with which I see clients holding this erroneous belief that "anger = aggression" leads me to believe that the blurred line between anger and aggression, rather than being a case of misunderstanding at the personal level, is much more of a collective social construct around which many Americans (at least) carry a great deal of confusion.

American culture has a truly confusing relationship with anger and aggression. We decry aggression, yet Americans are ravenous consumers—to the tune of several billion dollars a year—of entertainment media that portray aggression. Christianity is held to be the founding religion of America. The Christian God says, "Thou shalt not kill" (Exodus, 20:13) yet Americans seek as many ways around this as possible—war, capital punishment, etc. Even our rhetoric is aggressive. From our "War on Poverty" in the 1960s to the "War on Terrorism" at the dawn of the twenty-first century, our language demonstrates that Americans believe the best way to solve a problem is to declare war on that problem. It speaks to the powerful pull that aggression has on us that when it comes to aggression what we *say* and what we *do* are often two very different things.

As powerful as anger and aggression are, defining these words can be quite difficult. Jungian analyst Jan Wiener (1998) states, "As analysts, it seems to me that we tend to use the word anger in an ambiguous and over-general way when it is actually a subtle, complex affect with many nuances of meaning" (p. 493). This problematic confusion is inherent in any attempt to find solutions to problems of aggression.[6] Papadopoulos (1998) describes this difficulty well in a lengthy passage on the destructiveness of aggression that bears repeating:

> Destructiveness is an equally widespread phenomenon affecting most of us, in its various shapes and forms, and yet we tend to find it difficult to get a proper grip on it. By simply condemning it, we do not get closer to the phenomenon and thus we cannot begin to understand it. We seem to get caught up in a debilitating conundrum: on the one hand, we cannot afford to "normalize" destructiveness while, on the other hand, we cannot delve more deeply into it in order to understand it more fully, unless we adopt a less judgmental stance. This impossible situation has multifarious repercussions; one of them is exemplified by our attitudes toward the out-break of new wars. *After each eruption of violent hostilities or war we believe that we shall never forget it, that we shall learn from the horrible experience and thus avoid any future repetitions. Yet, when the next outbreak occurs we react with remarkable dismay as if we did not expect it to happen.* It seems that there is a protective function in human beings which enables us to "forget" painful memories of war and react with the wrath of naive ignorance when conflict recurs. It is as if humanity needs to keep cleansing itself from the horrors of war by constantly "forgetting" them and thus renewing its virginal innocence. (p. 208; italics added)

Understanding aggression and developing effective solutions for it requires us to walk the fine line between normalizing the destructive qualities of aggression and condemning aggression harshly. Walking this line is a very tricky task, indeed. To support us in walking this line, I would like to take a moment to discuss the distinction between anger and aggression.

Anger is a *feeling*, an emotion that takes place in the mind, body, and spirit. Aggression is outwardly directed hurtful *behavior*.[7] Aggression comes, at least in part, from anger, but they are not the same. It is possible to feel anger and choose not to act hurtfully on that feeling. It is possible to own the anger, learn to manage it, and find more constructive and life-affirming ways of behaving. Let us first explore aggression in a little more depth, and then turn our attention to anger.

Since the time of Freud, a great deal has been written about aggression in modern psychology. Psychological writers have used the term aggression in various ways, at times using it solely with a negative connotation while at other times using the term with both positive and negative connotations. Giving multiple meanings to aggression occurs not only in the professional literature but also in general American society.

A further complication is the multiple meanings that American culture gives to the term "aggression." Aggression can mean "hurtful" or "violent" on one hand (for example, "his aggression cost us a broken window"), or it can mean "active," "energetic," and "enthusiastic" (for example, "she sold so aggressively this month that she became the top salesperson in her district"). Sometimes the line between the two meanings is not always clear in American culture. On one hand, we are told that it is not appropriate to be aggressive, in the sense of being hurtful to another. On the other hand, the American sports world praises the "aggressive player." Many of the young men with whom I work who play football inform me that their coaches have either directly or indirectly told them to: 1) hit another player as hard as possible in order to do the most damage; and 2) try and get away with as much as possible when the referee is not looking.[8]

In this chapter, and in the clinical work that I do, I use the word aggression in the sense of being hurtful or violent. Here I will focus on the negative aspect of aggression and define aggression simply as "any type of intentionally hurtful behavior." For purposes of working with adolescents and children, I have chosen to use the word aggression in the negative sense so as to (hopefully) avoid confusion. Furthermore, I attempt as much as possible to use language that is developmentally appropriate for a particular adolescent or child (i.e., "aggression," "violence," "hurtful," "mean," and so forth).

Anger—as stated above—is a feeling, an emotional state, involving mind, body, and spirit. One metaphor that I use with the families with which I work is that emotions are like the weather, in that we have little control over when emotions come to us and when they leave us. Paraphrasing Shakespeare, a feeling is neither good nor bad but thinking makes it so. We judge a rainy day to be good or bad depending upon our perspective. If I am a gardener, I may welcome a rainy day to help my roses grow. If I have a day's vacation and I am planning to go to the beach, then a rainy day is an unwelcome event. There are certainly some emotions that we enjoy the experience of over other emotions, but emotions are not good or bad by themselves.[9] Even in young children emotions are highly complex, and can be intensely felt. Regarding emotions, Damasio (1999) states,

> Human emotion is not just about sexual pleasure or fear of snakes. It is also about the horror of witnessing suffering and about the satisfaction of seeing justice served; about our delight in the sensuous smile of Jeanne Moreau or the thick beauty of words and ideas in Shakespeare's verse; about the world-weary voice of Dietrich Fischer-Dieskau singing Bach's *Ich habe genug* and the simultaneously earthly and otherworldly phrasings of Maria Joao Pires playing any Mozart, any Schubert; and about the harmony that Einstein sought in the structure of an equation. In fact, fine human emotion is even triggered by cheap music and cheap movies, the power of which should never be underestimated. (p. 36)

Anger is frequently a feeling that covers over other types of feelings. And the feelings that are covered by anger are usually those feelings that are not accepted by a person's environment (i.e., these feelings are *shameful* to feel.). For example, in American culture, it is *not* culturally acceptable for a male to feel weak, afraid, or ashamed. It *is* culturally acceptable for a male to feel anger, and at times it is practically culturally mandated for a male to act out that anger aggressively in order to "save face." In the American culture, for males (and for a growing number of females) in some situations *not* to respond aggressively to an attack is to be seen as weak and powerless. In the beginning stages of therapy, most of the adolescents with whom I work who are referred for "anger management" problems can usually only identify one feeling: anger.[10] They may have multiple ways to describe it (i.e., "pissed off," "mad," "upset," "frustrated," "annoyed"), yet the root emotion of anger is the same.

Aggression, as we have said, is a behavior. I have control over my behavior because I have the ability to make choices about my behavior.[11] I can be angry, and I may or may not choose to be aggressive. It is generally accepted that emotions may be occurring in us that are un- or non-consciously experienced (see Damasio, 1999, p. 37). Some small to middle-range physical behaviors may also occur un- or non-consciously (i.e., a client may unknowingly clench and unclench her hand every time she talks about person X in her therapy session). However, despite the claims by many adolescents with whom I have worked, it is unusual for complicated sequential behavior (i.e., picking up a chair, screaming, and throwing it through a window) to occur without conscious thought and/or choice.

Anger and the behavior that one chooses to express feelings of anger are *always* situated in a context, and as such are subject to affect by multiple factors, including but not limited to factors of gender, race, culture, intellectual ability, prior experience, perceived level of possible consequences and many others. In fact, it is often the context of the situation that determines the "goodness" or "badness" of an action (Crum, 1987; Linden, 1988).

The Paradigm of Individualism

A paradigm is a way of looking at the world. Every culture has a paradigm from which it operates. There is nothing wrong with paradigms per se, as we need paradigms to make sense of the world. Paradigms, by definition, provide us with the language to reveal certain aspects of our experience, while at the same time concealing other aspects of our experiences. Difficulties arise when we begin to hold a particular worldview as the one and only way of seeing the world. Such is the case currently with the paradigm of individualism, which is the present reigning paradigm for Western thought. This paradigm can be traced back to and ". . . grounds itself in the philosophical assumptions and attitudes of classical Greece" (Wheeler, 1996, p. 24). Wheeler further notes that the paradigm of individualism is marked by

> . . . the habit of thinking that starts with the (mostly unexamined) assumption that the separateness, the isolation even, of our own awareness and consciousness is the basis and bedrock of reality and human experience, whereas connection and community, however important they may be, are somehow only instrumental and secondary to individual integration and individual satisfaction . . . (p. 24)

In short, the paradigm of individualism holds that self exists apart from and prior to relationship. As a consequence, relationships and relational aspects of life are seen as having less importance than the individual. In contrast, the Gestalt phenomenological field model (and other phenomenological constructivist models)

> sees the individual as constructing sense of self and other out of a prior field of relationship and organizing perception and behavior in an ongoing subjective/constructive activity that is best understood from the point of view of *phenomenology*, the study of the subjective organization of experience . . . (Wheeler, 1996, p. 39; italics in original)

Our current paradigm has supported us to make incredible advances. Examples of these advances include placing people on the moon, creating the Internet, and developing medical cures for many devastating illnesses. However, as the paradigm of individualism holds relational aspects to be less important, it has also supported us in poisoning a good portion of our environment (relationship with nature); brought us to the brink of nuclear war (relationship with each other); and brought about the ennui that so typifies the Western world (relationship with ourselves). And each of the above examples can be viewed as acts of aggression. We are destroying Earth and poisoning it for future generations. Money directed to military spending and war is money that is unavailable to the powerless and marginalized populations of our world. And we do violence to people when we do not support other people (or ourselves) by creating a "stimulating and fulfilling environment" (Elias, 1997, p. 125).[12]

Our adherence to the paradigm of individualism does us immense disservice when it comes to aggression because the paradigm *demands* that we ignore the contextual issues around aggression and place all the blame on the individual perpetrator(s) of aggression.

Another metaphor comes to mind here, which is the mythological motif of walking along a bridge made by the razor-sharp edge of a sword. We walk the razor's edge here, and can easily err on one side or the other. The side we usually err on is to completely and totally place the responsibility for aggression on the individual perpetrator(s) without considering contextual issues. And to a point—this is well and good. We as humans are responsible for our behavior, and no single life events or group of life events "causes" (in a direct, linear fashion) someone to act out aggressively. We slip off one side of the sword edge by focusing solely on the individual because doing so all but eliminates our ability to address and to change the underlying factors that are contributing to and supporting the aggression.

People often become upset when contextual factors are brought up in discussions of aggression. This is because contextual factors are often used as excuses to rationalize aggression. For example, American law has the notorious "Twinkie defense" where a man attempted to blame his violent behavior on the consumption of too many yellow confectionary treats. It is important to be clear that setting up consequences or justice for a perpetrator of a *past* offense is different from seeking solutions to avoid *future* offenses . . . and future victims. If a person or group of people has chosen to be violent toward another person or group of people, then those who perpetrated the aggression should receive fair and just consequences for their behavior. By viewing that person or group of people as isolated instances, though, we do little to prevent the aggression from occurring again.

To instead turn toward those who use aggression, and to seek to understand them, is not—as some would hold—to coddle them or to excuse their behavior. To either coddle or excuse aggressive behavior is to err and to continue the cycle of aggression that occurs in our world. To turn toward aggression and to develop a relationship with it in order to understand and resolve aggression—not merely in a cognitive sense of "understand"—but to understand holistically, is to reclaim and renew our relationship with aggression, and to begin to resolve aggression in our world.

Finally, it is important to remember that the paradigm of individualism is a *Western* worldview. It holds true for American adolescents who use violent behavior. These comments are not intended to describe Middle Eastern worldviews. I will leave the potential application of the paradigm of individualism outside Western culture to those who have experience in other cultures. However, it is also important to remember that nothing occurs in a vacuum. To examine terrorism and only look at "them" is a logically flawed approach. "Them" is only half of the equation. It is inescapable that the Western paradigm of individualism has created numerous scenarios throughout the global community that support, encourage, and even provoke terrorism. We in the West have to clean our own house if aggression in the world is going to change.

Shame

The concept of shame has already surfaced several times in the present work. Recall that I felt ashamed when I noticed that my experience in the aftermath of the terrorist attack of September 11, 2001, was markedly different from what I was hearing about other people's experience. Also, we saw that feelings of anger often serve to cover up feelings that are perceived as more shameful. Let us now turn our attention to shame and its relationship to aggression.

At one time or another, we have all felt shame. Lee (1996) identifies shame as a relational phenomenon and states:

> *Shame* is the experience that what is me is not acceptable, that this is not my world. As such, shame signifies a rupture (or threat of a rupture) between the individual's needs and goals on the one hand and environmental receptivity to those needs and goals on the other. (p. 9; italics in original)

We all deal with shame in different ways at different times. We deal with shame in ways that can range from life giving and healing to destructive and hurtful.

Lee (1996) notes, "The link between shame and rage is well documented . . ." (p. 13). A common way in which people manage feelings of shame is to become angry. At first glance, the connection between anger and shame may be counterintuitive. For many, the typical reaction to shame is, as Tangney, Miller, Flicker, and Barlow (1996) note, "a desire to escape or to hide—to sink into the floor and disappear" (p. 1258). However, as Tangney, Wagner, Fletcher, and Gramzow (1992) note,

> The consistent theme emerging from these and other case studies and clinical observations . . . is that, rather than curbing hostile and aggressive impulses, shame tends to *initiate* a particular type of anger episode, namely, an irrational and generally counterproductive rage reaction. (p. 672; italics added)

Shame, rage, and the ensuing aggression are certainly breaking our world apart in many ways. Shame and shaming are so fundamental to the structure of Western psychology that we must explore another vantage point in order to best understand and address shame. Wheeler (1996) notes

> . . . the dynamics and experience of shame can be seen and understood *only* from the point of view of a different paradigmatic map of human nature and process altogether—one based on relationship as a coequal pole with individuality as organizing dimensions of life. (p. 25; italics in original)

One of the strongest ways that shame is supported in our current paradigm is that it is shameful to feel shame. This holds true especially for males in our Western culture (Canada, 1998; Jennings & Murphy, 2000; Wheeler, 2000; Wheeler & Jones, 1996). For the Western male, as Hollis (1994) notes,

> Every man will recall times when, as a boy, as a youth, or even last week, he dared reveal himself and was shamed and isolated. He learns to stuff that shame, mask it in male bravado and cover, cover, cover. Along the way he is frequently degraded and unable to speak his pain, his protest. (p. 73)

As mentioned above, shame—given the right conditions—can lead to rage. Let us say that I am in an argument with a friend. She says something about which I am ashamed (of course, at the time of the argument, I may not even be aware that I am ashamed of this topic). In an instant, I have felt the shame, pushed it away, and gone through a dance in my head in which I have convinced myself that my friend is really the one with the problem. In my anger—and if the shame is deep enough, my rage (the feeling that serves to cover the shame), I may lash out at my friend— most likely about a topic that I (at some level) know that may be shameful to her, that is, I *countershame* her.

In a relationship where there is little trust and/or poor communication— whether that relationship consists of a couple, a work group, an organization, or a nation—the shame/countershame cycle can rapidly spiral into more and more verbal attacks, and even, if conditions support it, into physical attacks. In a comment relevant to the current discussion, Lee (1996) also notes,

> . . . consider the many revolutionary thinkers who maintain that violent revolution is the only way to throw off the internal shackles of inferiority and shame. . . . their strategy is seen as advocating a common deshaming strategy—a shift from shame to rage. However, while this strategy, which is typically evoked in the midst of experiencing overwhelming shame, can temporarily interrupt the experience of shame, ultimately it only perpetuates and increases the accumulated shame. (pp. 11–12)

Lee's words hold true not only for "revolutionary leaders" but for other leaders as well. In American culture, to be victimized is to be in a shameful position.[13] Lee's "common deshaming strategy" of shifting from shame to rage is a strategy that is used by many Americans, including teens and political leaders. The basic sentiment of this position is, "I feel powerless when I am a victim. I feel very ashamed when I am powerless. I will feel powerful at any cost—even at the cost of serious aggression. So—if you hurt me, I will hurt you back—worse." If I were referred an adolescent who was spending only $10 a day to aggressively "get back" at someone who victimized him or her, he or she would most likely be in therapy for a long period of time, if not incarcerated outright. Yet the American government's response to the September 11 terrorist attack is to spend $30 million *a day* on aggression,[14] declaring war not only on those who attacked America, but also on *all* terrorism. By declaring the "War on Terrorism," America has figured out a way to distance itself from the shame of victimization, but in a way that only, in Lee's words, "perpetuates and increases the accumulated shame."

Negative Projections: Throwing a Long Shadow

Looking at aggression as something strange, different, or foreign is an act of making aggression "other"—existing only in *other* people, in *other* places, for *other* reasons. We readily forget the words of the Roman poet Terence: "*Homo sum, humani nihil a me alienum puto*" ("I am a person; and nothing human is foreign to me."). Instead, we are all too ready to accept the shaky premise that somehow, in some way, the people who commit aggression are fundamentally different from ourselves.

The psychological term for attributing characteristics onto other people that we do not wish to recognize in ourselves is called *projection.* One way to understand projection is to consider a movie projector showing a movie onto a blank screen. The content of the movie has more to do with the movie projector than with the screen. So too projection—when we psychologically project onto another—has more to do with ourselves than the other person.[15]

The Gestalt perspective of psychology holds that projection can be either positive or negative. Gestalt theory holds that it is important to honor the way we "do" projection, as each person has creatively adapted projection in ways that serve them in their life. That we do project is not the question. The question is: How do we project? Is projection done with consciousness and awareness or is it done with a lack of awareness?

The positive aspect of projection can be seen in the ability to empathize with another human being. In order to place myself in another person's shoes, I need some ability to be able to understand what he is going through—both affectively and cognitively. When I witness my friend Joseph being yelled at unjustly, my heart can go out to him. I know that when I am yelled at unjustly I feel hurt and misunderstood. I can imagine that Joseph is feeling similar feelings and I can act accordingly to support Joseph.

However, demons arise when I project a part of myself that I am uncomfortable with onto another. If I have difficulty expressing my anger, then I may experience those who are able to express their anger, positively or negatively, as foreign or strange to me. Then it is easy for me to become judgmental in my observations about the other person who expresses anger. This is the negative aspect of projection.

Significantly, there is a part of each of us that yearns to believe that the world of aggression—including terrorism and juvenile violence—is a world that has nothing to do with our own, and *should* have nothing to do with our own—except when the worlds collide and we, or someone we know, are victimized by terrorism, juvenile aggression, or some other form of aggression. In fairy tales, this stance is that of the king/queen/mother/father/guardian character, who would keep the adventure (and the story) from happening. This character wishes to maintain the status quo with a naively dichotomized view of the world—that "we" are the "good guys," always just, compassionate, and fair, and that "they" are the "bad guys," always evil, deceitful, and hurtful. This naive perspective often comes at a price— the price of liveliness (Von Franz, 1995).

Shame enters into the picture when the blame is placed on others. Tangney et al. (1992) note that in four independent studies of adults, there was "a consistent positive relationship between proneness to shame and a tendency to externalize blame . . ." (p. 672). "Externalizing blame" is another way of describing projection. Tangney et al. further note that "Such externalization of blame may ameliorate the pain of shame in the short run, but it can lead either to subsequent withdrawal from the blamed person or to an *exacerbation of the hostile, humiliated fury*. . . ." (p. 672; italics added)

All of us have violent thoughts and images—no matter how unwanted—that pass through our consciousness from time to time. Each one of us, given the "right" circumstances or conditions could and would act violently. The Swiss psychiatrist C. G. Jung called our unacceptable side the *shadow*. Jung (1966) described the shadow as "the dangerous aspect of the unrecognized dark half of the personality" (p. 96). Von Franz (1995) described the shadow simply as "all that is within you which you do not know about" (p. 4). In *Pigs Eat Wolves*, his wonderful amplification of the story of the "Three Little Pigs," Charles Bates (1991) says the following about the wolf:

> The wolf is the designated evil one. . . . He represents everyone's dark side, the shadow . . . We could say he is the despised self. . . . Culture forms a wolf by compelling us to develop certain sides of ourselves and deny others. . . . We form our own wolf by ignoring or repressing everything we do not want to see or know. The wolf is our darkness, holding our unacceptable instincts, fears, anger, violence, insecurity, sexuality, and so on. There we hide away thoughts of revenge, jealousy, animal behaviors that are socially inappropriate, thoughts of incest, rage, greed, physical abuse. (p. 11)

We frequently manage the shadow side of ourselves, which often includes much of our aggression, by suppressing it as much as possible. While this suppressing of aggression is done for appropriate social purposes, it can also be overdone and result in disconnecting ourselves from a basic awareness of our own aggression, thus making it easier to project our anger and aggression onto others. Jung (in Campbell, 1971) also notes "certain features" of the shadow "offer the most obstinate resistance . . . and prove almost impossible to influence" (p. 146). These resistances, he notes,

> are usually bound up with projections, which are not recognized as such, and their recognition is a moral achievement beyond the ordinary. While some traits peculiar to the shadow can be recognized with-

out too much difficulty as one's own personal qualities, in this case both insight and good will are unavailing because the cause of the emotion appears to lie, beyond all possibility of doubt, in the *other person.* No matter how obvious it may be to the neutral observer that it is a matter of projections, there is little hope that the subject will perceive this himself. *He must be convinced that he throws a very long shadow before he is willing to withdraw his emotionally-toned projections from their object.* (p. 146; first italics in original, second italics added)

Projection can occur at either the personal or collective level. America collectively "throws a very long shadow" regarding aggression. Through our unwillingness to wrestle with our own relationship with aggression, we project our anger and hatred onto those who act aggressively in the external world. One common example of the collective level of projection can be seen in how American society views juvenile aggression. When there were a number of school shootings by teenagers several years ago, much effort was made by American culture (read: adults) to distance our responsibility from the violence caused by teens. Newspapers and magazines decried the "violent teen culture" of video games, movies, and television shows. One magazine even ran a cover page showing "The Monsters Next Door," with the face of a teenager split in half—one half smiling and happy, one half dark and sinister. The same process is occurring currently with our treatment of the people who engage in terrorism. The projection of all of my aggression onto another person allows me to create an object rather than a living, breathing, feeling person. And it is far easier to be aggressive toward an object (a "monster") than to a real person.

Labeling: A Form of Projection

The act of labeling has both positive and negative aspects. Space does not allow for a discussion about the positive aspects of labeling, except to offer the metaphor that cancer needs to be identified as cancer before it can be treated properly. The negative aspects of labeling, which we will focus on here, can be very destructive.

I have had the experience of working with families where one (or both) of the parents will describe their teenager as "sociopathic" or "sadistic." I have also heard the same labels used after school shootings, such as at Columbine, and after September 11.[16] It is a mistake to label groups of people, whether terrorists or adolescents, from a distance as sociopaths, sadists, or any other mental health diagnosis.

Hazelwood and Michaud (2001) describe seven behaviors that are commonly confused with sexual sadism, but which are not sexual sadism. Among these behaviors they list "pathological group behavior" and "state-sanctioned cruelty." A similar argument can be made with regard to both terrorism and juvenile violence. Again, while either behavior is incredibly hurtful and damaging, it would be a mistake to label the individual terrorists or adolescents as sociopathic (having an antisocial personality). While sociopaths, terrorists, and violent adolescents belong to a group of people who engage in hurtful behavior, it does not logically follow that terrorists (or violent adolescents) are sociopaths.[17] This is a logical fallacy of the *undistributed middle* (Hurley, 1985, p. 219). The fallacious syllogism goes something like this:

> All terrorists (violent juveniles) engage in hurtful behavior.
> All sociopaths engage in hurtful behavior.
> Therefore, all terrorists (violent juveniles) are sociopaths.

Which is similar to saying:

> All Fords are cars.
> All Chevys are cars.
> Therefore, all Fords are Chevys.

The second syllogism, while clearly fallacious, is also fairly innocuous. No one is injured or pushed aside if someone were to confuse a Ford with a Chevy. However, the first syllogism, regarding terrorism, is not only fallacious but also dangerous, as it serves only to widen the projective canyon between those who engage in terrorism and those who are victimized by terrorism. Little if any dialogue can occur between groups of people when one group believes the other group is sociopathic. Labeling a group of people as sociopathic or sadistic only serves to objectify that group, setting the stage for more aggression.[18]

Denying Aggression: A Way to Support Projection

In America, throwing a long shadow allows us to deny our own aggression and thereby supports our aggressive stance in the world. In America, we live in an aggressive culture (Elias, 1997), yet we often tend to react to aggression (whether juvenile aggression or terrorism) as something strange or different.

Our denial of our own aggressive culture is another way that our aggression becomes projected onto others. And the resulting aggression that follows is hurtful not only to those who are *outside* American society who are direct recipients of American violence (i.e., those people on whom we wage war), it is also incredibly hurtful to those *inside* American society who are powerless and/or marginalized. One such powerless group is American children and adolescents. On a daily basis I see the impact of America's aggressive stance on the children and adolescents with whom I work.

Collectively speaking, America's children are growing up in an extremely dangerous environment, and are at high risk to be traumatized. It is important to remember that while no single factor *causes* aggression, there are certainly a number of factors that have been identified as *contributing to* aggression. Research has shown that a particularly troubling effect of early trauma is that it leads to a significantly higher propensity for aggression later in life (Brooks-Gunn, Klebanov, Liaw, & Duncan, 1995). Yet, when we hear of an adolescent or child who is acting out violently, we frequently engage in a great deal of projection and blaming—looking at the juvenile as an individual aberration rather than a whole person responding to a vast number of factors, often including an inability to feel safe—either at home, school or other places.[19]

Again, being a child or teenager in America today is very dangerous. Let us take a moment to examine the impact of daily aggression on our children. To examine only three issues (there are many), let us look at the issues of: 1) children and guns; 2) children and poverty; and 3) children and sexual assault. Here are some disturbing statistics concerning America's children from the Centers for Disease Control and Prevention (2000), the Children's Defense Fund (2000), and the National Center for Children in Poverty:[20]

Guns and Children in America

- From 1979 to 1998, 84,000 children and teens have been killed by gunfire (36,000 *more* than the total number of American soldiers killed in Vietnam).

- Children are *twice* as likely as adults to be victims of violent crimes and are more likely to be killed by adults than by other children.

- Nearly three times as many children under the age of 10 died from gunfire as the number of law enforcement officers killed in the line of duty.

- More children and teens died from gunfire than from cancer, pneumonia, influenza, asthma, and HIV/AIDS *combined.*

- Compared with 25 other industrialized countries, American children (under 15 years of age) are:

  - *Sixteen (16) times more likely to be murdered with a gun*

  - *Eleven (11) times more likely to commit suicide with a gun*

  - *Nine (9) times more likely to die in a firearm accident*

- In the year 2000, for the first time since 1988, the number of child gun deaths per year dropped below 4,000 (the official number of child gun deaths in 2000 was 3,761).

One in Six: Children and Poverty in America

According to the National Center for Children in Poverty's (NCCP) Web site, one in six American children lives in poverty (2001). The NCCP also finds that:

- *America's children are more likely to live in poverty than Americans in any other age group.* Despite significant improvements since 1993, there are more children in poverty today than there were two decades ago.

- *More than 12 million American children live in poverty, 4.2 million under the age of six.*

- *The number of children living in poverty has increased by 1.6 million since 1979.*

- *The United States' child poverty rate is substantially higher*—often two to three times higher—than that of most other major Western industrialized nations.

- *7 percent of America's children live in extreme poverty* (8 percent of U.S. children under age six), in families with incomes below 50 percent of the poverty line. (In 1999, the extreme poverty line was $6,145 for a family of three.)

- Finally, *39 percent of American children live in or near poverty* (41 percent of U.S. children under age six), in families with incomes below 200 percent of the poverty line ($26,580 for a family of three).

Sexual Assault and Children

The National Center for Juvenile Justice (2000) reports that out of all sexual assault victimizations reported to law enforcement from 1991–1996, *67 percent were less than 18 years old.* The age breakdown is as follows:

- 1 percent were 54 years old or older
- 7 percent were more than 34 years old
- 12 percent were 25 to 34 years old
- 14 percent were 18 to 24 years old
- 67 percent were under 18 years old

Of those children under 18 years old who were sexually victimized:

- 33 percent of all victims were 12 to 17 years old
- 34 percent of all victims were under 12
- 14 percent of all victims were under 6

To summarize, we can see that American children are twice as likely as adults to be a victim of a violent crime; are more likely to be killed by an adult than another child; under the age of 10 years old have a 300 percent greater chance of being killed than a police officer on active duty; are almost twelve times as likely to die from firearms than in twenty-five other industrialized nations; have a 20 percent chance of living at or below the accepted poverty line; and have a much greater chance of being sexually victimized or living in poverty than at any other point in their lives.

Consequently, it is not an extreme conclusion to draw that it is not safe to be a child in America today. While these statistics are vitally important to our under-standing of the issue of juvenile aggression, they often lie silent in the background of any popular discussion about juvenile aggression. These statistics reflect the pri-orities of our domestic agenda. It is likely that statistics concerning our foreign agenda show similar denial around aggression. One wonders about the factors that lie silent in the discussion of terrorism. Most likely they are equally complex in their multiplicity.

While the statistics show that America is a violent nation as far as our children are concerned, there is curiously little awareness about this problem, either in the media or in other important areas in America, such as the political arena (kids don't vote!). When American media focus on aggression, they focus exclusively on individual acts of aggression, which only serves to perpetuate the notion that personal responsibility is the sole factor that affects aggression, thus continuing to support the paradigm of individualism. American politicians tend to use the violent actions to advance their own positions, frequently with vocal outpourings of empathy for the victims.

With denial of childhood victimization by both the American political and media systems, it is not a far reach to conclude that there is denial in the general American public. And denial of our own aggression creates a ground that is ripe for projection of our shadow of aggression onto the "other." Consequently, Americans bear some collective responsibility in co-creating an atmosphere of aggression in our world. When our foreign and domestic policies contribute to an atmosphere that supports aggression, then we need to take responsibility for our role in the creation of these aggressive policies if we expect to resolve the problem of aggression in our world.

The Role of Power

Another commonality between terrorists and juveniles with aggression problems is their relationship to power. Both terrorists and juveniles with aggression problems are one-down relative to power. They are *not* the ones with the authority in a given situation.[21] Let us look at the definitions for terrorism. *Webster's New Universal Unabridged Dictionary* (1996) defines *terrorism* as: 1) The use of violence and threats to intimidate or coerce, esp. for political purposes. It defines *political* as: 1) exercising or seeking power in the governmental or public affairs of a state, municipality, etc. 2) having a definite policy or system of government.

People who repeatedly have the experience of being unempowered in the political system in which they live are more at risk to perform acts of terrorism. People who engage in terrorism do not have power in whatever system they are operating, and use "violence and threats" to gain more (or sufficient) power that will allow them to do whatever it is that they wish to do. Like so many other things, terrorism is in the eye of the beholder. As the victors write history, it is rare that actions of the victor in any particular conflict will be recorded as terrorism. For example, as an American, I have never heard the Boston Tea Party of the American Revolutionary War described as terrorism. Yet—surely that is what it must be under the definitions that we are using for this present work.

Terrorism is a response given within certain political systems. If we broaden the concept of political systems to include the family, then we can view juvenile aggression as a terrorist-like response to the familial political system. In every family, there is a base of power, and a style of governing that family. Some families are totalitarian, some are complete anarchy—most families are somewhere in between.

In healthy, functioning families, children and adolescents do not have power in the family system equal to the parent. Being a child or adolescent is usually synonymous with having little or no power.[22] For example, in America adolescents are generally told where to live and where to go to school by their parents. The adolescents are managed by tight rules in academic, work settings, and organized extracurricular activities. Consequently, an adolescent who has the experience of not having his or her voice heard and/or needs attended to is ripe to become a terrorist—hurtful and aggressive.[23]

CONCLUSION

Let us revisit the group that we dropped in on at the start of this chapter and examine how the factors that we have discussed above apply to juveniles who have aggressive behavior problems. First, allow me to provide a little more background about our clinical groups. At our community mental health center, my colleague and I run two groups. The first group is for adolescent males who have used sexually aggressive behaviors. The second group is for adolescents who use verbal or physical aggression. Our clinical experience has led us to structure our groups to have a more significant level of familial involvement than typically occurs in these types of groups. We recognize that aggression is as much a family problem as an individual problem, and that targeting only the adolescent for intervention is often a recipe for failure.

On September 12, 2001, we presented to both groups the exercise described at the beginning of this chapter. That description was a brief composite of both groups. The first and second questions ("What did you experience regarding the terrorist attack?" and "What have you heard others experiencing as a result of the attack?") were geared toward increasing awareness around victim impact both at the interpersonal and intrapersonal levels. The third question ("What kinds of thoughts or feelings do you think the terrorists had before they attacked?") was intended to tap into the projections that our group members had around the motivation for terrorists.

The final question ("How have you been a terrorist in your own family?") was intended to supportively challenge the families to recognize the ways in which each one of them supports and/or contributes to the aggression in their families. After discussing the final question, we taught that the thoughts and feelings that the terrorists may have had were no different from the many thoughts and feelings that each one of us in the group has had at times. We began to tie the terrorists' thoughts/feelings list back into the various concepts that we have been teaching in both groups, including how the use of "thinking errors" supports aggression.[24]

We wanted to continue to press home the understanding that all of us engage in thoughts, feelings, and behaviors on the same continuum of aggression, at the extreme end of which are terrorist actions. We wanted to educate the families that people respond to being victims of aggression—both personally and collectively—in similar ways whether we are talking about a terrorist attack on the World Trade Center, a school shooting, or a screaming match between a parent and adolescent. When we witness aggression, we tend to blame one person or the other—whomever we see as being "at fault." And we often want to lash out at that person. Frequently because we are uncomfortable with our own relationship with aggression, we turn our backs on those who hurt others—seeing them as somehow "different" than we are. And, as described in the section above on projection, by seeing aggression as something foreign to ourselves we perpetuate the continuation of aggression. Instead, by seeing that we are part of the context that supports aggression, we can understand the aggression better and act to resolve it more effectively.

From what we have discussed above, we can see that contextual factors are very important in understanding aggression. In particular, we looked at the five factors of: 1) misunderstanding the difference between feeling anger and acting on it; 2) the paradigm of individualism; 3) shame; 4) the process of negative projection; and 5) the role of power. It is tempting to put these factors in a linear order and to talk about which factor caused what other factor(s). This approach, however, does not do justice to the complexities and interrelatedness of the factors. Rather than understanding the five factors in a linear fashion, it is more helpful to understand them as five factors among others in a complex systemic relationship.

These factors combined support us in believing that we can place full and complete responsibility onto those who are aggressive, while allowing ourselves to remain virginally pure—or at least to do so in our minds. We tell ourselves that we have no responsibility for the "monsters next door," because we had nothing to do (or so we believe) with the creation of the monster. If we have no hand in the creation of these alien monsters, then we hold no fault in causing—and possibly hold a moral imperative to bring about—the destruction (or at least containment) of these monsters.[25]

One of humanity's major tasks in the twenty-first century is to find a more conscious place for anger and aggression in our society—to bring our dragon of aggression out of hiding.[26] Pretending that anger and aggression belong to someone else through projection simply does not work anymore. As Bridges (2001) states:

> Remember the story of Sleeping Beauty? The curse that put the young woman to sleep was invoked by the "wicked" spirit that wanted to hurt her because the spirit had been left off the invitation list to her parent's wedding. On a literal level the exclusion is understandable ("Who needs a troublemaker at a wedding?"), but what the story is saying at its deeper levels is that attempting to exclude the bad and increasing the good simply increases the destructive power of whatever was excluded. (p. 188)

Resolving aggression and destruction at any level—in our family, in our neighborhood, in our country, in our world—is extremely difficult and requires a multidisciplinary collaboration. In the words of Wilber (1997),

> In other words, if you and I are going to live together, we have to inhabit, not just the same empirical and physical space, but also the same intersubjective space of mutual recognition. We are going to have to fit, not just our bodies together in the same objective space, but our subjects together in the same cultural, moral and ethical space. We are going to have to find ways to recognize and respect the rights of each other and the community, and these rights cannot be found in objective matter, nor are they simply a case of my own individual sincerity, nor are they a matter of functionally fitting together empirical events: they are rather a matter of fitting our minds together in an intersubjective space that allows each of us to recognize and respect the other. Not necessarily *agree* with each other, but *recognize* each other—the opposite of which, simply put, is war. (Wilber, 1997; original author's italics)

When we project our shadow onto the world, we do so at our own peril.

I have met the terrorist, and I am he.

Who is the terrorist in *your* world?

REFERENCES

Alighieri, D. (1954). *The inferno.* (J. Ciardi, Trans.). New Brunswick, NJ: Rutgers University Press.

American Psychiatric Association. (1994). *Diagnostic and statistical manual of mental disorders* (4th ed.). Washington, DC: Author.

Bates, C. (1991). *Pigs eat wolves—Going into partnership with your dark side.* Saint Paul, MN: Yes International Publishers.

Bridges, W. (2001). *The way of transition: Embracing life's most difficult moments.* New York: Perseus Publishing.

Brooke, R. (2000). Jung's recollection of the life-world. In R. Brooke (Ed.), *Pathways into the Jungian world: Phenomenology and analytical psychology* (pp. 13–24). New York: Routledge.

Brooks-Gunn, J., Klebanov, P., Liaw, F., & Duncan, G. (1995). Toward an understanding of the effects of poverty upon children. In H. E. Fitzgerald, B. M. Lester, & B. Zuckerman, (Eds.), *Children of poverty: Research, health, and policy issues.* New York: Garland Publishing.

Bushman, B., & Baumeister, R. F. (1998). Threatened egotism, narcissism, self-esteem, and direct and misplaced aggression: Does self-love or self-hate lead to violence? *Journal of Personality and Social Psychology, 75,* 21–39.

Campbell, J. (Ed.) (1971). *The portable Jung.* New York: Penguin Books.

Canada, G. (1998). *Reaching up for manhood: Transforming the lives of boys in America.* Boston: Beacon Press.

Children's Defense Fund. http://www.childrensdefense.org

Crum, T. (1987). *The magic of conflict: Turning a life of work into a work of art.* New York: Simon & Schuster.

Damasio, A. (1999). *The feeling of what happens: Body and emotion in the making of consciousness.* New York: Harcourt Brace.

Elias, R. (1997). A culture of violent solutions. In J. Turpin & L. Kurtz (Eds.), *The web of violence: From interpersonal to global* (pp. 118–147). Urbana, IL: University of Illinois Press.

Goodchild, V. (2000). Eros and chaos: The mysteries and shadows of love. In R. Brooke, (Ed.), *Pathways into the Jungian world: Phenomenology and analytical psychology* (pp. 199–215). New York: Routledge.

Hillman, J. (1975). *Re-visioning psychology.* New York: Harper & Row.

Hazelwood, R., & Michaud, S. G. (2001). *Dark dreams: Sexual violence, homicide and the criminal mind.* New York: St. Martin's Press.

Hollis, J. (1994). *Under Saturn's shadow: The wounding and healing of men.* Toronto: Inner City Books.

Hurley, P. J. (1985). *A concise introduction to logic.* Belmont, CA: Wadsworth Publishing.

Jennings, J., & Murphy, C. (2000). Male-male dimensions of male-female battering: A new look at domestic violence. *Psychology of Men and Masculinity, 1,* 21–29.

Jung, C. G. (1966). *Two essays on analytical psychology.* New York: Bollingen Foundation.

La Cerva, V. (1996). *Pathways to peace: Forty steps to a less violent America.* Cordova, TN: Heal Foundation Press.

Lee, R. (1996). Shame and the gestalt model. In R. Lee & G. Wheeler (Eds.), *The voice of shame: Silence and connection in psychotherapy* (pp. 3–21). San Francisco: Jossey-Bass.

Lee, R., & Wheeler, G. (Eds.) (1996). *The voice of shame: Silence and connection in psychotherapy.* San Francisco: Jossey-Bass Publishers.

Linden, P. (1988, Autumn). Being in movement: Intention as a somatic meditation. *Somatics Journal, 54–59* (available online at www.being-in-movement.com).

Linden, P. (1998). Tools for harmony. *Aikido Journal, 25,* 46–49 (available online at www.being-in-movement.com).

National Center for the Analysis of Violent Crime. FBI Academy. Quantico, VA.

O'Toole, M. E. (1999). *The school shooter: A threat assessment perspective.* National Center for Children in Poverty. http://cpmcnet.columbia.edu/dept/nccp/

Papadopoulos, R. K. (1998). Destructiveness, atrocities and healing: Epistemological and clinical reflections. *The Journal of Analytical Psychology, 43,* 455–477.

Tangney, J., Miller, R., Flicker, L., Barlow, D. (1996). Are shame, guilt, and embarrassment distinct emotions? *Journal of Personality and Social Psychology, 70,* 1256–1269.

Tangey, J., Wagner, P., Fletcher, C., Gramzow, R. (1992). Shamed into anger? The relation of shame and guilt to anger and self-reported aggression. *Journal of Personality and Social Psychology, 62,* 669–675.

Von Franz, M. (1995). *Shadow and evil in fairy tales.* Boston: Shambhala Press.

Webster's New Universal Unabridged Dictionary (1996). New York: Barnes & Noble Books.

Wilber, K. (1997). *The eye of spirit: An integral vision for a world gone slightly mad.* Boston: Shambhala Publications.

Wheeler, G. (1996). Self and shame: A new paradigm for psychotherapy. In R. Lee & G. Wheeler (Eds.), *The voice of shame: Silence and connection in psychotherapy* (pp. 23–58). San Francisco: Jossey-Bass.

Wheeler, G. (2000). *Beyond individualism: Toward a new understanding of self, relationship and experience.* Cambridge, MA: GIC Press.

Wheeler, G. (2001). The self in the eye of the father: A gestalt perspective on fathering the male adolescent. In M. McConville & G. Wheeler (Eds.), *The heart of development: Gestalt approaches to working with children, adolescents and their worlds* (pp. 122–152). Cambridge, MA: The Gestalt Press.

Wheeler, G., & Jones, D. (1996). Finding our sons: A male-male gestalt. In R. Lee & G. Wheeler (Eds.), *The voice of shame: Silence and connection in psychotherapy* (pp. 61–99). San Francisco: Jossey-Bass.

Wiener, J. (1998). Under the volcano: Varieties of anger and their transformation. *The Journal of Analytical Psychology, 43*, 493–508.

Wynn, J. (2001). *Inside Rikers: Stories from the world's largest penal colony.* New York: St. Martin's Press.

SUPPLEMENTARY BIBLIOGRAPHY

National Funding Collaboration on Violence Prevention Information and Resources. www.peacebeyondviolence.org.

National Youth Violence Prevention Resource Center Information and Resources for Parents/Guardians, Professionals & Teens (sponsored by the Centers for Disease Control & Prevention). www.safeyouth.org.

Paul Linden's articles cited above and other articles he has written are available for free download at Paul's website: www.being-in-movement.com.

Tim Warneka is available for consultation and training. Visit Tim on the Web at: www.clevelandtherapists.com/psyche-and-soma.html or email Tim at: Tim@clevelandtherapists.com.

NOTES

1.   Nothing is written in a vacuum, and I would like to thank the following people for thoughts, feedback, discussion, and support on several editions of this chapter: Paul Linden, Mary E. Warneka, Bob Lee, James Johnson, Katerine Osatuke, Kirste Carlson, Phil Emminger, Gary Saltus, Diane Wakeley, Pete Smith, Barb Pagon, Janis Woodworth, and Tom Warneka. Special thanks to my colleague and mentor, Debbie Gurney, who co-created the exercise that opens the chapter, and taught me most of what I know about working with adolescents. Thanks to the music of Pat Metheny. My deepest thanks go to my family for

supporting my writing—Beth, Christopher, and Bridget. Of course, all mistakes and errors are my own.

2. The phrase "adolescents who use violent behavior," although cumbersome, is an important distinction from "violent adolescents" or similar phrases that are frequently used in the American media and other venues of speech. It is important to remember that these are adolescents—people—first and foremost, and that they do particular behaviors. Distinguishing between people and behavior is very important if we are not to objectify (and do violence toward) other people. This distinction holds equally true for people who engage in terrorism. People who engage in terrorism are as much mothers and fathers, brothers and sisters as anyone else.

3. All names, dates, and identifying information presented in this chapter have been changed to protect confidentiality.

4. The germinal ideas on the concepts of the paradigm of individualism and shame came from the work of Gestaltists Gordon Wheeler and Bob Lee (see: Lee, 1996; Lee & Wheeler, 1996; Wheeler, 1996; Wheeler, 2000; Wheeler, 2001; and Wheeler & Jones, 1996). For a related Jungian perspective, see Hillman (1975).

5. While much more needs to be explored and written on the five factors, I would refer the interested reader to the works of Wheeler and Lee (see above footnote) for further discussion regarding the interplay of shame and the paradigm of individualism.

6. For example, because the Western worldview does not support much exploration of the transpersonal domain, there has been little discussion of the transpersonal issues surrounding anger and aggression. Space does not permit a discussion of these issues in the present work except to echo Goodchild's (in Brooke, 2000) concern that "Until we find again appropriate religio-cultural channels for these transpersonal energies that move through our world and live in us as powerful affects seeking an individual ethical response, we will continue to destroy ourselves and dismember each other, like Pentheus, in ways, both individual and collective, that have become all too familiar today." (p. 207)

7. Paul Linden (personal communication, 2002) notes that both anger and aggression are behaviors, the former being an internal behavior and the latter an external behavior.

8. Imagine a cultural worldview in which a referee was not required in sports, and players were truly responsible for their own actions. Imagine further a sporting culture that held in highest regard the players who took full responsibility for their fouls, errors, and mistakes. Impossible? Healthy children play self-governing sports and games all the time. (And yet we adults, in our narcissism, frequently place children at the bottom of our moral and ethical models).

9. In the present discussion of emotions and thoughts, I want to be clear about the importance of recognizing that both have physiological underpinnings. One encouraging avenue of treatment (further discussion of which is beyond the scope of the present work) that I have been pursuing for a number of years is incorporating somatic education into my clinical work. As everything about human existence has a physiological component, it only makes sense to bring the body into the work in a conscious manner. The somatic work that I practice has it roots in the Japanese martial art of Aikido ("The Art of Peace") and is very much informed by the work of Paul Linden, Ph.D. (1988, 1998), creator of Being In Movement® somatic education.

10. There seems to be a strong correlation between the ability to be aware of affective states and the ability to be aware of somatic states. Most of the teens who enter therapy at our center have a paucity of awareness at either level.

11. Having a physiological component, we have more control over when emotions come to us and when they leave us than we ordinarily are aware of, but the predominant

cultural view is that emotions come and go like the weather, over which we have no control at all. Adolescence is an emotionally stormy period of time under the best of circumstances. The experience of many (traumatized) adolescents with whom I have worked is that emotions can be very overwhelming. Consequently, I have found it clinically helpful for the population I work with to make the rather black-and-white distinction between the capriciousness of emotions and the choicefulness of behavior. The reality, of course, is much more convoluted.

12.   While Elias's comments concerned children, they are equally valid for adults.

13.   Ask any therapist who has worked with a male who has been sexually abused. While sexual abuse is horrifically shaming for men and women, in Western culture it is so shaming for a male to have been victimized that the male's shame often becomes a barrier that prevents healing.

14.   Reported by President George Bush in his State of the Union address of January 29, 2002.

15.   One of the difficulties in identifying projections in others is the fact that one may be projecting oneself. This can be a serious occupational hazard for mental health professionals—in supporting our clients in understanding their projections, we have to be careful about our projections.

16.   In currently accepted diagnostic language, the term used to describe sociopathy is anti-social personality disorder (American Psychiatric Association, 1994). The only currently accepted diagnosis for sadism is sexual sadism.

17.   This is not to say that neither terrorists nor adolescents *cannot* be sociopaths (although current diagnostic criteria requires a person to be eighteen years old before they can be diagnosed with an antisocial personality disorder (American Psychiatric Association, 1994). One can, in the case of adolescents, speak of characteristics of personality disorders (although there is disagreement in the field as to whether this is appropriate or not.). It is a mistake to apply the label of sociopath to a group of people from a distance. We cannot logically and/or accurately make inferences on the psychological makeup of an individual (i.e., is this person a sociopath?) based on group behavior (i.e., engaging in terrorist activity or juvenile violence). More in-depth individual assessing would need to be done to determine if a particular terrorist was a sociopath, or in the case of an adolescent, showed sociopathic characteristics.

18.   Again, this discussion is in no way meant to minimize the horror and/or atrocity of the attacks of September 11, 2001. The people who attacked the United States objectified the Americans they killed. I see no merit, advantage, or healing in objectifying in return the people who attacked America.

19.   Nothing in this chapter should be read to absolve an individual for personal responsibility for violent behavior. I, along with many other therapists, am very clear in working with aggressive individuals that I support legal consequences (including incarceration) for behaviors that violate our laws. By considering contextual factors, I do not wish to further contribute to a victim mentality that anyone who engages in aggressive behavior may hold. Personally, after hearing the life stories of many of the adolescents who are referred to me, I often find myself being surprised—not at the aggressive behavior that they committed—but why they are not more aggressive than they are. I doubt that I could live through what some of these kids have lived through and not become very violent.

20.   Space does not allow for a thorough discussion of the impact of violence in the media on violent behavior in children, other than to highlight La Cerva's (1996) observation that "by the time today's children finish high school, they will have been exposed to not only 16,000 murders but hundreds of thousands of violent acts—none of which occurred in

their immediate environment." (p. 121)

21. A discussion concerning the relationship between power and aggression could take up an entire chapter of its own. Space does not allow for a fuller discussion of abuses of power, such as when adolescents have too much power in a particular family system (when the power is abdicated by the parent(s)) or when nations engage in terrorist-like activities in order to maintain their power base. Both of these areas of study need to be explored further.

22. Again, space does not permit a fuller discussion of those unhealthy families where the teens have too much power (or too much self-esteem). See Bushman, B., & Baumeister, R. F. (1998).

23. The scenario of one (or more) parent(s) who choose(s) to govern the family with violence, although a fascinating area of study, is outside the realm of this chapter. This scenario has some relationship to the present question, certainly, as many of the adolescents seen in so-called anger management programs come from familial environments wherein many of the members (including the parents) use violence as a primary method of solving problems. And for many of these families, violence has been a method of solving problems for generations.

24. "Thinking errors" are formally called cognitive distortions in the literature of cognitive behaviorism. A thinking error is self-talk that we use to support avoiding responsibility for our actions. Blaming, lying, denying, justifying, minimizing, and rationalizing are all examples of thinking errors.

25. Domestically imprisoning people is not the sole answer either. Wynn (2001) notes that in the 1970s, there were 200,000 people incarcerated in the United States. By the year 2000, America had 2,000,000 people behind bars—an increase of more than 1,000 percent in less than 30 years. Wynn notes that New York City spends $175 per day ($68,000 annually) to incarcerate someone at Rikers—which is "more than eight times what it spends to educate a child in public school, or as much as a college education" (p. 9). Further, Wynn reports that in 1985, America spent just under $13 billion for prison operation. In 2000, America spent $40 billion—which is more than it spent on university construction in that same year (p. 10).

26. Creating a place for understanding the role of anger and aggression in our lives requires a deeply embodied experience. And by "understanding" I do not mean simply a cognitive understanding, but I mean a fuller, deeper understanding—Brooke's (2000) "primordial mode of engagement" (p. 4)—an understanding that holistically incorporates all of ourselves into that understanding. I have found some success when working with adolescents who use aggressive behavior in using a somatic treatment approach based on the Japanese martial art of Aikido. While a discussion of my treatment approach is beyond the scope of this chapter, I would invite any interested reader to visit my Web site or contact me for more information or to share thoughts.

7

Preventing Terrorism: Raising "Inclusively" Caring Children in the Complex World of the Twenty-First Century

Ervin Staub

How do children become caring, helpful, and altruistic? I will discuss the socialization practices by adults and the experiences that children require to achieve this. I want to start, however, with several issues relevant to raising caring children who are unlikely to engage in terrorism.

First, it is possible for children to learn to care about others' welfare, but to restrict their caring to members of their own group. This group may be a family or extended family, a tribe, a religious or ethnic group, a nation, or defined in some other way. This makes it easier for caring children, who become caring adults, to turn against people outside the group. My concern will be with the development of caring both for members of one's "ingroup" and for people outside one's group, that is, with the development of "inclusive" caring. A strong differentiation between "us" and "them," a negative view of those outside the group, and scapegoating of others for life problems and ideologies that identify some others as enemies of the right way of life—these practices not only lead to an absence of caring for the "other," but contribute to the possibility of violence, including terrorism.

Second, caring for others' welfare develops through experiential learning. While children can be effectively instructed and guided by words, and this may even develop an "experiential understanding" that contributes to a positive orientation to self and others, caring cannot be developed by verbal communication alone.

This is especially the case when, through harsh treatment or abuse, children have experienced other people not caring about them. Explanation and verbal guidance must be supported by experiences in interaction with people.

Third, for children to learn to care about other people and their needs, it is essential that their own fundamental needs be satisfied. Like Abraham Maslow and many other psychologists and social scientists, I have stressed in my work for well over a decade the importance of fundamental ("basic") human needs. These needs, shared by all human beings, must be satisfied at least to a moderate degree, in order for people to lead fulfilled, satisfying lives.

The satisfaction of these needs provides the preconditions for the development of caring about and helping other people; frustration of these needs generates hostility and creates a basis for aggression. These needs include the need for security, the need for a positive sense of self or identity, the need for a feeling of effectiveness and some reasonable control over one's life, the need for positive connection to other people (individuals and community), the need for some degree of autonomy, and the need for a worldview that provides a meaningful comprehension of the world and of one's place in it. As these needs are fulfilled to a reasonable extent, the need for transcendence, for going beyond a focus on one's own self, also becomes important. Sometimes people in difficult times, with their basic needs frustrated, engage in pseudo transcendence. They relinquish a burdensome self by giving themselves over to an ideology or movement (Staub, 1996b, 1999, in press-a, in press-b).

SOME OBSTACLES TO RAISING INCLUSIVELY CARING CHILDREN AND CONTRIBUTORS TO TERRORISM

It is possible to reasonably identify, on the basis of research and theory in the last few decades, what children require to become inclusively caring persons (Eisenberg, 1992; Eisenberg & Fabes, 1998; Staub, 1979, 1996a, in press-a, in press-b). But for children to receive that kind of socialization and experience requires adults who want to and are capable of providing this. This is partly a matter of personality and past experience. For example, adults who have been neglected and badly treated as children may have neither the inclination nor the skills to provide the warmth and guidance needed (Staub, 1996a, in press-a, in press-b). But the child rearing required for inclusive caring is also a matter of the culture and the social and political conditions under which adults live. I will very briefly note some conditions that interfere with adults' ability to raise inclusively caring children, or that provide children with experiences that limit their caring in general, or restrict it to members of their own group.

Poverty

When poverty is not extreme, it probably does not, by itself, limit adults' ability to provide the affection, need satisfaction, and guidance (see below) required for children to become caring people. Except under extreme conditions of poverty, poor people can be as happy as wealthier people (Myers, 1992); they may also be able to be loving parents and caretakers of children.

However, when the economic condition of poor people deteriorate, this may affect their ability to fulfill both biological needs and the basic psychological needs noted above. The poor may feel less secure, less good about themselves, less effective, less able to control their lives, and so on. I have suggested that difficult life conditions—which may include severe economic decline, political disorganization, and great social change—frustrate basic needs and are one of the starting points for an evolution toward mass killing or genocide (Staub, 1989, 1999). Such conditions tend to give rise to scapegoating and destructive ideologies. They make less likely parenting that helps to develop caring, especially inclusive caring (Staub, 1996b).

Justice and Injustice, Repressive Political Systems, and Culture Change

Poverty and deteriorating economic conditions are especially likely to affect people when they see others as much better off than they are. The experience of great injustice would make less likely child rearing that gives rise to inclusive caring.

Repressive political systems make it difficult if not impossible to deal with injustice and improve the economic conditions and rights of groups that live in poverty. They create anger and hostility that, when they cannot be expressed, may be channeled toward targets that are physically less dangerous and psychologically more accessible than the repressive authorities at home, which often claim they represent tradition and are carriers of cultural or religious virtues. Repressive systems also make it difficult to deal with the impact of culture change. Such systems are monolithic; they allow the expression of only limited values and beliefs and inhibit the free exchange of ideas.

To live in the modern world, to gain the material benefits, educational opportunities, and much else it has to offer, requires an integration of new and old. This is difficult under the best of conditions. The psychological demands of living with change are great. In traditional societies that have repressive systems, the struggle to reconcile tradition and change, the clash of the old and the new, engagement with discrepant values and beliefs, is especially difficult if not impossible. The accommodation between old and new or the transformation required to integrate them may not take place. Confusion of identity, problems in connecting with other people, feelings of ineffectiveness, and especially difficulty with having a coherent understanding of reality may result. When the repressive system is highly effective, which in terms of communication and information is increasingly difficult in the contemporary world, individuals' problems may become acute if and when they encounter the outside world.

Poverty has extraordinary power, especially when combined with relative deprivation, a feeling of powerlessness to improve one's life, and great culture change—when the process of accommodation, transformation, and integration of old and new cannot take place. These factors often occur together. They may lead people to turn to ideologies, visions of a better life, that help them deal with the psychological impact of their experience. These ideologies may be nationalistic, religious, or something else. In addition to providing hope for a better future, they can give followers an understanding of the world and a sense of personal significance. But they also identify enemies of the ideology and as a result have an important role in mass killing and genocide, as well as a powerful role in terrorism—whether we look at the terrorism of Palestinians, Osama bin Laden and his supporters, Basques, or other nationalist movements.

Many of the conditions described here make it more difficult but still allow people to raise children in ways that develop caring. But they make practices that develop inclusive caring much less likely. For the latter to happen, the conditions must change. There must be greater equality, shared suffering, and mutual support in the face of life problems, integration of the new and the old, and so on. At the very least, people must create more inclusive ideologies, positive visions in the face of difficult conditions that do not create divisions between us and them—ideologies that people can strive to fulfill by peaceful means.

IMPORTANT SOCIALIZATION PRACTICES

Warmth and Affection Versus Harsh Treatment and Hostility

The experience of warmth, nurturance, and affection are central to the development of caring about other people and their welfare (Yarrow & Scott, 1972). An essential form of warmth and nurturance by parents and other caretakers is responsiveness to infants' and young children's needs. The satisfaction of these needs for food, stimulation, contact, interaction, and affection contributes to the development of secure attachment (Bretherton, 1992; Staub, 1996a, in press-a). Their satisfaction leads children to feel effective, to value themselves, and to feel connected to other people. It leads them to value other people.

In contrast, harshness, rejection, punitiveness, and abuse make the development of caring about others' welfare and helping others unlikely. Whatever is the adults' reason for such treatment of a child, inherent in it is a devaluation of the child. Such treatment frustrates the needs for positive identity, security, effectiveness and control, and positive connection. It teaches the child to fear and mistrust people (Staub, 1996a, 1996b, in press-a).

Warmth and affection require sensitivity in perceiving and responding to the needs of a growing child (Staub, 1996a; in press-a). For example, a young child coming home from school may be upset about something that has happened. Sensitive affection would lead a parent or caretaker both to perceive this and to consider the child's sensitivity in talking about it. The child may be ashamed of something that has happened. If it is a problem in school with other children or a teacher, the child may be concerned that parental intervention will humiliate him or her. Genuine affection and nurturance does not simply mean a certain amount of warmth, or of physical affection; they require sensitive responding to the needs and feelings of the child.

Structure and Guidance at Home and in School

Young children require predictable environments for growth and development. They require organization and structure not only in their external world, but also—with help from parents or caretakers—in their internal world. For example, parents help young children organize their emotions. They teach the child what different emotions are, help the child to modulate intense emotions, soothe the child when distressed, and reassure the child when afraid. They even help the young child to keep pleasurable excitement within controllable limits. Through all this, the parent or caretaker provides an essential structure. The parent needs also to help the child organize tasks and other activities. Such structuring—or as Vygotsky called it, scaffolding (see Rogoff, 1990)—can help the child develop internal structure, which then guides the child in his or her reactions and actions.

An important form of guidance is reasoning with children. Rules are an essential form of structure and guidance. Rules can be arbitrarily set and enforced in an authoritarian manner. Alternatively, rules can be set on the basis of values. Children can be told what these values are and how the rules relate to them. This makes it more likely that children will accept the rules, make them their own, and follow them in a cooperative manner.

An especially important form of reasoning for the development of caring and helping has been referred to as induction. Induction means explaining to the child the consequences of his or her behavior for other people (Eisenberg, 1992; Eisenberg & Fabes, 1998; Hoffman, 1970, 1975, 2000; Staub, 1979, 1996a, in press-a). When a child says or does something hurtful—whether to strangers, peers, or parents—the painful consequences of this, the feelings of hurt and distress, physical pain, and so on, are laid out.

Actions can affect a person's body, feelings, or thoughts. Pointing out the consequences of his or her actions makes a child aware of others' inner worlds. It helps the child to see his or her own power in influencing others' welfare. It helps promote the capacity to take others' role. It helps the child develop empathy and a feeling of responsibility for others' welfare. All these have been found importantly involved in people helping others. Positive induction, or pointing out to children the positive consequences of their actions on others' welfare, is also valuable (Staub, 1979).

Another important form of guidance is modeling. The actions of adults in the child's environment, especially important adults, have great influence. So do story characters, whether in fairy tales, other types of stories, movies, or on television. Modeling teaches the child what is normal, expected, and right. It helps the child to learn the consequences of different actions on other people, as well as the reactions that different behaviors generate.

Schools are very important in all these aspects of socialization. Schools set rules for children for their interaction with teachers and peers, for attending to tasks, for living in a social world. They provide structure and guidance of many kinds. Teachers and other adults in schools can be warm and affectionate, cold and indifferent, or harsh and punitive, with consequences similar to such variations in parents.

Schools are also important in offering opportunities for participation. Children can develop a feeling of importance and responsibility by participating in significant ways in the life of the school. For example, even very young children can participate in creating rules for the classroom. In the course of discussing how various rules might affect them, their peers, teachers, and their learning in the classroom, children can learn independence of judgment.

The creation of community in the classroom is also very important (Staub, in press-a, in press-b). Some children, starting at an early age, become marginal in their classroom. This is especially likely to happen with children who most need connection and community, because they have not had it in their families. Their marginality, their lack of connection to their peers and to learning in the classroom, can lead them to turn to deviant peers. This is one of the avenues through which children, as they grow into adolescents, move into gangs. When their experiences at home and in schools and their interaction with peers fail to fulfill their basic needs for identity, positive connection, and a sense of effectiveness, they are likely to turn to other groups that will satisfy these needs. These are basic needs that, starting in early adolescence, become developmentally especially important (Staub, 1996b).

A column in the *New York Times* by Thomas L. Friedman (2002) discusses the terrorists of September 11, 2001, in ways that relate to issues of socialization and experience. They were from middle-class families in the Arab world, educated young men who went to Europe for more education. There they joined a local prayer group or mosque where they became radicalized, and went off to get training in Afghanistan. The narrowness of the experience and worldview with which they grew up, the clash between that world and the world they encountered in Europe, and what Friedman described as a lack of respect that Muslims experience in Europe joined in making the influence of the mosques especially potent.

A number of factors probably all entered into the formation of these terrorists: the ideology of a strict religion, as practiced at home and as preached in the mosques to which they turned; the difficulty of integrating their past understanding of the world with their new experiences in a much different world; the lack of satisfaction of basic needs in Europe, such as positive identity (respect) and connection to the world around them; and the sharp lines between us and them that these influences would have created. However, not all young men from the same Arab countries who go to Europe become terrorists. For a more thorough understanding of them, we would also need to know the experiences of these young men in their families, and the joint influence of those experiences and the larger contexts of their lives.

The Role of Discipline

Affection, structure, and guidance go a long way in gaining children's cooperation. However, they don't always go all the way (Baumrind, 1975). While it is important to allow children a great deal of autonomy, and increasing autonomy with increasing age, it is also important to get them to abide by rules that express the values of their parents, teachers, or other caretakers.

While discipline is very important, it is essential that it not be harsh, negative, and punitive. As I have noted, children who experience harsh treatment from an early age on, who experience rejection, frequent physical punishment, and other expressions of hostility from parents, are likely to become hostile and aggressive (Dodge, 1993; Huesmann, Eron, Lefkowitz, & Walder, 1984; Staub, 1996a, 1996b, in press-a). Their basic needs unfulfilled, they will lack a positive sense of self and come to see other people in a negative light.

Moderate, positive forms of discipline are important to use but hard to devise. They can include communication to children about what consequences will follow undesirable actions. Sparingly used, they can include withdrawal of privileges. In school, getting children involved in discussing certain kinds of discipline problems and in deciding on consequences can be useful. However, children can be overly punitive to each other, a punitiveness that ought to be moderated.

Acknowledging and affirming positive behavior and ingenuity in devising mild forms of discipline techniques is important. However, the more children's needs are fulfilled starting early in their lives, and the more they are guided through explanation and other positive means, the less extensively will discipline have to be used.

Learning by Doing

A central avenue for children to learn to become caring and helpful is engagement or participation in helpful acts. In a number of studies, my students and I involved children in making toys for poor hospitalized children, or had older children teach younger children (Staub, 1975, 1979). We found that such engagement in helping increased children's later helping. There is other evidence that shows this kind of learning of caring and helpful behavior by doing (Eisenberg & Fabes, 1998; Staub, 1979; Whiting & Whiting, 1975).

Children also learn to be aggressive through engagement in aggressive behavior. There is evidence with adults that harming people makes it easier to harm people again, and/or to a greater extent. There is also evidence, from the study of genocide, that as members of a perpetrator group harm others, they change. Increased harming of the victims, increased violence, becomes easier and more likely (Staub, 1989). This is also likely to be true of children. When children repeatedly engage in aggressive acts, they are likely to change. For them as well, aggression will become easier and more likely.

Us and Them: The Origins of Inclusive Caring

Among rescuers, people who endangered their lives in Nazi Europe to help persecuted Jews, many were found to draw a less sharp line between "us," their own group, and "them," people outside their group, than others in a similar situation who did not help. This group was composed of individuals who grew up in families with parents who, through words and actions, engaged with people outside their own group; as children, these rescuers learned to respect and value people beyond their narrowly defined group (Oliner & Oliner, 1988).

Children can learn to care about other people, but at the same time to draw a sharp line between members of their own group and those outside the group. Or they can learn to include people beyond their group in the realm of humanity. They can learn to care about their welfare and act in their behalf. Parents can promote this by the way they guide their children, including efforts to promote relationships with children belonging to different groups.

In most societies, some subgroups of society are the objects of devaluation, prejudice, and discrimination. They may be identified as a group because they are ethnic minorities, or they have a different religion, or hold currently unpopular political views, or are people who have come to occupy a lower status in society. The negative attitude and behavior toward them may have developed in the distant historical past or in response to recent circumstances in society. Almost inevitably, the cultural devaluation of a group is transmitted to children by the culture: by literature, the media, word of mouth, and the attitude and action of adults. Existing devaluation and the tendency to devalue are likely to be strengthened by the social and political conditions described earlier.

In schools, it has been found that cooperative learning promotes positive relations among children belonging to different ethnic and racial groups (Aronson, Stephan, Sikes, Blaney, & Snapp, 1978; Hertz-Lazarowitz & Sharan, 1984). For example, a group of children may be put together to work on a shared task. To fulfill this task, each of them has to learn some material and teach it to others in the group. Each child is thus a learner as well as a teacher (Aronson et al., 1978).

Deep engagement among members of groups is essential both to overcoming devaluation and to promoting inclusive, caring, cross-cutting relations (Pettigrew, 1997; Staub, 1989). Such deep engagement can take the form of joint projects, whether business projects, or members of different groups cleaning up neighborhoods together, or cultural exchanges. Schools provide extensive opportunities both for learning to care about others through participation and engagement, and for cooperative learning and cross-cutting relations.

The Development of Moral Courage

We are frequently witnesses or bystanders not only to other people's pain and suffering, but also to harm inflicted on them. This harm may be inflicted through discrimination, prejudice, or violence. Harm may be inflicted on groups of people in our society or in some other part of the world. Even in the latter case, we as individuals, our nation as a whole, and individuals and nations around the world are witnesses or bystanders to this. People can be passive bystanders or respond actively.

People often remain passive bystanders because it is difficult to speak out. Speaking or acting sometimes requires physical courage. Frequently it requires moral courage, the willingness to stand up for and act on one's values. In the course of growing up, many children suffer due to exclusion, taunting, ridicule, or other forms of persecution by their peers (Olweus, 1993). Others frequently remain passive bystanders (Staub & Spielman, 2000). Some who were initially passive get drawn in and become perpetrators. In turn, children who have themselves suffered are often passive bystanders when this is done to others. All this leaves psychological wounds, as many students in my courses have reported when encouraged to write about personal experiences in the course of exploring psychological research and theory on these issues.

The willingness of teenagers to speak out and oppose are of essential importance when a group of their peers contemplates some action that harms others or causes damage. The willingness of adults (as well as adolescents) to speak and act is crucial when a society begins to victimize a minority in its midst (Staub, 1989, 1999), or when antagonism develops toward outsiders, with the possibility of persecution, mass killing, or terrorism. The issue of bystandership is present in children's lives from an early age and remains present in their lives as adults.

How can moral courage develop, the courage to speak out and take action consistent with one's values and beliefs? Moral courage is a requirement for helping in many contexts. Teachers involving children in the creation of rules for the classroom is one important avenue to the development of moral courage. In the course of this, children can learn to express their views and beliefs, to discuss and argue, to present their points of view, to stand up for what they believe. Similar things can happen in the family as well. The example of moral courage provided to the children by parents, teachers, and other people is also central to developing moral courage of their own.

CONCLUSIONS

I have described here some central principles for raising children so that they will become caring, helpful, and altruistic people. There are no exact recipes for raising children. While the principles are important, different parents, teachers, and caretakers who want to follow such principles will do so in their own ways.

Learning about such principles and developing skills in practicing them are of great value. But they can be insufficient. Frequently, adults have had experiences in their own lives that make it difficult for them to effectively act on such principles. These experiences may include harsh treatment and abuse that they themselves have suffered. It may include current difficulties in their lives, economic problems, or lack of social support. For many adults to act on these principles may require personal transformation, that is, finding ways to change themselves and their ways of perceiving, experiencing, and reacting to events. This requires special procedures and experiences (Staub, in press-a; Staub & Pearlman, 1996).

To create conditions in which these principles can be fulfilled can also require societal changes that provide sufficient support for adults involved in raising and socializing children (Staub, 1996b). And it can require social and political changes that allow people and help develop in people a valuing of the "other" rather than restricting the focus to the self and generating hostility to people outside the group. The creation of such changes is essential for a better world (Staub, 1999, in press-b; Staub & Pearlman, 2001). The role of nations is central in this. Especially powerful nations, such as the United States, and the international community, as "active bystanders," can exert positive influence in promoting pluralistic and just societies that affirm individuals and help fulfill basic needs.

REFERENCES

Aronson, E., Stephan, C., Sikes, J., Blaney, N., & Snapp, M. (1978). *The jigsaw classroom.* Beverly Hills, CA: Sage Publications.

Baumrind, D. (1975). *Early socialization and the discipline controversy.* Morristown, NJ: General Learning Press.

Bretherton, I. (1992). The origins of attachment theory: John Bowlby and Mary Ainsworth. *Developmental Psychology, 28,* 759–775.

Dodge, K. A. (1993). Social cognitive mechanisms in the development of conduct disorder and depression. *Annual Review of Psychology, 44,* 559–584.

Eisenberg, N. (1992). *The caring child.* Cambridge, MA: Harvard University Press.

Eisenberg, N., & Fabes, R. A. (1998). Prosocial development. In W. Damon (Ed.), *Handbook of child psychology, fifth edition.* Vol. 3: N. Eisenberg (Ed.). *Social, emotional, and personality development.*

Friedman, T. L. (2002, January 27). The 2 Domes of Belgium. *New York Times,* p. 13.

Hertz-Lazarowitz, R., & Sharan, S. (1984). Enhancing prosocial behavior through cooperative learning in the classroom. In E. Staub, D. Bar-Tal, J. Karylowski, & J. Reykowski (Eds.), *Development and maintenance of prosocial behavior* (pp. 423–445). New York: Plenum.

Hoffman, M. L. (1970). Moral development. In P. H. Mussen (Ed.), *Carmichael's manual of child development.* New York: Wiley.

Hoffman, M. L. (1975). Altruistic behavior and the parent-child relationship. *Journal of Personality and Social Psychology, 31,* 937–943.

Hoffman, M. L. (2000). *Empathy and moral development: Implications for caring and justice.* New York: Cambridge University Press.

Huesmann, L. R., Eron, L. D., Lefkowitz, M. M., & Walder, L. O. (1984). Stability of aggression over time and generations. *Developmental Psychology, 20,* 1120–1134.

Myers, D. G. (1992). *The pursuit of happiness.* New York: William Morrow and Company.

Oliner, S. B., & Oliner, P. (1988). *The altruistic personality: Rescuers of Jews in Nazi Europe.* New York: Free Press.

Olweus, D. (1993). *Bullying at school: What we know and what we can do.* Oxford: Blackwell Publishers.

Pettigrew, T. F. (1997). Generalized intergroup contact effects on prejudice. *Personality and Social Psychology Bulletin, 23,* 173–185.

Rogoff, B. (1990). *Apprenticeship in thinking.* New York: Oxford University Press.

Staub, E. (1975). To rear a prosocial child: Reasoning learning by doing, and learning by teaching others. In D. DePalma & J. Folley (Eds.), *Moral development: Current theory and research*. Hillsdale, NJ: Erlbaum.

Staub, E. (1979). *Positive social behavior and morality: Socialization and development* (Vol. 2). New York: Academic Press.

Staub, E. (1989). *The roots of evil: The origins of genocide and other group violence*. New York: Cambridge University Press.

Staub, E. (1996a). Altruism and aggression in children and youth: Origins and cures. In R. Feldman (Ed.), *The psychology of adversity*. Amherst, MA: University of Massachusetts Press.

Staub, E. (1996b). The cultural-societal roots of violence: The examples of genocidal violence and of contemporary youth violence in the United States. *American Psychologist, 51*, 117–132.

Staub, E. (1999). The origins and prevention of genocide, mass killing, and other collective violence. *Peace and Conflict: Journal of Peace Psychology, 5*, 303–336.

Staub, E. (in press-a). *A brighter future: Raising caring and nonviolent children*. New York: Oxford University Press.

Staub, E. (in press-b). *The psychology of good and evil*. New York: Cambridge University Press.

Staub, E., & Pearlman, L. (1996, November). Trauma and the fulfillment of the human potential. Workshop presented at the meeting of the International Society for Traumatic Stress Studies. San Francisco.

Staub, E., & Pearlman, L. (2001). Healing, reconciliation and forgiving after genocide and other collective violence. In S. J. Helmick and R. L. Petersen (Eds.), *Forgiveness and reconciliation: Religion, public policy and conflict transformation*. Radnor, PA: Templeton Foundation Press.

Staub, E., and Spielman, D. (2000). Students' experience of bullying and of other aspects of their lives in middle school. Unpublished manuscript, Department of Psychology, University of Massachusetts at Amherst.

Whiting, B., and Whiting, J. W. M. (1975). *Children of six cultures*. Cambridge, MA: Harvard University Press.

Yarrow, M. R., & Scott, P. M. (1972). Imitation of nurturant and nonnurturant models. *Journal of Personality and Social Psychology, 8*, 240–261.

8

Preventing Future Terrorist Activities Among Adolescents Through Global Psychology: A Cooperative Learning Community

Sherri McCarthy

The threat of terrorism has been undermining our sense of security, control, and predictability since the tragedies of September 11, 2001. This is true for people of all ages, but is particularly salient for adolescents, whose vulnerability to fear, anxiety, trauma, and stress is heightened due to physiological and psychological development. The same factors that make adolescents particularly vulnerable to the psychological impact of stress also make them particularly susceptible to developing attitudes and "scripts" that will lead to either their own participation in future terrorist activities or their adherence to values that will prevent engagement in such activities.

By consciously incorporating strategies into the education and socialization of adolescents and young adults that are designed to minimize tendencies toward stereotyping that lead to prejudice, hate, and violence, we can prevent the spread of terrorism in the future. The content area of psychology seems to be a natural venue for accomplishing this goal. At the community college or university level in the United States, Introductory Psychology is one of the most commonly required courses in a variety of degree programs, including education, business, nursing, liberal arts, criminal justice, and social sciences. It is also a popular and commonly available elective at the high school level. In many other countries, it is a required course during high school or secondary education (McCarthy, 1999a). Thus, integrating elements into the psychology curriculum that decrease the likelihood of future participation in terrorist activities by students is an effective prevention strategy.

This chapter first briefly summarizes relevant research in the areas of developmental and social psychology that support this assertion. Then, promising educational strategies to incorporate into classrooms are reviewed. Finally, the Global Psychology project, which was developed through the American Psychological Association (APA) P3 Project (McCarthy, 2001), Division 2, and the First International Conference on Psychology Education (Karandashev, 2002) in St. Petersburg, Russia, is described.

WHY ADOLESCENCE IS A CRITICAL DEVELOPMENTAL WINDOW FOR PREVENTING FUTURE TERRORISM

In the psychological literature, adolescence is generally defined as the transitional period between childhood and adulthood. Adolescence begins when the physical capability to reproduce is present and ends when a role implying adult status has been achieved (Muuss, 1996). The age boundaries are not exact, and vary somewhat from culture to culture. Some societies, in fact, may not include a period of adolescence (Schlegel & Barry, 1991), but it can be assumed that adolescence begins around the age of 12 and ends around the age of 25, with some individual variation, in most countries today. A protracted period of adolescence is seen primarily in highly industrialized nations where advanced education is required to enter the workplace and economic independence from parents is seen as a "rite of passage" into the adult world.

During this period, which occurs primarily during high school and early college years for the majority of youth, many critical attitudes and behaviors are solidified. Erikson (1968) postulated that adolescence was a period of pivotal importance, when one's identity was formed. Adolescents wrestle with such important issues as "What do I stand for?," "Who am I?," and "What do I want to do with my life?" The answers to these questions derived during adolescence allow individuals to commit not only to an occupational direction but also to a value system (Marcia, 1991). The struggle for identity may be an ongoing process throughout our lives, but it is particularly intense during adolescence. The advent of formal operational thought, as explained by Piaget (Inhelder & Piaget, 1958), promotes self-reflection and can even be expressed as a particular form of egocentrism (Elkind, 1985) in which adolescents assume they are the central focus of others' attention. The physical changes of puberty, including the increased levels of adrenaline that fuel the growth spurt and the advent of hormonal changes, heighten perceptions and intensify feelings. Experiences seem more intense. Memories become more deeply rehearsed and processed.

Identity Development and Attitude Formation

For the reasons explained above, attitudes formed during the stage of identity formation that occurs during adolescence are likely to be long-lasting, even permanent, and to exert a great influence on behavior. One's self-concept, as determined initially during adolescence, is critical to regulating behavior in the future. One's sense of possible selves (Markus & Nurius, 1986), based on experiences, modeling, and information acquired during this period, can influence the likelihood of engaging in or refraining from terrorist activities. The attitudes toward others established during adolescence can lead either toward or away from a tendency to stereotype members of groups (religious, ethnic, economic, or cultural) to which one does not belong. Hate and prejudice are built on these stereotypes, and experiences during adolescence will either exacerbate or prevent the development of these attitudes. Educational strategies aimed at the prevention of developing these attitudes are especially useful during these times of development. Integrating into high school and college curricula strategies to prevent the formation of stereotypes that lead to prejudice and hate is critical if we wish to prevent future terrorism.

Media Influence

Evidence of the effect the media has on the attitudes and behavior of children and adolescents is well documented (Murray, 1980). Research over the past four decades (Bandura, 1968; Bandura, Ross & Ross, 1963; Banks, 1971) has established that television plays a role in developing attitudes toward members of groups. The vicarious modeling that occurs influences behavior among adolescent viewers and influences identity development. The roles that Web-based entertainment, video games, and music play are certainly similar. If young viewers are not educated to think critically about what they see, to question it, and to actively separate "entertainment" from "reality," they are not likely to do so.

It is important to stress, however, that media are best used as a tool to prevent terrorism rather than as a scapegoat for its occurrence. Certainly any movie, series, game, or song that presents members of other religious, racial, or geographic groups as "enemies" or "subhuman" must share in the blame for creating a mindset that leads to terrorism, and concerned citizens around the world should actively boycott and prevent such uses of media. Our present challenge is to use the media to provide programming, experiences, and models to youth that illustrate the fallacy of assuming that those who believe, look, think, or act differently should be attacked, discredited, or otherwise discounted. Using this powerful tool to stress human similarities across cultures and to highlight that individual differences are positive rather than negative is essential if we are to prevent youth from embracing terrorism.

Peer Influence

The peer group becomes increasingly important during adolescence. In the United States, adolescents are likely to spend well over 50 percent of their time with age-mates (Csikszentmihalyi & Larson, 1984). Obviously, all of the time in school occurs with age-mates, but American teenagers also average more than twenty hours a week outside the classroom with peers, compared with two to three hours reported in Japan and Russia (Savin-Williams & Berndt, 1990). Peer relations can be either positive or negative, depending upon what occurs. At best, such unsupervised interaction with peers can result in a bridge into adult social roles and an opportunity to develop friendships, develop social skills, and gain emotional support. At worst, it can reinforce the ingroup/outgroup dynamics that lead to prejudice and hate, antisocial behavior, and lack of attachment to society at large. What makes the difference?

Diversity versus homogeneity of the group with which an adolescent primarily associates is one important variable. An adolescent who interacts positively with peers from a variety of backgrounds (socioeconomic, cultural, geographical, and religious) is more likely to develop an acceptance of individual differences and a wariness of stereotyping, while an adolescent who interacts only with peers who are similar is more likely to develop a mistrust of other groups. Such experiences during youth may even affect physiological responses of the amygdala and result in differential processing of emotional cues based on race or group (Hetherton, 2002; Phelps et al., 2000) later in life. It is important to engage adolescents in positive, prosocial activities with diverse groups of friends. The tendency of adolescents to gravitate toward "rival gangs" based on race, economic factors, or attitudes should be counteracted to avoid the development of the "mindset" that leads to the ability to engage in terrorist belief systems and activities.

Role Models and Social Learning

The powerful role of social learning, based on identification with and imitation of others perceived as "high status" members of the community, has been well-established for decades (Bandura, 1962, 1965, 1969, 1971). Adolescents look to sports figures, political leaders, actors, and musicians, as well as family members and peers, to find "models." They use these models to help determine their own potential beliefs and actions—their "possible selves." The more consistent the modeling, especially among those with whom adolescents interact on a daily basis, the more powerful it is. If the models available to youth espouse values and attitudes that lead to prejudice, hate, mistrust of other groups, and violent resolutions to problems, future terrorists are molded. Recent experiences in Northern Ireland and the Middle East illustrate this, as do occurrences such as the Oklahoma bombing and recent high school shootings in the United States. If, instead, the models espouse acceptance of diversity, nonviolent problem-solving strategies, and humanitarian values, terrorism is prevented. Educational and societal interventions need to provide such models to adolescents.

Attributions, Stereotyping, and Prejudice

Social psychologists conducting studies that have focused on person perception, causal attribution, and attitude formation have provided us with insight regarding how stereotypes form and how this can lead to prejudice, discrimination, and acts of violence toward others. Much of this is rooted in attribution theory. Attributions are inferences that people draw about the causes of their own behavior, the behavior of others, and events. In some cases, due to faulty logical processes, negative modeling, unsavory media influence, and other methods that lend themselves to propaganda, attributions may occur based on appearance alone. Physical features, combined with one's beliefs about what such features imply, are one of the most common ways impressions of others are formed (Bull & Rumsey, 1988). For example, "He stole the wallet because he is black, and all blacks are poor criminals" and "She is on welfare because she is Mexican and all Mexicans are lazy" are not farfetched attributions to many adolescents, depending upon how they have been socialized. "That person is a terrorist because he is Muslim" is another potential attribution that might occur if appropriate safeguards against media and models are not enacted.

Attributions contribute to perceiver expectancies. These expectancies then influence behavior toward others. This confirmation bias has been evidenced in many studies (Cohen, 1981; Fiske, 1993; Fiske & Taylor, 1991; Snyder, Tanke & Berscheid, 1977) and seems related to stereotype formation and prejudice. When individuals encounter groups they view with prejudice, they are likely to see what they expect (Stephan, 1989). Behavior toward others can, in turn, influence the behavior of others. This is the self-fulfilling prophecy phenomenon described by Merton in 1948 and since documented empirically (Rosenthal, 1985). Adolescents are especially susceptible to this phenomenon since they are still unsure of their identities. As Swann and Ely (1984) demonstrated, self-fulfilling prophecy is most likely to occur when target persons are uncertain about their self-views.

Other common errors of attribution are also worth noting. Defensive attribution (Lerner & Miller, 1978) is the tendency to blame victims for their own misfortune. Several studies (Kristiansen & Giuletti, 1990; Salminen, 1992; Thornton, 1992) have illustrated this error. The fundamental attribution error (Ross, 1977) is the tendency to explain the negative behavior of others in terms of personal rather than situational factors, while one's own negative behavior is viewed as situationally determined. The reverse pattern characterizes positive acts—i.e., situational for others and personal for self.

Other cognitive distortions that are related to the formation of attitudes that may lead to terrorism include categorization and stereotyping. Individuals perceive those like themselves (on dimensions such as appearance, age, race, gender, religion, occupation, nationality, or some other salient dimension) as an "ingroup." Those who are not similar are perceived as an "outgroup." People usually have less favorable attitudes toward members of the outgroup (Meindl & Lerner, 1984). This group categorization is likely a feature of the human brain that is "hard-wired in." Efficiency of processing is dependent upon categorization. Basic logical processes rely on it. Even safety and survival are rooted in the ability to quickly distinguish a predator from a non-predator. Metacognitive awareness of this process, and how it functions, is essential to prevent stereotyping and prejudice. Stereotypes are widely held beliefs that membership in a certain group automatically bestows certain characteristics. The most prevalent stereotypes seem to be based on physical appearance, gender, age, and ethnicity (Eagly, Ashmore, Makhijani & Longo, 1991; Fiske, 1993). Stereotyping, in turn, leads to prejudice—the formation of a negative attitude toward all members of a particular group.

In addition to faulty attributions, categorization, and stereotyping, two other avenues that researchers have demonstrated lead to prejudice are competition for resources and threats to social identity. As the economy shifts to an increasingly capitalistic, global base and Western society continues to encroach on other cultures, it becomes apparent that these two avenues are increasingly likely to be taken. As for the first avenue, more than half a century ago, Sherif's experiments (Sherif, Harvey, White, Hood & Sherif, 1988) clearly demonstrated that competition led not only to prejudice against members of competing groups, but also to violence against those members. However, simple competition for resources is certainly not the only cause for striking out against others who are perceived as different. If individuals perceive that their group is being threatened, they often look for scapegoats in other groups (Pettigrew, 1978) and strike out against these groups. A perceived threat to the group is often seen as even more devastating than a personal threat (Bobo, 1988). These findings seem to provide a strikingly clear explanation for the rise of the occurrence of terrorist acts against the West in traditional Mideastern societies. The ongoing struggle over Northern Ireland and racial turbulence and aversive racism (Dovidio & Gaertner, 1998) in South Africa and the United States, as well as tribal and religious warfare throughout the world, can be explained in these terms. If the trend toward an increasingly global, competitive, and capitalistic economic base continues, it is logical to predict that such conditions will create more, not less, of a propensity toward acts of terrorism due to increasing perceived threat and increasing prejudice.

Threat to one's social identity is the second avenue that accounts for prejudice and acts of violence. This may be more relevant to "domestic" acts, such as the U.S. school shootings in Colorado, California, Arkansas, and elsewhere, than to global acts, although it certainly impacts those as well. Although no real "profile" for adolescents has emerged from the efforts of U.S. criminal justice agencies to identify potential "school shooting terrorists," the one characteristic common to most cases is that of a rather isolated Caucasian male. In an educational environment increasingly tuned into diversity and cultural differences, it may be this group that has the least social identity and perceives the most threat. According to social identity theory (Tajfel, 1982; Turner, 1987), self-esteem is determined in part by the "collective self," which is tied to group membership. Salient groups include nationality, gender, religion, occupation, and so forth. Threats to both individual and group identity lower self-esteem and motivate individuals to engage in acts designed to restore it. Threats to group, or social, identity are most likely to provoke responses that foster prejudice, discrimination, or violence (Crocker & Luhtanen, 1990). A common way to deal with threats to one's social identity is through outgroup derogation—insulting, discounting, and otherwise harming others who are perceived as threatening (Branscombe & Wann, 1994). Social isolation and lack of a cohesive ingroup make such behavior even more likely.

Because of the heightened sensitivity and the struggle for identity that adolescence spurs, teens and young adults are even more likely to be susceptible to these reactions than adults. However, this is one situation where "knowledge is power," and Socrates' admonition to "Know thyself" can be a useful tool for understanding and regulating such behavior. Providing young adults with an understanding of these human tendencies seems crucial, and a psychology curriculum seems a natural place to include such content. A curriculum that not only points out such important information about human tendencies, but also breaks down barriers between groups and brings students into positive interactions with members of the outgroups by whom they feel threatened is an even more powerful tool. Systematically applying interventions to reduce fear and prejudice while increasing self-understanding among youth seems to be our wisest course in combating future terrorism.

Interventions for Reducing Prejudice

As alluded to above, making individuals mindful of the ways in which stereotypes are formed and prejudice results is a powerful cognitive tool for diminishing the condition. Siegler has shown that providing adolescents with information that addresses specific flaws in their reasoning encourages them to use more advanced rules (Siegler, 1991). Incorporating instruction in contextualized logic into the curriculum (McCarthy, 1998a) and focusing this instruction on disconfirmation of stereotypes and prejudice is a promising strategy. Devine's (1989) strategy of shifting from automatic to controlled processing or Langer's (Langer, Bashner, & Chanowitz, 1985) recommendation of incorporating "mindful" rather than "mindless" processing might be achieved in this way.

An even more powerful strategy for reducing prejudice is through controlled intergroup contact. As Fazio and others have demonstrated (Dovidio, 2002), the best predictor of reduced prejudice as measured by indirect, spontaneous means is the amount of contact with other groups that has occurred early in life. Aronson (2001) has demonstrated for decades how use of cooperative learning in schools, using heterogeneous grouping, not only benefits student learning but also reduces contention among groups. His classic work on "jigsaw classrooms" (Aronson, Stephan, Sikes, Blaney, & Snapp, 1978) is relevant for reducing school violence and acts of terrorism against individuals perceived as outgroup members.

Simply bringing members of potentially hostile groups into contact, however, is not sufficient. If not appropriately directed, such contact may actually exacerbate hostility and prejudice. Instead, the contact needs to be controlled to allow for positive interaction. Brewer and Brown (1997) demonstrate several requisites for intergroup contact that reduces stereotypes and prejudice. These requisites include that: 1) individuals from several groups must work together toward a common goal; 2) there must be a successful outcome or product from the cooperative efforts; 3) group members must have the opportunity to establish meaningful connections with one another that have the potential to develop into long-term friendships; and 4) the contact must be structured so that each individual is perceived as of equal status to the project. If these guidelines are followed, prejudice is reduced and acts of hate toward members of the group previously perceived as hostile are diminished.

Given the research summarized above, it seems clear that assignments that meet these criteria should be incorporated in classrooms around the world if we wish to reduce the likelihood of violent, terrorist acts among our youth and citizens of tomorrow.

Channeling Anger Constructively

Anger seems to be a common state among many. Whether created by fear, insecurity, dissatisfaction, frustration, or a combination of these states, many adolescents experience anger. Anger expresses itself in many different ways. It may be directed inward, resulting in substance abuse, eating disorders, self-mutilation, or even suicide. It may be directed outward, resulting in violent and antisocial acts toward others such as bullying, delinquency, gang violence, school shootings, or acts of terrorism. Anger among youth seems to be on the rise, and constructive forms of dealing with this anger are lacking.

It may be that anger is simply a form of energy that fuels action, and destructive acts are thus simply evidence of individuals who have not been provided, through education and life experiences, with the tools for more creative or artistic expression (McCarthy & Gold, 2002). Youth see only destructive acts in their environments and, lacking other options, social learning results in participation in destructive acts to release emotion.

As a result, shootings at school are becoming frighteningly commonplace. Juvenile arrests for violent or aggressive acts have increased dramatically in recent years. In 1975, 1,273 juveniles were arrested for murder (Goldstein & Lick, 1987) . By 1993, the number had nearly tripled, to 3,284, and it continues to rise. Juvenile courts, originally designed to deal with problems such as truancy and shoplifting, have been handling more than 1.5 million cases a year since 1992.

Violent acts committed by juveniles have risen in number far more rapidly than the number of juveniles in the population (Schatz & Eddington, 1995). Gang violence continues to increase. Terrorism is another expression of inappropriately expressed anger directed at society and, in particular, against individuals seen as members of outgroups.

Viable treatments to curb the aggressive behavior of adolescents need to be incorporated not only into offender rehabilitation but also into mainstream education (McCarthy & Gold, 2002). A major challenge facing counselors and educators is designing interventions that reduce violence and aggression. Psychology has devoted a considerable amount of study to the emotion of anger. From definitions and speculations on cause that date back to the work of William James in the last century and the James-Lange theory of emotion, to current cross-cultural research into facial expression and bodily responses, psychology has explored and attempted to define the emotion of anger. A vast literature base on causes, correlates, and definitions of anger exists. In addition to definitions, psychology has provided several methods for measuring individual differences in anger, aggression, and hostility (Tagney et al., 1996). Observational techniques such as event sampling, tallying, and observer rating scales are common. Many tests have also been developed to predict the likelihood of aggressive acts and to assess perceived levels of aggression (McCarthy, Gold, & Garcia, 1999).

Research indicates that improvements gained by traditional behavior modification programs decrease when the program is withdrawn (Marriott & Iwata, 1984). Barfield and Hutchinson (1989) noted that a group setting that used a variety of teaching and experiential modalities offered helpful alternatives to habitual maladaptive expressions of anger by adolescent boys in residential treatment and tended to have lasting impact after their release. LeCroy (1984) found that clients in residential treatment centers who received anger management training reduced the frequency of angry outbursts. In addition to decreasing observed aggressive behaviors, the training also resulted in clients reporting other positive benefits, such as an increased ability to relax. Bistline and Friederick (1984) found long-term and stable reduction of perceived anger and observed aggressive acts due to implementing cognitive-behavioral techniques of stress inoculation to control anger.

Kellner and Tutin (1995) developed an anger management training strategy that aimed to teach adolescents more about the physiology, consequences, and triggers of anger, as well as to help them develop coping strategies to manage their feelings and reduce aggressive acts. This strategy also incorporated cognitive-behavioral techniques such as assertiveness training, communication skill building, guided relaxation, self-talk, thought-stopping, and mediation. In addition, it used Gestalt techniques of role-playing, primal screams, art therapy, and the empty chair.

In a study on the use of anger management training with twelve adolescents in residential treatment, Dangel, Deschner, and Rasp (1989) found that observed aggressive acts were reduced. Wilcox and Dowrick (1992) also reported progress beyond that expected from the regular treatment program when anger management training was utilized. They recommended that adaptations of their methods for use with adolescents might prove beneficial.

Anger management training appears to be a helpful strategy for providing coping skills to incarcerated adolescents with a history of violent crimes and aggressive behaviors. It is likely that such training would be even more beneficial if available to all, so that appropriate coping skills could be developed *before* antisocial acts result from unmanageable and/or unacknowledged anger.

PROGRAMS THAT SHOW PROMISE

In light of the research summarized above, five major areas need to be addressed in the education of youth if we wish to reduce the likelihood of terrorism. First, education needs to provide adolescents and young adults throughout the world with tools for understanding, acknowledging, managing, and constructively expressing anger. Second, positive role models and mentors who display appropriate social skills, express anger constructively, and do not engage in acts of hate against others need to replace dysfunctional family and media role models.

Third, the curriculum needs to include information and learning activities that develop metacognitive awareness in students so that categorization, stereotyping, and prejudice are understood and counteracted in daily thought processes. Fourth, cooperative learning strategies that provide the opportunity to work with individuals from divergent backgrounds in order to successfully accomplish common goals need to characterize education.

Lastly, the members of these divergent groups need to come not just from a particular community but from the global community. Students need to interact with and learn with youth from a variety of countries, cultures, belief systems, lifestyles, and backgrounds. Education needs to become not just a regional or even a national enterprise, but a global endeavor.

Anger Management

Use of cognitive-behavioral strategies to help adolescents and adults manage anger constructively has proved effective in a variety of settings (Beck & Fernandez, 1998). Making such training available to adolescents is important to avoid proliferating acts of terrorism and violence. Ideally, counselors should offer anger management groups for all adolescents in public schools. At the very least, teachers should incorporate a few useful strategies into their classrooms to help adolescents recognize and deal with anger. A few promising techniques for classroom use (McCarthy & Gold, 2002) are:

1. Develop group trust through kinesthetic activities such as the "blind fall" exercise, in which each group member takes a turn at being blindfolded and "falling" from a chair into the arms of other group members. This may be modified by instead asking the blindfolded member to sit down, trusting that another member will place a chair in the appropriate place at the appropriate time. Trust activities conducted with a group of diverse peers help to overcome the sense of isolation that may later express as anger at others and acts of violence. Activities such as these help to build group trust and rapport. Devoting time and attention to building rapport is essential for anyone who works with youth—teachers, counselors, law enforcement officials, and therapists alike.

2. Develop credibility through shared stories, limited self-disclosure, and shared experiences. Acknowledge that anger is not taboo, and model strategies for dealing with anger. Using stories and poetry as a form of bibliotherapy is also useful. Allowing youth to read about and analyze the actions of others, through literature, can be a pow-

erful tool. Capture the imagination with literature. Have adolescents develop their own metaphors, stories, and poems to express anger. Use journals to record events and feelings, and encourage that these be shared with the group. Use the experiences and actions shared as discussion starters for problem-solving activities.

3. Art and music therapy are great tools for developing anger management skills among adolescents. Develop the concept of art, music, and literature as constructive forms of releasing pent-up emotion. Develop team poetry, have students write new lyrics to songs, discuss key scenes from movies, draw cartoons—there are many options. The key is providing many venues and allowing each student to find those that work best. Focus on expression, not technique. Painting a picture, making a movie, composing a song, drawing a cartoon, dancing, writing a poem—any avenue of positive expression should be accepted and encouraged. In a very basic sense, it may be that anger is a lack of imagination. Rather than going "back to basics" and continuing to cut art and humanities education from school curriculums, providing such education should be seen as a useful part of developing humanity. It is far better to allow adolescents to learn how to express pain with a paintbrush than with a gun.

4. Teach relaxation techniques. Counting, self-hypnosis, meditation, or various exercises from martial arts are all appropriate. Teaching adolescents how to focus on relaxing provides them with a valuable tool for learning emotional control.

5. Role-play problematic situations. Examples of bullying, misuse of authority, and being treated without respect are common for most adolescents. Acting out situations that can result in anger, and practicing various coping strategies, develops problem-solving skills and serves as a foundation for positive habits.

6. Reframe passive stressors into active stressors, and help students feel in control of their own lives and reactions. Develop lessons and activities that shift the locus of control to students. Provide for choices in assignments and projects. Build group decision making into all activities. Utilize physical and experiential exercises whenever possible. Work with guided imagery. Building the imagination and increasing the behavioral repertoire, while modeling proactive, social behavior, is the best inoculation you can provide.

Though certainly not a cure-all or panacea, systematic inclusion of anger-management training, relaxation training, coping skills, and life skills into the curriculum for all adolescents is a potentially valuable strategy to reduce the likelihood of future terrorist acts among students.

Mentoring Programs

Studies of resilience (Groberg, 2000) have consistently demonstrated that the best inoculation against tragic outcomes for at-risk youth is the presence of at least one caring adult mentor who takes an active interest in life decisions. Whether the mentor is a family member, teacher, neighbor, coach, or other community member doesn't seem to matter. What does seem to matter is that each adolescent has one adult with whom he or she feels comfortable talking honestly about life events and decisions, whom he or she respects and whom he or she wishes to emulate. Creating opportunities for youth and adults to interact in non-threatening, equal-status ways helps encourage the development of these valuable relationships.

Another strategy that has been explored recently gives adolescents the task of writing a personality profile of a particular adult whom the students have interviewed or heard speak. This adult may be a community member who attended the same school as the student, a person currently working in a field of interest to the student, or an elderly adult from a local geriatric center (Beyersdorfer & Schauer, 1992; Hamilton, 1990). Although systematic research to determine whether such assignments enhance resiliency has not yet been conducted, based upon principles of identification, modeling, and transfer of knowledge, such methods may be fertile avenues for future exploration.

Job-shadowing though career exploration units is another option for developing relationships. The use of the Internet in instruction offers even more possibilities. Students may communicate with authors or public figures they admire, relatives who are a great distance away, sports and entertainment figures, and other adults. If integrated into instruction appropriately, this provides a great opportunity for developing mentoring relationships that help youth maintain a connection to society and an acceptance of diversity.

Critical Thinking Skills and Metacognitive Awareness

Metacognition—the ability to think about one's thought processes—is an essential process to allow us to recognize and disconfirm stereotypes. It is one of a cluster of skills that are included in critical thinking or reasoning processes. These processes need to be explicitly taught to adolescents if they are not apparent through modeling in the social and family arenas.

Our current mainstream society, at least in the United States, does not seem to offer many examples of hypothetical-deductive thought to the majority of the populace. Correspondingly, lack of critical thinking skills in American high school and college students is currently viewed as a problem by educators, businesses, and society at large (Arons, 1985; Barnes, 1992; Hartley, 1990). This suggests that experience with some of the fundamental processes that are required for critical thought are not being transmitted through education or socialization at present.

Reintroducing logic, one of the requisite skills for critical thought, into the curriculum during the first two years of high school—when students are developmentally tuned to efficiently process the information—may, therefore, improve thinking skills (McCarthy, 1998). Improved thinking skills should, in turn, lead to a greater likelihood of acquiring formal operational thought and also generalize to an awareness of the invalid assumptions inherent in most stereotypes that lead to prejudice.

Two common problems in logic instruction are that: 1) teachers focus on relating the skills presented only to their own subjects, thus limiting transfer of knowledge to other areas by students who do not make such connections independently; and 2) instruction in logic is inconsistently utilized from teacher to teacher, school to school, and district to district. Although logic is commonly included to some degree in district curriculums, it is not consistently presented, and few means are available to systematically introduce, teach, and practice logical reasoning skills from year to year (Miller, 1993). Consequently, because instruction is content-tied and sporadic, students may have difficulty transferring it to daily life. It may be viewed as an isolated "fact" rather than a strategy useful in daily life.

Teaching logical reasoning skills in conjunction with course content seems to be the preferred method, and is supported by research. However, availability of materials to teach logic at the high school level in this way is limited. The most effective units studied have been developed by teachers for use specifically in their own classrooms. However, many teachers receive no training in formal logic during their own educations, and are therefore unable to appropriately integrate it into their classrooms. Even those who are trained to do so may not have sufficient time to develop units in logic to accompany their teaching. Thus, finding a means to include logic in the curriculum is a current concern for public school curriculum developers and teacher trainers (Hathurn, 1993). Although many high schools offer instruction in metacognition and logic in some form, such as elective courses in psychology, philosophy, semantics, and formal logic, these courses typically are only available to high-achieving students (McCarthy, 1998b).

Some researchers (Martin, 1983a, 1983b) suggest that the best way to improve critical thinking skills among students is to train teachers in formal logic, metacognition, and thinking skills so they are able to impart these skills to students in whatever area they teach. This seems compatible with the suggestion that students be exposed to logical reasoning throughout their schooling, in all subject areas, so that they are able to internalize the thinking strategies involved. Modeling is a powerful tool for teaching. Just as infants must hear language used constantly before they begin to speak, children may need to watch logical reasoning skills being applied continuously before they are able to think critically. Ensuring that all teachers understand, apply, and consistently model logical reasoning skills in their classes may be an appropriate means of assisting students to learn critical thinking skills.

Another option is to establish national requirements for a course that includes formal logic in public high schools. Perhaps the most efficient place to include formal logic in the high school curriculum would be in a required psychology course at the freshman level, covering metacognition, life skills, career exploration, social psychology (with particular attention paid to the processes of stereotyping and prejudice), and human development, as well as units on the various components of formal logic as part of a "thinking skills" unit. Lessons on categorization, hierarchical organization, intensional and extensional meanings, propositional logic, Venn diagramming, hypothesis testing, and inductive, deductive, and analogical reasoning could be presented in the context of how the human brain organizes information. Transferring this knowledge to other classes and activities would thus be encouraged; logic would be viewed as a thinking skill we use consistently in all areas of our lives rather than in just math or science.

Such a reintroduction of logic into the high school curriculum would be efficient not only from the standpoint of knowledge transfer, as noted above, but in other ways, as well. The required psychology class could meet one of the social studies requirements most high schools have. Psychology instructors, provided they are certified in the discipline and have had sufficient training, will already be familiar with formal reasoning and the scientific method, so required in-servicing will be minimal. Many of the current materials aimed at teaching critical thinking in logic courses were written by psychologists, so psychology instructors will be familiar with the perspectives presented and the terminology used.

High school psychology classes are an appropriate place to infuse logic and metacognition into the curriculum. Students could study *why* and *how* they reason in the context of learning about the human brain. Psychology courses in high school, though currently available to more students than the electives of philosophy and semantics, are generally elective courses in the current high school system. Changing psychology courses in high schools to a "required" status, as they already are in some countries, and using these courses to provide instruction in logical reasoning, critical thinking, and metacognition to *all* students, along with life skills and human development training, might be an effective means of returning logic to the curriculum. This return of logic would likely result in overall improvements in the critical thinking skills for the next generation and a reduction in terrorist activities.

Global Cooperative Learning

As previously mentioned, cooperative learning techniques have proved to be very effective in reducing racial tension (Aronson, 2001) and improving achievement. A logical next step seems to be to implement cooperative learning activities among students around the globe. Technology currently makes this activity quite feasible. The Global Psychology Project, described below, is one current model for realizing this goal.

A DESCRIPTION OF THE GLOBAL PSYCHOLOGY PROJECT

As American Psychological Association President Phillip Zimbardo (2002) recently pointed out, psychology should occupy a central position at all levels of education, since most major problems facing our nation involve psychological causes. Solving these problems requires changing attitudes, values, behaviors, and lifestyles. Terrorism certainly qualifies as one of these major problems, and the Global Psychology

Project is a current strategy to utilize psychology education as the avenue to reach adolescents and young adults to prevent future outbreaks.

Critical thinking skills and the ability to function well in a global environment are essential products of a useful education in the twenty-first century. Psychology is a course offered at pre-university and university levels that offers, within its content, opportunities for improving scientific reasoning, critical thinking, and human relations. This project will bring together leaders in psychology education from around the world to create an electronic learning community to improve thinking skills and international understanding, assess the success of this, and expand it to other disciplines.

Secondary and university general psychology teachers from several countries will meet periodically to facilitate electronic dialogue and create group projects that enhance the development of critical thinking skills among students. Specifically, the project will encourage acceptance and tolerance while broadening the knowledge of psychology as a natural science, with implications for improved critical thinking in all areas. The project will utilize technology to encourage acceptance of and tolerance for diversity, support a move toward internationalization of education, and encourage faculty development through exchange of ideas. It will encourage institutional partnerships and international cooperative mentoring relationships. The overall objectives are to:

1. determine current curriculum, materials, and practices of secondary and university general psychology instructors from countries throughout the world and compare this database to define best practices for teaching critical thinking and human relations skills within the content of the discipline;

2. develop a productive exchange of ideas and information among master teachers, educational leaders, and students internationally;

3. with this group, develop a curriculum that enhances critical thinking and tolerance for and understanding of diversity based on the research conducted as part of item 1 above, and incorporate this curriculum into general psychology courses that are delivered, in part, in a Web-based interactive forum;

4. assess the success of the project in improving critical thinking and global understanding; and

5. if warranted, expand the model into other disciplines through teacher training and other venues.

Secondary objectives are the enhancement of technological literacy among educators and students and the development of international partnerships among institutions of higher education and secondary public schools around the world.

This project began as part of the American Psychological Association's (APA) P3: Psychology Partnership Project: Academic Partnerships to Meet the Teaching and Learning Needs of the 21st Century. P3 was designed to promote and facilitate the development of partnerships among psychology teachers at high schools, community colleges, four-year colleges, universities, and research universities with graduate programs and between psychology teachers and other professionals in community agencies and business organizations. P3 began in 1996 as a multi-year, multi-phase project resulting from discussions between Virginia Andreoli Mathie, then president of the Society for the Teaching of Psychology; Randy Ernst, then chair of APA's Teachers of Psychology in Secondary Schools (TOPSS); and Jill Reich, executive director of the APA Education Directorate. In July 1999, P3 brought 118 participants to a two-week forum at James Madison University. The participants were selected for their expertise in relevant areas and included 90 invited teachers (of whom I was one) from 34 states plus the District of Columbia. Observers from regional, national, and international professional associations as well as several graduate students also attended.

The breakdown of teachers was as follows: five university professors from predominantly graduate level training (myself included); twenty-four high school psychology teachers; nineteen community college teachers; and forty-two college/university teachers from predominantly undergraduate training. In addition, a few psychologists working in mental health institutions were included, along with several members of the business community.

Participants were divided into groups to brainstorm and design projects, based on research on the current changes in schools in the United States, to improve public education. Many of the issues apparent in the research are not specific to the United States, however, and they likely apply to Europe, Russia, Australia, and much of the rest of the world as well. For example, there will be an increasing number of high school graduates by 2004 and if current trends continue, a larger percentage of these students will be going on to higher education. The U.S. Department of Education predicts that college enrollment will grow from 14.3 million in 1996 to approximately 16.1 million in 2008, with projected increases in full-time students from 8.1 million to 9.6 million (National Center for Education Statistics, 1999).

The number of full-time employees who require training is growing rapidly (Davis & Botkin, 1994; Oblinger & Verville, 1998). Futurists estimated that by 2002 there would be over 28 million new learners from the workforce in higher education (Dolence & Norris, 1995). National Center for Education Statistics (1999) reported that in 1995 there were 3.3 million men and 3.8 million women who were full-time undergraduate college students. Projections for 2007 are that there will be 4.2 million men and 5.4 million women who are full-time undergraduate students. The U.S. Census Bureau (1999) projects that the percentage of non-Hispanic whites in the U.S. population will drop from approximately 73 percent to approximately 52 percent by 2050 (Holiday et al., 1997). This is problematic, in part, since many of the growing population of students are not well prepared for higher education (Hansen, 1998). A sizeable percentage of students who graduate from high school and enter college lack the basic skills needed to be successful, especially critical thinking skills (McCarthy, 1999b). This supports the need for changing education strategies, developing critical thinking skills, and increasing understanding of diversity among educators and students alike.

As a corollary to this, increased workforce (and student) mobility requires distance education and distributed learning options to be more fully developed. Institutional boundaries will be transparent, with students conceivably enrolled in multiple levels at the same time (Dolence & Norris, 1995; Duderstadt, 1999). In fact, with the increasing presence of educational institutions such as the University of Phoenix (1999), they have already become so.

These trends have implications for how we assess what students have learned and how we teach students. We need a more seamless curriculum across levels. To meet the needs of an increasingly international marketplace, we need broader connections to the international education community. "Information Age" students demand individualized education that is offered at a time, place, and pace that students select and one that evaluates students on their mastery of skills rather than on seat-time (Dolence & Norris, 1995). Knowledge and the ability to gather, understand, synthesize, analyze, and use information are becoming the primary source of economic advantage in the global economy (Dolence & Norris, 1995; Oblinger & Verville, 1998). Businesses are becoming increasingly complex yet also need to adjust quickly to the rapid pace of change and to greater globalization of the economy and greater global interdependence. Training and learning will become integral to the work environment. We must make education more applicable to this world and pay more attention to the outcomes of instruction and to developing competencies that will have lifelong value.

The Internet revolutionized the way we communicate and transfer knowledge and information. In the educational arena, technology has expanded the possibilities for multimedia, asynchronous, individualized education. It is also changing how we do research. Technology now makes the research enterprise open to many more people through electronic access. It has created virtual research environments (Dolence & Norris, 1995). As we more clearly define the knowledge, skills, and attitudes we want students to have when they leave us, we may find that, as teachers, we can provide this information more economically online and have more time to focus on our tutor and mentor roles. Our research activities will likely be more applied, more directly tied to the mission of the university, more interdisciplinary, and more likely done in collaboration with the private sector and the international community (Plater, 1995).

It is imperative to develop educational materials that address needs of a curriculum that is more coordinated across academic levels, countries, and continents. A logical way to accomplish this is to develop instructional technology materials based on sound learner-centered principles that can be used to develop student thinking skills and connect students to their peers around the world. Based on these findings, the group that I worked with during the P3 seminar developed a framework for "The International Partnerships Project in Psychology." The following Web sites (available as of March, 2002) contain additional information on P3 and on the International Partnership group: http://www.apa.org/ed/p3.html; http:

//www.icope2002/narod.ru/; http://www.geocities.com/globalpsychology/; and http://www.globalpsych.cjb.net.

As I see it, critical thinking, international understanding and tolerance for diversity, and technological literacy are the three most important legacies we can leave to our students for the world of tomorrow if we wish to minimize the likelihood of acts of terrorism. This project plants the seeds to make better use of Web-based technology to increase international collaboration on teaching and research, to design professional development opportunities that keep us current in our fields, and to increase opportunities to develop interdisciplinary perspectives. It promises to prepare us to work with more culturally diverse students, keep us on the cutting edge of emerging pedagogical techniques, and keep us more attuned to the fast-changing global marketplace. Students now must be prepared for jobs that require the ability to gather, understand, synthesize, analyze, and use information as well as the ability to work with people much different from themselves. Our current education systems do not seem to be up to the task (Paul, 1992). This project is eminently worthwhile, and it offers the opportunity for the institutions of higher education most involved with its implementation to acquire long-lasting recognition as global partners that are bringing public education into line with the changing needs of the twenty-first century for the good of the planet as a whole.

Examples of two preliminary assignments that students have completed with each other illustrate the power of this strategy to make connections and overcome stereotypes. Two high school psychology instructors, Carlo Prandini of Bologna, Italy, and Frank Hollingsworth of Pittsburgh, Pennsylvania, worked together to plan a curriculum in developmental psychology for their classes. The unit focused on rites of passage from adolescence to adulthood and included information on physical, social, cognitive, and emotional development. As part of the unit, the Italian students and the American students collaboratively developed a questionnaire about what events characterize someone as an adult. They included such items as marriage, childbearing, and financial independence. Both groups of students gave out the questionnaires in their respective communities. They compared results and found that the data gathered from two different countries were nearly identical. They also engaged in Web-based discussion with each other about what it means to become an adult. This dialogue and exchange familiarized students in both countries with the common experiences they shared. Learning was enhanced and, more importantly, stereotypes were disconfirmed. Imagine a similar exchange going on between students in India and Pakistan, for example, or Afghanistan and the United States. Similar collaborative learning activities on the Internet can result in future friendships and increased understanding of members of other groups.

Another project, at the university level, carried out by Professor Victor Karandashev of Vologda State Pedagogical Institute in Vologda, Russia, and myself, at Northern Arizona University, asked students to compare their perceptions of the history of psychology. Graduate students from both universities developed papers explaining how they understood the history of the discipline and the major figures responsible for various branches of psychology. They then compared their papers and discussed the similarities and differences they had in their understanding of the history, and how these differences could be explained by their experiences in their respective cultures. Again, a simple learning activity was expanded to include an added dimension of social understanding. Firsthand experience—even if virtual— with members of other countries and cultural groups resulted in disconfirmation of stereotypes and a sense of connection.

These are just two examples of the many activities that can be developed to connect adolescents and young adults around the world with each other. These connections will help to break down barriers. They will make it far more difficult for the psychological profile that creates a terrorist to develop.

Future Goals and Directions

Preliminary groundwork has already been laid for this project. I will present a timeline, indicating what has been done so far and what will occur, to explain the plan.

1996–1999: APA P3 Project (described above) establishes the groundwork for this project (see http://www.apa.org/ed/p3.html).

1999–2000: Contacts are made with interested psychology educators and psychologists around the world. A homepage linking together interested participants is developed (see http://www.geocities.com/globalpsychology/).

2001: A survey is distributed internationally to determine curriculum, materials, and interests of psychology teachers. Responses are gathered from more than sixty countries and regions, including Africa, Asia, North America, South America, Europe, and the Pacific Rim. An international conference planning committee is established and connected via a listserv for discussions. Preliminary publicity is begun. External funding is solicited from APA, other organizations funding collaborative education projects between the United States and the European Union and Asia, and private businesses.

2002: Publicity and solicitation of external funding continues. University and secondary (high school) teachers of psychology from around the world attend the St. Petersburg, Russia International Conference on Psychology Education (ICOPE) in June (see http://www.icope2002/narod.ru/ for more information). There, through structured activities, they develop teaching activities for their students that will require them to collaboratively complete assignments with their peers from around the world. These lessons, tied into psychology curriculum, will focus on development of critical thinking skills, breaking down stereotypes and diminishing prejudice, stimulating tolerance for diversity and international understanding, and human relations skills. After the conference, participating teams from around the world gather baseline data on students' critical thinking skills, stereotypes, international understanding, and tolerance for diversity and then implement the lessons in their classrooms.

2003: Teaching activities are monitored and refined as they are delivered electronically. Dialogue with teachers, student reactions, and student products are gathered and analyzed. Publicity and increased ties to the global community continue. After a year of instruction, students again complete instruments that measure critical thinking skills, stereotypes, international understanding, and tolerance for diversity.

2004: Participating teams again meet in a structured one-week session to assess progress and refine the curriculum and the project. Using an "each one teach one" strategy and other outreach methods, the project will be expanded further within participating countries and to other countries. External support to expand the project to other disciplines and levels is solicited.

2005–2007: A model similar to the one described above will be used to expand the project into other disciplines (science, math, languages, etc.) and solidify a global curriculum aimed at improving critical thinking skills, reducing prejudice, expanding understanding and tolerance for diversity, and bringing future generations into a cooperative "one world" model.

The data gathered will include a rich base of information on curriculum and teaching practices from around the world. It will also provide comparative data on student mastery of critical thinking skills, tolerance for diversity, and tendencies to stereotype from several different countries. Qualitative information on curriculum development and teacher collaboration in an electronic environment will be generated. The disciplines of social and educational psychology will benefit from this data pool. Business, education, and other social sciences may also benefit. In an applied sense, the project will increase collaboration between education and the private sector and between countries around the world, to the benefit of society in a *truly* global sense. Most importantly, students will interact with peers from many backgrounds, geographic areas, and belief systems in a positive way. Such interaction will make it far less likely that these young people will be able to commit random acts of terror against a dehumanized outgroup. The groups will have faces and names, and contain friends.

As technology increasingly supports a global community, our discipline should take a key role in educating students in cross-cultural dynamics, human relations, and international affairs. A global curriculum, discussions among students from many different countries/cultural backgrounds, and a focus on international understanding are vital components of a sound education in psychology for the twenty-first century. International distance education partnerships and networking need to be developed to the greatest extent possible. Through efforts such as this, the likelihood of "terrorist mindsets" among future generations will be diminished.

REFERENCES

Arons, A. B. (1985). Critical thinking in the baccalaureate curriculum. *Liberal Education, 71*, 141–158.

Aronson, E. (2001, April 20). *Nobody left to hate: Teaching compassion after Columbine.* Paper presented at the 2001 Annual Convention of the Rocky Mountain Psychological Association, Reno, NV.

Aronson, E., Stephan, C., Sikes, J., Blaney, N., & Snapp, M. (1978). *The jigsaw classroom.* Beverly Hills, CA: Sage.

Bandura, A. (1962). Social learning through imitation. In M. R. Jones (Ed.), *Nebraska symposium on motivation.* Lincoln: University of Nebraska Press.

Bandura, A. (1965). Influence of models' reinforcement contingencies on the acquisition of imitative responses. *Journal of Personality and Social Psychology, 1*, 589–595.

Bandura, A. (1968). What TV violence can do to your child. In O. N. Larsen (Ed.), *Violence and the media.* New York: Harper and Row.

Bandura, A. (1969). Social learning theory of identificatory processes. In D. A. Goslin (Ed.), *Handbook of socialization theory and research.* Chicago: Rand McNally.

Bandura, A., Ross, D., & Ross, S. (1963). Imitation of film mediated aggressive models. *Journal of Abnormal and Social Psychology, 67*, 601–607.

Bandura, A. (1971). *Social learning theory.* New York: General Learning Press.

Banks, S. (1971, October 28). Testimony presented before the Federal Trade Commission on behalf of the Joint Committee of the Association of National Advertisers and the American Association of Advertising Agencies, Washington, DC.

Barfield, C. K., & Hutchinson, M. A. (1989). Observations on adolescent anger and an anger control group in residential and day treatment. *Residential Treatment for Children and Youth, 7*, 45–53.

Barnes, C. A. (1992). Critical thinking: An educational imperative. *New Directions for Community Colleges, 20*, 1.

Beck, R., & Fernandez, E. (1998). Cognitive-behavioral therapy in the treatment of anger: A meta-analytic approach. *Cognitive Therapy and Research, 22*, 63–74.

Beyersdorfer, J. M., & Schauer, D. K. (1992). Writing personality profiles: Conversations across the generation gap. *Journal of Reading, 35*, 612–616.

Bistline, J. L., & Frederick, F. P. (1984). Anger control: A case study of a stress inoculation treatment for a chronic aggressive patient. *Cognitive Therapy and Research, 8*, 551–56.

Bobo, L. (1988). Group conflict, prejudice and the paradox of contemporary racial attitudes. In P. A. Katz & D. A. Taylor (Eds.), *Eliminating racism: Profiles in controversy.* New York: Plenum Press.

Branscombe, N. R., & Wann, D. L. (1994). Collective self-esteem consequences of outgroup derogation when valid social identity is on trial. *European Journal of Social Psychology, 24*, 641–657.

Brewer, M. B., & Brown, R. J. (1997). Intergroup relations. In D. T. Gilbert, S. T. Fiske, & G. Lindzey (Eds.), *The handbook of social psychology.* Boston: McGraw-Hill.

Bull, R., & Rumsey, N. (1988). *The social psychology of facial appearance.* New York: Springer-Verlag.

Cohen, C. E. (1981). Person categories and social perception: Testing some boundaries of the processing effects of prior knowledge. *Journal of Personality and Social Psychology, 40*, 441–452.

Crocker, J., & Luhtanen, R. (1990). Collective self-esteem and ingroup bias. *Journal of Personality and Social Psychology, 58*, 60–67.

Csikszentmihalyi, M., & Larson, R. (1984). *Being adolescent.* New York: Basic Books.

Dangel, R., Deschner, J., & Rasp, R. (1989). Anger control training for adolescents in residential treatment. *Behavior Modification, 13*, 447–458.

Davis, S. M., & Botkin, J. W. (1994). *The monster under the bed: How business is mastering the opportunity of knowledge for profit.* New York: Touchstone.

Devine, P. G. (1989). Stereotypes and prejudice: Their automatic and controlled components. *Journal of Personality and Social Psychology, 56,* 5–18.

Dolence, M. G., & Norris, D. M. (1995). *Transforming higher education: A vision for learning in the 21st century.* Ann Arbor, MI: Society for College and University Planning.

Dovidio, J. F. (2002, January 5). *Why can't we just get along? Aversive racism and interracial distrust.* Paper presented at the 24th Annual National Institute on the Teaching of Psychology, St. Petersburg, FL.

Dovidio, J. F., & Gaertner, S. L. (1998). On the nature of contemporary prejudice: The causes, consequences and challenges of aversive racism. In J. Eberhardt & S. T. Fiske (Eds.), *Confronting racism: The problem and the response* (pp. 1–32). Newbury Park, CA: Sage.

Duderstadt, J. J. (1999). Can colleges and universities survive in the information age? In R. N. Katz and Associates (Eds.), *Dancing with the devil: Information technology and the new competition in higher education* (pp. 1–26). San Francisco, CA: Jossey-Bass Publishers.

Eagly, A. H., Ashmore, R. D., Makhijani, M. G., & Longo, L. C. (1991). What is beautiful is good but . . . : A meta-analytic review of research on the physical attractiveness stereotype. *Psychology Bulletin, 110,* 107–128.

Elkind, D. (1985). Egocentrism redux. *Developmental Review, 5,* 218–226.

Erikson, E. H. (1968). *Identity, youth and crisis.* New York: Norton.

Fiske, S. T. (1993). Social cognition and social perception. *Annual Review of Psychology, 44,* 155–194.

Fiske, S. T., & Taylor, S. E. (1991). *Social cognition.* New York: McGraw-Hill.

Gershner, V. T., & Snider, S. L. (1998). Classroom internet integration: A collaborative adventure. *Technology and Teacher Education Annual, 1012–1015.*

Goldstein, A. P., & Lick, B. (1987). *Aggression replacement training: A comprehensive intervention for aggressive youth.* Champaign, IL: Research Press.

Groberg, E. (2000, July). *Resilience.* Paper presented at the 58th Annual Convention of the International Council of Psychologists, Padua, Italy.

Hamilton, S. F. (1990, April). *Linking school learning with learning on the job.* Paper presented at the Annual Meeting of the American Educational Research Association, Boston, MA.

Hansen, E. J. (1998). Essential demographics of today's college students. *AAHE Bulletin,* 3–5.

Hartley, N. K. (1990). *An analysis of the professional development needs of Colorado vocational educators.* Denver, CO: Colorado State Community College and Occupational Education System.

Hathurn, M. (1993, March 8). Personal communication between author and curriculum specialist for Phoenix Union High School District, Phoenix, AZ.

Hetherton, T. F. (2002, January 4). *The social mind: Neuroscience in personality, social and developmental psychology.* Paper presented at the 24th Annual National Institute on the Teaching of Psychology, St. Petersburg, FL.

Holiday, B. G., et al. (1997). *Visions and transformations: The final report, Commission on Ethnic Minority Recruitment, Retention, and Training in Psychology.* Washington, DC: American Psychological Association.

Inhelder, B., & Piaget, J. (1958). *The growth of logical thinking from childhood to adolescence: An essay on the construction of formal operational structures.* New York: Basic Books.

Internet Society (1999). International connectivity. Retrieved on March 9, 1999, from http://www.isoc.org/infosvc/map.gif.

Karandashev, V. (2002). ICOPE: International Conference on Psychology Education. See http://www.icope2002/narod.ru/.

Kellner, M. H., & Tutin, J. (1995). A school-based anger management program for developmentally and emotionally disabled high school students. *Adolescence, 30,* 813–825.

Kristiansen, C. M., & Giuletti, R. (1990). Perception of wife abuse: Effects of gender, attitudes toward women and just-world beliefs among college students. *Psychology of Women Quarterly, 14,* 177–189.

Langer, E., Bashner, R., & Chanowitz, B. (1985). Decreasing prejudice by increasing discrimination. *Journal of Personality and Social Psychology, 49,* 113–120.

LeCroy, C. W. (1984). Anger management or anger expression: Which is most effective? *Residential Treatment for Children and Youth, 5,* 29–39.

Lerner, M. J., & Miller, D. T. (1978). Just world research and the attribution process: Looking back and ahead. *Psychological Bulletin, 85,* 1030–1051.

Marcia, J. E. (1991). Identity and self-development. In R. M. Lerner, A. C. Petersen, & J. Brooks-Gunn (Eds.), *Encyclopedia of adolescence* (Vol. 1). New York: Garland.

Markus, H., & Nurius, P. (1986). Possible selves. *American Psychologist, 41,* 954–969.

Marriott, S. A., & Iwata, M. (1984). Group anger control training for junior high school delinquents. *Cognitive Therapy and Research, 8,* 299–311.

Martin, D. S. (1983a, November). *Can teachers become better thinkers?* Paper presented at the Annual Conference of the National Staff Development Center, Tulsa, OK.

Martin, D. S. (1983b, February). *Thinking skills: A critical new role in teacher education.* Paper presented at the Annual Meeting of the American Association of Colleges for Teacher Education, Detroit, MI.

McCarthy, S. (1998a). Teaching logic to adolescents to improve thinking skills. *The Korean Journal of Thinking and Problem Solving, 8,* 45–66.

McCarthy, S. (1998b). The need for logic instruction in public schools. *The Korean Journal of Thinking and Problem Solving, 8,* 2.

McCarthy, S. (1999a). Les défis de l'enseignement de la psychologie au 21ème siècle: La point de vue des États-Unis. *Pratiques Psychologique.*

McCarthy, S. (1999b). Student preferences for electronic instructional options in a community college introductory psychology class. *Community College Journal of Research and Practice, 23.*

McCarthy, S. (2000). Teaching style, philosophical orientation and the transmission of critical thinking skills in U.S. public schools. *The Korean Journal of Thinking and Problem Solving, 10,* 1.

McCarthy, S. (2001). International perspectives on teaching critical thinking and problem solving. *Teaching of Psychology.* Mahwah, NJ: Lawrence Erlbaum.

McCarthy, S., & Gold, A. (2002, January 24). *Using anger management training to reduce violence in public schools.* Paper presented at the 8th National Conference on Alternatives to Suspension, Expulsion and Dropping Out of School, Orlando, FL.

McCarthy, S., Gold, A., & Garcia, E. (1999). Effects of anger management training on aggressive behavior in adolescent boys. *Journal of Offender Rehabilitation.*

Meindl, J. R., & Lerner, M. J. (1984). Exacerbation of extreme responses to an outgroup. *Journal of Personality and Social Psychology, 47,* 71–84.

Miller, K. (1993, April 12). Personal communication with author by mathematics department chairperson at South Mountain High School, Phoenix, AZ.

Murray, J. P. (1980). *Television and youth: Twenty-five years of research and controversy.* Stanford, WA: Boys Town Center for the Study of Youth Development.

Muuss, R. E. (1996) *Theories of adolescence* (6th ed.). New York: McGraw-Hill.

National Center for Education Statistics (1999). Department of Education Statistics, 1997. Retrieved on March 8, 1999, from http://nces.ed.gov.

Oblinger, D. G., & Verville, A. L. (1998). *What business wants from higher education.* Phoenix, AZ: American Council on Education/Oryx Press.

Paul, R. (1992). *Critical thinking: What every person needs to survive in a rapidly changing world.* Santa Rosa, CA: Foundation for Critical Thinking.

Pettigrew, T. F. (1978). The ultimate attribution error: Extending Allport's cognitive analysis of prejudice. *Personality and Social Psychology Bulletin, 5,* 461–476.

Phelps, E. A., O'Connor, K. J., Cunningham, W. A., Funayama, E. S., Gatenby, J. C., & Banaji, M. R. (2000). Performance on indirect measures of race evaluation predicts amygdala activation. *Journal of Cognitive Neuroscience, 12,* 729–738.

Plater, W. M. (1995). Future work: Faculty time in the 21st century. *Change: The Magazine of Higher Learning, 27,* 22–33.

Rosenthal, R. (1985). From unconscious experimenter bias to teacher expectancy effects. In J. B. Dusek, V. C. Hall, & W. Meyer (Eds.), *Teacher expectancies.* Hillsdale, NJ: Erlbaum.

Ross, L. D. (1977). The intuitive psychologist and his shortcomings: Distortions in the attribution process. In L. Berkowitz (Ed.), *Advances in experimental social psychology* (Vol. 10). New York: Academic Press.

Salminen, S. (1992). Defensive attribution hypothesis and serious occupational accidents. *Psychological Reports, 70,* 1195–1199.

Savin-Williams, R. C., & Berndt, T. J. (1990). Friendship and peer relations. In S. S. Feldman & G. R. Elliott (Eds.), *At the threshold: The developing adolescent.* Cambridge, MA: Harvard University Press.

Schatz, A., & Eddington, M. (1995). *What can we do about violence? A Bill Moyers special, part 1: Juveniles locked up.* [videocassette]. Available from Films for Humanities and Sciences, Box 2053, Princeton, NJ 08543–2053.

Schlegel, A., & Barry, H., III (1991). *Adolescence: An anthropological inquiry.* New York: Free Press.

Sherif, M., Harvey, L. J., White, B. J., Hood, W., & Sherif, C. W. (1988). *The robber's cave experiment: Intergroup conflict and cooperation.* Middleton, CT: Wesleyan University Press.

Siegler, R. S. (1991). *Children's thinking* (2nd ed.). Englewood Cliffs, NJ: Prentice Hall.

Snyder, M., Tanke, E. D., & Berscheid, E. (1977). Social perception and interpersonal behavior: On the self-fulfilling nature of social stereotypes. *Journal of Personality and Social Psychology, 35,* 655–666.

Stephan, W. G. (1989). A cognitive approach to stereotyping. In D. Bartal, C. F. Graumann, A. W. Kruglanski, & W. Stroebe (Eds.), *Stereotyping and prejudice: Changing conceptions.* New York: Springer-Verlag.

Swann, W. B., & Ely, R. J. (1984). A battle of wills: Self-verification versus behavioral confirmation. *Journal of Personality and Social Psychology, 46,* 1287–1302.

Tagney, J. P., Hill-Barlow, D., Wagner, P. E., Marschall, D. E., Borenstein, J. P., Saftner, J., Mohr, T., & Gramzow, R. (1995). Assessing individual differences in constructive versus destructive responses to anger across the lifespan. *Journal of Personality and Social Psychology, 70,* 780–796.

Tajfel, H. (1982). *Social identity and intergroup relations.* London: Cambridge University Press.

Thornton, B. (1992). Repression and its mediating influence on the defensive attribution of responsibility. *Journal of Research in Personality, 26,* 44–57.

Turner, J. C. (1987). *Rediscovering the social group: A self-categorization theory.* Oxford: Basil Blackwell.

University of Phoenix (1999). General information. Retrieved on March 8, 1999, from http://www.uophx.edu.

U.S. Census Bureau (1999). Demographic projections. Retrieved on March 8, 1999, from http://www.census.gov/population/www/projections/natproj.html.

Wilcox, D., & Dowrick, P. W. (1992). Anger management with adolescents. *Residential Treatment for Children and Youth, 9,* 29–39.

Zimbardo, P. G. (2002, January). President's column: Going forward with commitment. *Monitor on Psychology, 33,* 5. Washington, DC: American Psychological Association.

SUPPLEMENTARY BIBLIOGRAPHY

Abramson, M. (1996). Partnership imperative: A critical appraisal. In M. Abramson, J. Bird, & A. Stennett (Eds.), *Further and higher education partnerships: The future for collaboration* (pp. 7–18). Bristol, PA: Society for Research into Higher Education and Open University Press.

Athey, T. H. (1998). Nontraditional universities challenge twenty-first-century higher education. *On the Horizon, 6,* 4–7.

Bullough, Jr., R., & Kauchak, D. (1997). Partnerships between higher education and secondary schools: Some problems. *Journal of Education for Teaching, 23,* 215–233.

Corl, K. A., Harlow, L. L., Macin, J. L., & Saunders, D. M. (1996). Collaborative partnerships for articulation: Asking the right questions. *Foreign Language Annals, 29,* 111–122.

Cowan, C. A., & Tsapatsarias, G. N. (1998). *Partnership programs: Middlesex Community College and Lowell Public Schools—A dynamic duo.* Lowell, MA: Middlesex Community College.

Graves, W. H. (1997). "Free trade" in higher education: The meta university. *Journal of Asynchronous Learning Networks [online serial], 1.* Available at http://www.aln.org/alnweb/journal/jaln_vol1issue1.htm.

Harris, M., & Wheeler, M. A. (1997). The PRIDE program at Bloomsburg University of Pennsylvania. *Multicultural Education, 5,* 20–22.

Katz, R. N. (1999). Competitive strategies for higher education in the information age. In R. N. Katz and Associates (Eds.), *Dancing with the devil: Information technology and the new competition in higher education* (pp. 27–50). San Francisco, CA: Jossey-Bass Publishers.

Keith, K. D. (1998, August). *Psychology on display: The Nebraska Wesleyan psychology fair.* Paper presented at the annual meetings of the American Psychological Association, San Francisco, CA.

Little-Reynolds, L., & Takacs, J. (1998). Distance collaboration and technology integration between two institutions. *Technology and Teacher Education Annual,* 366–369.

McClenney, K. M. (1998). Community colleges perched at the millennium: Perspectives on innovation, transformation, and tomorrow. *Leadership Abstracts, 11,* 8.

McGovern, T. V., & Reich, J. N. (1996). A comment on the quality principles. *American Psychologist, 51,* 252–255.

Wilbur, F. P., & Lambert, L. M. (1995). *Linking America's schools and colleges: Guide to partnerships & national directory* (2nd ed.). Boston: Anchor Pub. Co.

9

How Conflict Resolution Programming in Our Schools Addresses Terrorism Issues

Kathy Sexton-Radek

Many schools today offer conflict resolution programs that teach children and adolescents how to deal with problems including fear, anger, and violence—problems closely related to the experience of terrorism.

The focus on violence prevention among school-aged children addresses terrorism inasmuch as violence in their lives often involves a private terror. Surrounded by the familiar school setting, peers, and teachers, many students struggle inwardly with the irony of a terror that may be related to battery, intimidation, or abuse. The scope and physical/emotional gravity of this terror may be parallel to but distinguished in magnitude from a political terrorist attack. But violence, in both cases, is defined as a threat, attempt, or actual use of physical or emotional force or power against another person, or against a group or community, that results in or has a high likelihood of resulting in injury, death, or depression.

Alexander and Curtis (1995) commented that intervention programs have long-term effects on the likelihood of participation in delinquency; but these are undermined by continued exposure to other risk factors, such as violent neighborhoods (O'Donnell, 1995). This chapter focuses on the experience of violence in the schools. Terrorism-like issues of fear, intimidation, and abuse that are experienced by adolescent students, and subsequent conflict resolution programming are presented and evaluated. Recommendations are made, including that the hazards engendered by student life must also be prevented by community protection.

THE PROBLEM

Data collected from crime records reveal stark prevalence figures of 69 percent to 75 percent of crime type related to violence (Berton & Statt, 1996; Blemstein, 1995; Ellickson, Saner, & McGuigan, 1997). Battery is the most common of all violent crimes. Conclusions from analyses of national data sources on homicide and nonfatal crimes consistently indicate that those greatest at risk are adolescents and young adults. Furthermore, the most common perpetrator of violent crime against an adolescent/young adult is someone known to them. Adolescents are more likely to experience physically serious crimes such as simple or serious battery and homicide compared with the general population. A female, non-Hispanic black is the typical victim of these crimes. People at greatest risk of being offenders, namely adolescents and young adults, usually attack someone of the same demographic background.

Brendgen, Vitaro, Tremblay, and Lavoie (2001) identified proactive aggression as "cold blooded" offensiveness that did not require provocation. Approximately 15 percent of aggressive children engage in proactive aggression (Dodge, Lochman, Harnish, Bates, & Petit, 1977; Hill, Levermore, Twaite, & Jones, 1996; Lowry, Sleet, Duncan, Powell, & Kolbe, 1995). In a correlational study, Brendgen et al. (2001) reported that proactive aggression and delinquency-related violence were related and moderated by parental supervision. It has been proposed that proactive aggression, therefore, is fostered by parental endorsement—in such instances, aggression is modeled as an acceptable, successful means of goal achievement (Coley & Hoffman, 1996; Ewing, 1990; Weinburger & Gomes, 1998).

Figure 1 illustrates this violence cycle.

FIGURE 1. THE VIOLENCE CYCLE

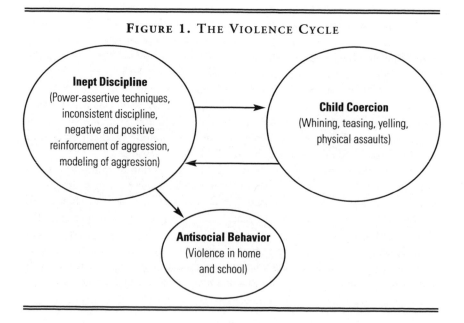

Inept Discipline
(Power-assertive techniques, inconsistent discipline, negative and positive reinforcement of aggression, modeling of aggression)

Child Coercion
(Whining, teasing, yelling, physical assaults)

Antisocial Behavior
(Violence in home and school)

Rosenthal (2000) examined the relationship between exposure to violence and psychological stress among adolescents. The study sampled 455 first-year students at an urban college who completed a questionnaire that contained items on exposure to community violence during high school and on their current level of psychological symptoms. Forty percent of the subjects in Rosenthal's study had been victimized and had statistically significant, positive correlations with psychological symptoms. The analyses were set up to distinguish exposure, victimization or not, and symptomatology. Rosenthal reported that 16 percent of the variance in anger and 4 percent of the variance in depression were accounted for by exposure to community violence. Rosenthal recommended routine screening to identify exposure to violence.

Blum, Beuhring, Shew, Bearinger, Sieving, and Resnick (2000) reported race/ethnicity differences in risk behaviors. Both black and Hispanic youths were more likely than white teens to engage in violence. Survey and interview methods were used with this nationally representative sample. Schwab-Stone et al. (1999) reported that exposure to violence (i.e., witnessing violence) was related to adolescents' internalizing symptoms first and externalizing behavior two years later. Page and Hammermeister (1997) reported a 15 percent increase in weapon carrying by youth in the last decade. The most prevalent reason reported for carrying the weapon was self-protection. Further, use of drugs and alcohol co-occur with weapon carrying and violent behavior (Cirillo et al., 1998). In a sample of conduct-disordered children, Stoolmiller, Eddy, and Reid (2000) reported decreases in observed violent behavior in aggressive children. In this school-based intervention, statistical analysis techniques allowed for a comparison across twelve schools to substantiate this finding.

Loeber and Stouthamer-Loeber (1998) wrote a position paper that addressed common "misperceptions concerning aggression in adolescents such as continuous display of aggression." In point of fact, a discontinuous relationship exists in that there are several different onset patterns of antisocial behavior during adolescence (Moffit, 1993). Paschall, Ennett, and Flewelling (1996) surveyed youth-based drug-abuse prevention programs and reported a higher prevalence for violent behavior among black males than among white males.

FACTORS CONTRIBUTING TO VIOLENCE

Social scientists have identified various factors contributing to the development of violence: lack of nonviolent child-rearing skills, belief in violence as an appropriate means of child discipline, poor caregiver/child attachment or bonding, early onset of verbal abuse, family discord, unaddressed mental health issues, substance abuse, lack of response to suspicious circumstances, family isolation, societal disenfranchisement, limited economic opportunities, lack of caregiver presence, lack of positive role models, excessive violence in the media, and lack of future orientation. It has been proposed that these factors inhibit the students' ability to effectively prob-

TABLE 1. YOUTH VIOLENCE FACT SHEET

- 92 percent of students say violence in schools nationwide is a serious problem, and 79 percent say it is on the rise.—*MTV Poll, 1998*

- 10 percent of students say they have seen guns in their school.
  —*MTV Poll, 1998*

- More than 6,000 students were expelled for bringing guns to school.
  — *U.S. Department of Education, 1997*

- Among students nationwide, 36.6 percent had been in a physical fight one or more times during the previous 12 months before the survey.
  — *Centers for Disease Control, 1997*

From: *American Psychological Association MTV Antiviolence Programming*

TABLE 2. SCHOOL VIOLENCE FROM THE STUDENT PERSPECTIVE

• Endure insults, put-downs, harassment that triggers anger and frustration.	• Validate feelings. • Develop alternatives to cope.
• Learn that they do not have to accept any type of intolerance.	• Aid in upgrading quality of relationships.
• Choice to use a weapon.	• Develop enhanced sense of self worth. • Examine options for what they can do proactively in situations.

lem-solve when in conflict (Calicchia, Moncata, & Santosfano, 1993; Borduin, Cone, Mann, & Henggeler, 1995; Lockman & Dodge, 1994).

Henggeler, Melton, Smith, Schoenwald, & Hanley (1993) wrote that a well-specified ecological intervention with individualized, empirically valid services would decrease violent behavior. They reported that the school is the most potent entity to provide this, given the impact and amount of time adolescents are students. Neapolitan (1981), however, stated that the potency of the intervention is best set with the family, in which violence is embedded and which sustains violent behavior in youth. Table 1 presents some facts on violence in schools. Table 2 summarizes features of school violence from the student's perspective and lists some approaches to address these features.

INTERVENTIONS PLANNED TO ADDRESS THE PROBLEM

Carruthers, Sweeney, Kindta, and Harris (1996) described the beginnings of conflict resolution training in the schools during the 1980s. Teachable moments were to be identified, according to Carruthers et al., to discuss the world at large and to encourage "peace lessons." Legislation and resources for school districts' implementation of conflict resolution followed this interest. Education of educators and the design of a curriculum followed (Dudley, Johnson, & Johnson, 1996; Johnson & Johnson, 1994; Lupton-Smith, Carruthers, Flythe, Goetter, & Modest, 1996; Minogue, Kingery, & Murphy, 1999; Moriarty, Kalill, & Benander, 2001). Levy (1989) proposed the structure of a curriculum that included theoretical as well as practical aspects of the topic. Conflict resolution curricula can be taught at all grade levels, according to Carruthers et al. (1996).

FIGURE 2. A DEVELOPMENTAL MODEL OF CR CURRICULUM

Figure 2 presents a developmental model of a conflict resolution (CR) curriculum (Patterson, DeBaryshe, & Randey, 1989). The sequence of materials, as proposed in this model, begins with a narrow scope of focus on issues of violence and then proceeds to topics of conflict, conflict resolution, and interpersonal relationships. The scope of coverage broadens as the students are educated through this sequence of topics. It is also assumed that developmental readiness (i.e., cognitive ability and social maturity) moderate the starting points in this sequence and the amount of topics that can be addressed.

For example, it has been my clinical experience that elementary and middle-school-aged children can proceed from the discussion of violence directly to conflict resolution topics. Sexton-Radek and Paul (2002) reported that high school and college-aged students are successful in completing the full sequence (Paul, Sexton-Radek, Adickas, & Fousek, 1999; Sexton-Radek, Slimmer, Lytle, McNeela, & Sadono, 1997). In a review of common themes of CR curricula, both positive and negative outcomes from conflict are addressed. Large global negative outcomes such as war and terrorist acts are approached in these curricula. Interpersonal conflict is more commonly responded to by American students with negative outcomes of conflict resulting in violence (Valois, McKeown, Garrison, & Vincent, 1995; Zhang, 1994).

A developmental model of CR curriculum for a day-to-day focus was presented by Carruthers et al. (1996). Developmental scientists proposed such a progression of skill-building instruction to be consistent with the needs and abilities of students (Horowitz & Boardman, 1994; Loeber & Farrington, 1997; Olweus, 1992; Thompson, 1996; Twemlow et al., 2001).

Carruthers et al. (1996) identified difficulties in the implementation of integrating CR curricula. Given that subject-based and student experiences have to be taken into account in such integration, incorporation of topic and issues pertinent to students' lives is paramount. Richman and Bowen (1997) stated that students with such learning experiences are better prepared, with an increased understanding of information and an enhanced ability to make connections between topics.

In a ten-week CR lesson unit given to 972 seventh- and eighth-grade students, O'Donnell et al. (1999) reported less violence in students receiving this instruction. O'Donnell et al. attributed the success of the intervention to the intensity of the experience and the community service component. Crespi (1996) underscored the need for intervention; the scope of violence is broad, with 3.49 million young people under age 21 arrested in 1993 alone. Tate, Repucci, and Mulvey (1995) identified the various types of interventions for violent delinquents. The cognitive-behavioral approaches are based on the hypothesis that a person's expectations and appraisals account for the violent behaviors. Violent individuals have constricted problem-solving skills and typically appraise situations negatively. These social-cognitive deficiencies lead to violent behavior where a neutral or any otherwise valenced situation is appraised negatively (Dodge, Lochman, Harnish, Bates & Petit, 1997; Dodge, Price, Bachorowski, & Newman, 1990). Accordingly, CR curricula focused on social and problem-solving skills are most effective.

Recent efforts have been made to build upon this effectiveness with the incorporation of other systems relevant to the student, such as community, peers, and family—and they are operating as cost-effective strategies. For example, Henggeler, Melton, Smith, Schoenwald, and Hanley (1993) used a CR intervention with chronic offending youth and reported a 20 percent reduction in the rate of arrests (68 percent) of those participating in the program. Astor, Behre, Wallace, and Fravil (1998) conducted a national survey of school social workers on school violence. The respondents were in support of social skills training for CR but felt that ecological interventions involving the students' systems and community would be equally effective. Carroll, Hebert, and Roy (1999) found a measured increase in awareness in adolescents after a one-hour discussion of their perception of violence. DuBois, Felner, Meares, and Krier (1994) provided evidence that the aggregation of high-risk youths in intervention programs resulted in escalations in problem behavior at school.

Designers of CR programs work to be effective within the system/field of focus. Plans for CR skill training and acquisition have the same intent, but the designs will vary.

TABLE 3. INTERVENTION SETUP STRATEGIES

Primary Prevention:

(Freshmen in High School)	Broad approaches that span an array of risk factors through a psychoeducational program.

Secondary Prevention:

(1st–4th-graders)	Mitigating the further development of aggression displays.

- Recognize the social basis of violence
- Target "at-risk" populations to inoculate the student against the harmful impact of environmental impediments

---

Table 3 describes intervention setup strategies. Paul, Sexton-Radek, Adickas, and Vairo (2002) approached the need identified by a Chicago inner-city school principal for CR interventions with incoming freshmen. A similar type of referral from a Chicago inner-city elementary school principal for first-graders was focused in a secondary prevention manner. The secondary prevention dealt with an already existing problem of bullying and violent acts by first-graders that had to be managed.

The contextual factor of media contributes to the development of violent behavior. Zimmerman (1996) noted that adolescents watch television approximately 23 hours a week and children (age 2–11) for 28 hours a week. This estimate becomes more alarming when a content review of shows reveals that during childhood and adolescence, viewers will observe an estimated 180,000 murders, rapes, armed robberies, and assaults (Zimmerman). The meta-analytic reviews on this topic have shown evidence of the positive association between exposure to violent content and higher levels of aggressive and antisocial behavior, at all ages and on all measures.

Everett and Price (1995) surveyed 726 public school students in grades seven through twelve. A positive association between poor grades and violent behavior in males was found, as well as between poor grades and weapon carrying. Cleary (2000) reported that all categories of suicide/violent behavior were most frequent, across both genders, in those who were victimized. A stratified sample of 1,569 students in grades nine through twelve was used in the Cleary study. School-based support for at-risk adolescents is linked to reduced psychological distress because the CR program buffers the effects of stress through a compensatory function (DuBois et al., 1994).

Moriarty, Kalill, and Benander (2000) reported a 30 percent reduction in violence incidents after a psychoeducational approach to violence.

Friedman and Wachs (1999) highlighted the theme of environment influencing behavior. They proposed a bioecological model in which assumptions about behavior are made and the impact of the environment is assessed. They explained that for development to occur, individuals need to be active on a fairly regular basis. An individual's development is also shaped by conditions and events that occur during the historical period in which they live. Additionally, the Friedman and Wachs model proposes that individuals influence their own development through their own choices and acts. This is often termed "human agency" (Bjarnason, Sigurdardottir, & Thorlindsson, 1998; Bowen & Bowen, 1999).

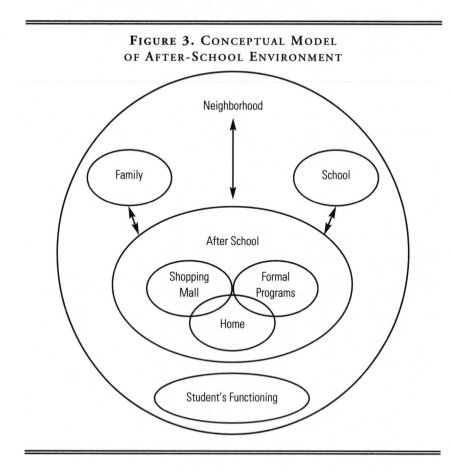

FIGURE 3. CONCEPTUAL MODEL
OF AFTER-SCHOOL ENVIRONMENT

In Figure 3, Bronfenbrenner (1993) has described the environments that influence a student's behavior. As the student progresses developmentally, this "human agency"—represented in each small circle, such as "Shopping Mall"—becomes varied in prominence in the student's life. Bronfenbrenner's developmental perspective highlights the areas of influence in an adolescent's life. Figure 2 provides an illustration of these factors. Formal programming such as CR interventions during school and after school has been designed as intervention with impact. School consumes six hours of adolescents' time, homework maybe two more hours; there is limited involvement in adult caretaking work, and therefore there is plenty of time for peers. "Friends' level of drug use was a strong predictor of drug use among populars, brains, normals and the Hispanic crowd but not among druggies or nerds" Bronfenbrenner (1993). The after-school environment may contribute to violent behavior with the many activities/options available to the adolescent.

Burt, Resnick, and Novick (1998) proposed the means of integrative services to assist adolescents from straying from a course to adulthood. Social services programs that serve the goal of assisting those who stray need further coordination and linkage. Additionally, a fragmentation occurs, according to Burt et al., where some types or populations are served and others are not. Delinquency, substance use, programmed parenthood (i.e., parenting by a teacher or neighbor), and school failure are considered to be common problems of adolescence.

Programs such as Big Brothers/Big Sisters provide an approach to service integration to a diverse group of people. Interviews with directors and a review of program documents provide varied ways of serving adolescents.

Murphy and Duncan (1997) provided a manual approach for practitioners working in school systems. The case studies and summaries provide a means of engaging students, moving them through a therapeutic process, and maintaining the empowered behavior they have acquired. The emphasis is on employing an exchange of power to the student for the behavior.

CR OUTCOMES

Intended outcomes of CR efforts include: reduction in the dropout rate, increase in attendance, decrease in grade retention rate, reduction in the number of suspensions, increase in standardized test scores, and reductions, in general, of violent behavior. We have measured outcomes in terms of changes in reported anger, teacher observations, and student's self-reported self-image (Paul, Sexton-Radek, Adickas, & Fousek, 1999).

Youth development efforts are aimed at increasing safety and structure in adolescent/young adult lives and instilling a sense of belonging, and of competence and mastery over their lives. A broad scope of youth development activities includes such things as non-school hours programming and job training and placement service to address these needs.

Self-focused interventions for adolescents provide an opportunity for self-regulation of prosocial and disruptive behavior. Tackling dysfunctional social and problem-solving skills in adolescents from a cognitive-behavioral perspective that targeted skill development was effective. Hritz and Gabau (1997) presented a community-based approach in which adolescents involved in gangs participated in an ex-gang-member–directed program that was modeled after the twelve-step program of Alcoholics Anonymous. Carruthers, Sweeney, Kindta, and Harris (1996) identified the need to set up a method of program evaluation in which school systems can easily measure the impact of the CR curriculum. An evaluation model that was termed "action research" was suggested for use in school districts. There were step-by-step approaches to collecting data and measuring outcome. Paul, Sexton-Radek, Adickas, and Fousek (1999) presented the utility of a six-week group intervention aimed at building skills for positive communication, resolving differences, and preventing violence. Analyses of pre- to post-intervention data substantiated the impact of the CR program delivery (Sexton-Radek & Paul, 2002).

Table 4. Findings from MEPS Testing

At pretest:

	Average of 1–2 means across stories	Average of 2 or more means across stories
Experimental Group	38%	53%
Control Group	38%	58%

At post-test:

	Average of 1–2 means across stories	Average of 2 or more means across stories
Experimental Group	35%	66%
Control Group	36%	64%

Fatum and Hooyle (1996) identified the use of a student forum in which participants in CR programs voiced their views. The collection of qualitative data provided a non-filtered expression of views that was valuable to the student participants' investment in the program and to the understanding of their views by administrators. For example, Fatum and Hooyle noted that some viewpoints of the students pointed to the consideration that today's youth may not regard aggression, fighting, and using guns as violence. Loeber and Farrington (1997) underscored the need for multisystem intervention with severe violence offenders.

The problem of violence in the schools presents a microcosmic view of terrorism issues. The fear of physical and/or emotional harm, intimidation, and physical and/or emotional abuse are evident. The facts and figures related to adolescent crime underscore the need for interventions within the school system as the source with the most impact. A large volume of CR intervention programming exists for this purpose. In the appendix that follows this chapter, materials distributed on the American Psychological Association Web site provide clear and succinct information points on CR. Some of the outcome studies suggest CR's effectiveness, although this research area is underdeveloped. In light of these presentations, several future directions in both areas of research and intervention are necessary to continue the vitality of this "good start" in conflict resolution.

UNRESOLVED ISSUES

Despite the advancements in CR curriculum design and implementation to address school violence, several important issues are unresolved. Action research aimed at further empirical investigation of curriculum design, match of curriculum to student population, and program evaluation of CR curriculums should be a future area of study. Specific tenets related to this are proposed.

- The importance of integrating CR management in core curricula
- How, cognitively and behaviorally, students are changed; the impact of the program
- The skills sustaining and applicable to the students' day-to-day life
- More precise identification of when and with whom the CR curricula should be done
- The extent of contribution of contextual factors
- Stability/linearity of violence being predicted from a higher number of early risk factors

REFERENCES

Alexander, R., Jr., & Curtis, C. M. (1995). A critical review of strategies to reduce school violence. *Social Work in Education. 17,* 73–82.

Astor, R. A., Behre, W. J., Wallace, J. M., & Fravil, K. A. (1998). School social workers and school violence: Personal safety, training and violence programs. *Social Work, 43,* 223–232.

Berton, M. W., & Statt, S. D. (1996). Exposure to violence and post-traumatic stress disorder in urban adolescents. *Adolescence, 31,* 489–498.

Bjarnason, T., Sigurdardottir, T. J., & Thorlindsson, T. (1998). Human agency, capable guardians, and structured constraints: A life style approach to the study of violent victimization. *Journal of Youth and Adolescence, 22,* 105–111.

Blum, R. W., Beuhring, T., Shew, M. L., Bearinger, L. H., Sieving, R. E., & Resnick, M. (2000). The effects of race/ethnicity, income, and family structure on adolescent risk behaviors. *American Journal of Public Health, 90,* 1879–1884.

Blemstein, A. (1995). Violence by young people: Why the deadly nexus? *National Institute of Justice Journal, 209.*

Borduin, C. M., Cone, L. T., Mann, B. J., & Henggeler, S. W. (1995). Multisystemic treatment of serious juvenile offenders: Long-term prevention of criminality and violence. *Journal of Consulting and Clinical Psychology, 63,* 569–578.

Bowen, N. K., & Bowen, G. L. (1999). Effects of crime and violence in neighborhoods and schools on the school behavior and performance of adolescents. *Journal of Adolescent Research, 14,* 319–342.

Brendgen, M., Vitaro, F., Tremblay, R. E., & Lavoie, F. (2001). Reactive and proactive aggression: Predictions to physical violence in different contexts and moderating effects of parental monitoring and caregiver behavior. *Journal of Abnormal Child Psychology, 29,* 293–304.

Bronfenbrenner, U. (1993). Environments in developmental perspective: A theoretical and operational model. In B. Brown (Ed.), *Measuring the peer environment of American adolescents* (pp. 59–90). Hillsdale, NJ: Erlbaum.

Burt, M. R., Resnick, G., & Novick, E. (1998). *Building supportive communities for at-risk adolescents: It takes more than service.* Washington, DC: American Psychological Association Press.

Calicchia, J., Moncata, S., & Santosfano, S. (1993). Cognitive control differences in violent juvenile inpatients. *Journal of Clinical Psychology, 49,* 731–740.

Carroll, G. B., Hebert, D. M., & Roy, J. M. (1999). Youth action strategies in violence prevention. *The Journal of Adolescent Health, 25,* 6–13.

Carruthers, W. L., Sweeney, F., Kindta, D., & Harris, G. (1996). Conflict resolution: An evaluation of the research literature and a model for program evaluation. *The School Counselor, 44,* 5–18.

Cirillo, K., Pruitt, B. E., Colwell, B., Kingery, P. M., Harby, R. M., & Ballard, D. (1998). School violence: Prevalence and intervention strategies for at-risk adolescents. *Adolescence, 33,* 319–330.

Cleary, S. D. (2000). Adolescent victimization and associated suicidal and violent behaviors. *Adolescence, 35,* 671–682.

Coley, R. L., & Hoffman, L. W. (1996). Relations of parental supervision and monitoring to children's functioning in various contexts: Moderating effects of families and neighborhoods. *Journal of Applied Developmental Psychology, 17,* 51–68.

Crespi, T. D. (1996). Violent children and adolescents: Facing the treatment crisis in child and family interaction. *Family Therapy, 23,* 43–50.

Dodge, K. A., Lochman, J. E., Harnish, J. P., Bates, J. E., & Petit, G. S. (1997). Reactive and proactive aggression in school children and psychiatrically impaired chronically assaultive youth. *Journal of Abnormal Psychology, 106,* 37–51.

Dodge, K. A., Price, J. M., Bachorowski, J., & Newman, J. P. (1990). Hostile attributional biases in severely aggressive adolescents. *Journal of Abnormal Psychology, 99,* 385–392.

DuBois, D. L., Felner, R. D., Meares, H., & Krier, M. (1994). Prospective investigation of the effects of socioeconomic disadvantage, life stress, and social support on early adolescent adjustment. *Journal of Abnormal Psychology, 103*, 511–522.

Dudley, B. S., Johnson, D. W. & Johnson, R. T. (1996). Conflict resolution training and middle school students: Integrative negotiation behavior. *Journal of Applied Social Psychology, 26*, 2038–2052.

Ellickson, P., Saner, H., & McGuigan, K. A. (1997). Profiles of violent youth: Substance use and other concurrent problems. *American Journal of Public Health, 87*, 985–991.

Everett, S. A., & Price, J. H. (1995). Students' perceptions of violence in the public schools: The Met Life Survey. *Journal of Adolescent Health, 17*, 345–352.

Ewing, C. P. (1990). *When children kill: The dynamics of juvenile homicide.* Lexington, MA: Lexington Books/D. C. Heath.

Fatum, W. R., & Hooyle, J.C. (1996). Is it violence? School violence from the student perspective: Trends and interventions. *The School Counselor, 44*, 28–34.

Friedman, S. L., & Wachs, T. D. (1999). *Measuring environment across the life span: Emerging methods and concepts.* Washington, DC: American Psychological Association.

Henggeler, S. W., Melton, G. B., Smith, L. A., Schoenwald, S. K., & Hanley, J. H. (1993). Family preservation using multisystemic treatment: Long-term follow-up to a clinical trial with serious juvenile offenders. *Journal of Child and Family Studies, 2*, 283–293.

Hill, H. M., Levermore, M., Twaite, J., & Jones, L. P. (1996). Exposure to community violence and social support as predictors of anxiety and social and emotional behavior among African American children. *Journal of Child and Family Studies, 5*, 399–414.

Horowitz, S. V., & Boardman, S. K. (1994). Managing conflict: Policy and research implementations. *Journal of Social Issues, 50*, 197–211.

Hritz, S. A., & Gabau, P. A. (1997). A peer approach to high risk youth. *Journal of Adolescent Health, 20*, 259–260.

Johnson, D. W., & Johnson, R. T. (1994). Constructive conflict in the schools. *Journal of Social Issues, 50*, 117–137.

Levy, J. (1989). Conflict resolution in elementary and secondary education. *Mediation Quarterly, 7*, 73–87.

Lochman, J. E., & Dodge, K. A. (1994). Social-cognitive processes of severely violent, moderately aggressive, and nonaggressive boys. *The Journal of Consulting and Clinical Psychology, 62*, 366–374.

Loeber, R., & Farrington, D. P. (Eds.) (1998). *Serious and violent juvenile offenders: Risk factors and successful interventions.* Thousand Oaks, CA: Sage.

Loeber, L. R., & Stouthamer-Loeber, M. (1998). Development of juvenile aggression and violence. *American Psychologist, 53*, 242–259.

Lowry, R., Sleet, D., Duncan, C., Powell, K., & Kolbe, L. (1995). Adolescents at risk for violence. *Educational Psychology Review, 7*, 4–39.

Lupton-Smith, H. S., Carruthers, W. C., Flythe, C., Goetter, E., & Modest, K. (1996). Conflict resolution as peer mediation: Primary, elementary, middle and high school students. *The Student Counselor, 43*, 379–391.

Minogue, N., Kingery, P., & Murphy, L. (1999). *Approaches to assessing violence among youth.* Roslyn, VA: Hamilton Fish National Institute on School and Community Violence.

Moffit, T. E. (1993). Adolescence-limited and life-course persistent antisocial behavior: A developmental taxonomy. *Psychology Review, 100*, 674–701.

Moriarty, A., Kalill, P. M., & Benander, M. (2001). The protocol approach to school violence. *Smith College Studies in Social Work, 71*, 279–299.

Moriarty, A., Kalill, P. M., Benander, M. (2000). *The protocol approach to school violence.* Smith College School for Social Work Conference, "Safe Schools Building Fortresses or Opening Doors to Community."

Murphy, J. J., & Duncan, B. L. (1997). *Brief interventions for school problems: Collaborating for practical solutions.* New York: Guildford Press.

Neapolitan, J. (1981). Parental influences on aggressive behavior: A social learning approach. *Adolescence, 16,* 831–840.

O'Donnell, C. R. (1995). Firearm deaths among children and youth. *American Psychologist, 50,* 771–776.

O'Donnell, L., Stueve, A., Sandoval, A., Duran, R., Atnafou, R., Haber, D., Johnson, N., Murray, H., Grant, U., Julien, G., Tang, J., Bass, J., & Piessens, P. (1999). Violence prevention and young adolescents' participation in community youth service. *Journal of Adolescent Health, 29,* 28–37.

Olweus, D. (1992). Bullying among school children: Intervention and prevention. In R. Peters, R. McMahon, V. Quincy (Eds.), *Aggression and violence throughout the lifespan* (pp. 100–125). Sage Publications.

Page, R. M., & Hammermeister, J. (1997). Weapon-carrying and youth violence. *Adolescence, 32,* 505–513.

Paschall, M. J., Ennett, S. T., & Flewelling, R. L. (1996). Relationships among family characteristics and violent behavior by black and white male adolescents. *Journal of Youth and Adolescence, 25,* 177–195.

Patterson, G. R., DeBaryshe, B. D., & Randey, E. (1989). A developmental perspective on antisocial behavior. *The American Psychologist, 44,* 329–335.

Paul, P., Sexton-Radek, K., Adickas, J. & Fousek, B. (1999). The use of service learning to promote understanding of gang-related issues faced by adolescents. *National Society for Experiential Education, 25,* 3–7.

Paul, P., Sexton-Radek, K., Adickas, J., & Vairo, K. (2002). Psychometric findings of the self-directed search with ethnic minority norms. Poster presentation at the Ninth Biennial Meeting of the Society for Research on Adolescence. New Orleans, Louisiana.

Richman, J. M., & Bowen, G. L. (1997). School failure: An ecological-interactional developmental perspective. In M. W. Fraser (Ed.), *Risk and resilience in childhood: An ecological perspective* (pp. 95–116). Washington, DC: National Association of Social Workers.

Rosenthal, B. S. (2000). Exposure to community violence in adolescence: Trauma symptoms. *Adolescence 35,* 271–284.

Schwab-Stone, M., Chen, C., Greenburger, E., Silver, D., Lichtman, J., & Voyce, C. (1999). No safe haven II: The effects of violence exposure on urban youth. *Journal of American Academy of Child & Adolescent Psychiatry, 38,* 359–367.

Sexton-Radek, K., & Paul, P. (2002). The use of interest inventories with at-risk for violence behavior adolescents. [Manuscript in review.]

Sexton-Radek, K., Slimmer, L., Lytle, J., McNeela, D., & Sadono, S. (1997, August). Service learning courses and action research. Poster presentation at the American Psychological Association Conference, Chicago.

Stoolmiller, M., Eddy, J. M., & Reid, J. B. (2000). Detecting and describing preventive intervention effects in a universal school-based randomized trial targeting delinquent and violent behavior. *Journal of Consulting and Clinical Psychology, 68,* 296–306.

Tate, D. C., Repucci, N. D., & Mulvey, E. P. (1995). Violent juvenile delinquents treatment effectiveness and implications for future action. *American Psychologist, 50,* 777–781.

Thompson, S. M. (1996). Peer mediation: A peaceful solution. *The School Counselor, 44,* 151–154.

Twemlow, S. W., Fonagy, P., Saceo, F. C., Gies, M. L., Evans, R., & Ewbank, R. (2001). Creating a peaceful school learning environment: A controlled study of an elementary school intervention to reduce violence. *American Journal of Psychiatry, 158,* 808–810.

Valois, R. F., McKeown, R. E., Garrison, C. Z., & Vincent, M. L. (1995). Correlates of aggressive and violent behaviors among public high school adolescents. *Journal of Adolescent Health, 16,* 26–34.

Weinburger, D. A., & Gomes, M. E. (1998). Changes in daily mood and self-restraint among undercontrolled preadolescents: A time series analysis of "acting out." *Journal of the American Academy of Child and Adolescent Psychiatry, 34,* 1473–1782.

Zhang, Q. (1994). An intervention model of constructive conflict resolution and cooperative learning. *Journal of Social Issues, 50,* 99–116.

Zimmerman, J. D. (1996). A prosocial media strategy: "Youth against violence: Choose to de-fuse." *American Journal of Orthopsychiatry, 66,* 354–362.

NOTE

The author graciously thanks Peggy Dumas for her perfect word processing help. Appreciation is owed to Mr. Ihles and Mr. Baier for providing trust and support for my interventions at John Hancock Academy. The author thanks Lynda Slimmer, Ph.D., Professor of Nursing and Director of Service Learning at Elmhurst College, for her continued support and inspiration.

APPENDIX: REACTIONS AND GUIDELINES FOR CHILDREN FOLLOWING TRAUMA/DISASTER

Compiled by Robin H. Gurwitch, Ph.D., Jane F. Silovsky, Ph.D.,
Shelli Schultz, Ph.D., Michelle Kees, Ph.D., & Sarah Burlingame, B.A.
Department of Pediatrics
University of Oklahoma Health Sciences Center

What to Expect after Trauma: Possible Reactions in Elementary School Students

1) Feelings of anxiety, fears, and worries about safety of self and others (more clingy to teacher or parent)

2) Worries about re-occurrence of violence

3) Increased levels of distress (whiny, irritable, more "moody")

4) Changes in behavior:
    a) Increased activity level
    b) Decreased concentration and/or attention
    c) Withdrawal
    d) Angry outbursts
    e) Aggression
    f) Absenteeism

5) Increased somatic complaints (e.g., headaches, stomachaches, aches and pains)

6) Changes in school performance

7) Recreating event (e.g., talking repeatedly about it, "playing" the event)

8) Increased sensitivity to sounds (e.g., sirens, planes, thunder, back-fires, loud noises)

9) Statements and questions about death and dying

In addition, at home parents may see:

1) Changes in sleep

2) Changes in appetite

3) Withdrawal

4) Lack of interest in usual activities

5) Increased negative behaviors (e.g., defiance) or emotions (e.g., sadness, fears, anger, worries)

6) Regression in behaviors (e.g., baby talk, bedwetting, tantrums)

7) Hate or anger statements

What to Expect after Trauma: Possible Reactions in Middle School Students

1) Feelings of anxiety, worries, and fears about safety of self and others

2) Worries about re-occurrence or consequences such as war, as well as worries about school violence

3) Changes in behavior:
    a) Decreased attention and/or concentration
    b) Increase in hyperactivity
    c) Changes in academic performance
    d) Irritability with friends, teachers, events
    e) Anger outbursts and/or aggression
    f) Withdrawal
    g) Absenteeism

4) Increased somatic complaints (e.g., headaches, stomachaches, chest pains)

5) Discomfort with feelings, particularly those associated with revenge

6) Increased likelihood to discuss the gruesome details

7) Repeated discussions of event

8) Increased sensitivity to sounds (e.g., sirens, planes, thunder, back-fires, loud noises)

1) Negative impact on issues of trust and perceptions of others, particularly of those that are "different"

2) Repetitive thoughts and comments about death and dying

In addition, at home parents may see:

1) Changes in sleep or appetite

2) Withdrawal

3) Lack of interest in usual activities (e.g., after-school activities, time with friends)

4) Increased negative behaviors (e.g., defiance) or emotions (e.g., sadness, fears, anger, worries)

5) Hate or anger statements

6) Denial of impact

What to Expect after Trauma: Possible Reactions in High School Students

1) Worries, fears, and anxiety about safety of self and others

2) Worries about re-occurrence or repercussions such as war or school violence

3) Changes in behavior:
   a) Withdrawal
   b) Irritability with friends, teachers, events
   c) Anger outbursts and/or aggression
   d) Changes in academic performance
   e) Decrease in attention and concentration
   f) Increase in hyperactivity
   g) Absenteeism

4) Discomfort with feelings, particularly revenge, but also those of vulnerability

5) Increased risk for substance abuse, including drinking

6) Discussion of events and reviewing of details

7) Negative impact on issues of trust and perceptions of others, particularly those that are "different"

8) Increased sensitivity to sounds (e.g., sirens, planes, thunder, backfires, loud noises)

9) Repetitive thoughts and comments about death or dying (including suicidal thoughts)

In addition, at home parents may see:

1) Changes in sleep or appetite

2) Withdrawal

3) Lack of interest in usual activities (e.g., after-school activities, time with friends)

4) Increased negative behaviors (e.g., defiance) or emotions (e.g., sadness, fears, anger, worries)

5) Hate or anger statements

6) Denial of impact

What to Expect after Trauma: Reactions in Teachers

1) Increased irritability and impatience with students and staff (decreased tolerance of minor student infractions—remember, they are trying to cope, too)

2) Difficulty planning classroom activities and lessons

3) Decreased concentration

4) Worries and fears that answers or responses to students could make things worse for them

5) Worries about re-occurrence and repercussions

6) Increased concern about school violence (e.g., hypersensitivity)

7) Feelings of discomfort with intense emotions, such as anger and fear

8) Denial that the traumatic event may impact the students

What Can I Do To Help? Guidelines for Teachers of High School Students

- Reinforce ideas of safety and security, even though many high school students will not verbalize fears around these issues. This may be needed multiple times, particularly in response to changes, loud sounds, or other events that may remind students of the tragedy. After any classroom discussion of the event, end the discussion with a focus on their current safety and a calming activity, such as having a moment of quiet reflection.

- Maintain a predictable class schedule and rules to provide support and consistency for the students.

- Listen to and tolerate your students retelling of events. Schedule specific times for discussion during the school day to allow for opportunities to express their thoughts and feelings about the tragedy; however, set limits on scary or hurtful talk (e.g., specific threats of retribution). This may need to be done in multiple classes.

- Encourage students to talk about confusing feelings, worries, daydreams, and disruptions of concentration by accepting feelings, listening carefully, and reminding students that these are normal reactions following a very scary event. Discuss students' perceptions of media descriptions of events. Information focused on safety will be important. For example, discuss what the US and other world leaders are doing to address safety. From this tragedy, opportunities for learning and discussion of world events are heightened.

- Some students might express hate toward a large group of people. It can be helpful to validate their strong feelings of anger. However, it will be critical to help students separate thoughts and feelings about the specific people who caused the tragedy from generalizing it to larger groups of people, including their classmates and other acquaintances (e.g., all people of Arab descent). It may be helpful to have discussions about how world leaders can help with reducing hate and preventing future violent acts.

- Students will often process the information about the events at unpredictable times throughout the day. As they try to develop an understanding for what has happened, they may ask questions that are initially shocking to adults, including questions that have gruesome details. Try to respond in a calm manner, answering the questions in simple, direct terms and help the students to transition back to their activity.

- Students will often misunderstand the information about the event as they are trying to make sense about what happened. For example, they may blame themselves, believe things happened that did not happen, believe that terrorists are in the school, etc. Gently help students develop a realistic understanding of the event.

- Students may ask the same types of questions repeatedly, which can be confusing and/or frustrating for teachers. Understand that students may need to hear the information multiple times before being able to Integrate and understand it. Give students time to cope with their fears.

- Expect some angry outbursts from students. Try to catch students before they "act out", taking them aside, helping them calm down and regain control of their behavior. In addition, redirect students who are being irritable with each other which could escalate to direct conflict.

- Do classroom activities that will reinforce the message that one person can make a difference to help and heal. Activities can include drawing pictures and sending cards or class projects of collecting pennies or aluminum cans or making origami cranes.

- Encourage some distraction times, which would include doing school work that that does not require high levels of new learning and enjoyable activities. Help students do activities that allow them to experience mastery and build self-esteem.

- Expect some brief (temporary) decline in students' school performance. Consider suspending standardized testing and classroom testing for the rest of the week. Also, consider reducing homework as the nation heals and the national routine is stabilized (e.g., parents are back to work, no additional threats).

- Provide reassurance to students that the feelings will get smaller and easier to handle over time.

- Protect students from re-exposure to frightening situations and reminders of trauma. This includes limiting teacher-to-teacher conversations about the events in front of students.

- Maintain communication with other teachers, school personnel, and parents monitor how students are coping with the demands of school, home, and community activities. Should difficulties coping with the event persist and interfere with students' functioning, consider seeking help from a mental health professional. In addition to helping those who are clearly angry or depressed, monitor students who are withdrawn and isolated from others.

- Remain aware of your own reactions to students' trauma, as well as your own reactions to the trauma. It is okay to express emotions to your students, such as "I am feeling sad about what happened." However, if you are feeling overwhelmed with emotion, it is important to take care of yourself and to seek support from other teachers and staff.

What Can I Do To Help? Guidelines for Teachers of Middle School Students

- Reinforce ideas of safety and security. This may be needed multiple times, particularly in response to changes/loud sounds/or other events that may remind the students of the tragedy. After any classroom discussion of the event, end the discussion with a focus on their current safety and a calming activity, such as taking deep breaths, working together on an art project, or having a moment of quiet reflection.

- Listen to and tolerate your students retelling of events, as well as playing out the events. Maintain a predictable class schedule and rules to provide support and consistency for the students. Schedule specific times for discussion during the school day to allow for opportunities to express their thoughts and feelings about the tragedy. This may need to be done in multiple classes; however, set limits on scary or hurtful talk (e.g., specific threats of retribution).

- Encourage the students to talk about confusing feelings, worries, daydreams, and disruptions of concentration by accepting the feelings, listening carefully, and reminding the students that these are normal reactions (any of these feelings are okay) following a very scary event. Discuss students" perceptions of media descriptions of events. Information focused on safety will be important. For example, the President of the USA and other "helping people" (e.g., the firefighters, military, police, doctors) are all working together to make us safe (give examples). Review of school safety rules may also be helpful.

- Some students might express hate toward a large group of people. It can be helpful to validate their strong feelings of anger. However, It will be critical to help the students separate thoughts and feelings about the specific people who caused the tragedy from generalizing it to larger groups of people, including their classmates or other people they might know (e.g., all people of Arab descent). It may be helpful to have discussions about how world leaders can help with reducing hate and preventing future violent acts.

- Students will often process the information about the events at unpredictable times throughout the day. As they try to develop an understanding of what has happened, they may ask questions that may be initially shocking to adults, including questions that have gruesome details or focus on death. Try to respond in a calm manner, answering the questions in simple and direct terms and helping the students transition back to their activity.

- Use simple direct terms to describe what happened, rather than terms designed to "soften" the information, which inadvertently further confuses the students. For example, use the term "died," rather than "went to sleep."

- Students will often misunderstand information about the event as they are trying to make sense of what happened. For example, they may blame themselves; may believe things happened that did not happen, may believe that terrorists are in the school, etc. Gently help students develop a realistic understanding of the event.

- Students may ask the same types of questions repeatedly, which can be confusing and/or frustrating for the teacher. Understand that students may need to hear the information multiple times before being able to integrate and understand it. Give the students time to cope with fears.

- Expect some angry outbursts from students. Try to catch students before they "act out," by taking them aside, and helping them calm down and regain control of their behavior. In addition redirect students who are being irritable with each other which could escalate to direct conflict.

- Do classroom activities that will reinforce the message that one person can make a difference to help and heal. Activities can include drawing pictures and sending cards or class projects of collecting pennies or aluminum cans or making origami cranes.

- Encourage some distraction times, which would include doing school work that that does not require high levels of new learning as well as enjoyable activities. Help students do activities that allow them to experience mastery and build self-esteem.

- Expect some brief (temporary) declines in the students' school performance. Consider suspending standardized testing and classroom testing for the rest of the week. Also, consider reducing homework as the nation heals until the national routine is stabilized (e.g., parents are back to work, no additional threats).

- Provide reassurance to the students that feelings will get smaller and easier to handle over time.

- Protect students from re-exposure to frightening situations and reminders of trauma. This includes limiting teacher-to-teacher conversations about the events in front of the students.

- Maintain communication with other teachers, school personnel, and parents to monitor how the students are coping with the demands of school, home, and community activities. Should difficulties coping with the event persist and interfere with the students' functioning, consider seeking help from a mental health professional. In addition to helping those who are clearly angry or depressed, monitor students who are withdrawn and isolated from others.

- Remain aware of your own reactions to student's "trauma." It is okay to express emotions to your students, such as "I am feeling sad about what happened." However, if you are feeling overwhelmed with emotion, it is important to take care of yourself and to seek support from other teachers and staff.

What Can I Do to Help? Guidelines for Elementary School Teachers

- Reinforce ideas of safety and security. This may be needed multiple times, particularly in response to changes, loud sounds, or other events that may remind the students of the tragedy. After any classroom discussion of the event, end the discussion with a focus on their current safety and a calming activity, such as taking deep breaths, working together on an art project, or holding hands and singing a quiet song.

- Maintain a predictable class schedule and rules to provide support and consistency for the children.

- Listen to and tolerate your students retelling of events, as well as playing out the events. Schedule specific times for discussion and play during the school day to allow for opportunities to express their thoughts and feelings about the tragedy; however, set limits on scary or hurtful play.

- Encourage students to talk about confusing feelings, worries, day-dreams, and disruptions of concentration by accepting the feelings, listening carefully, and reminding students that these are normal reactions (any of these feelings are okay) following a very scary event. Information focused on safety will be Important. For example, the President of the USA and other "helping people" (e.g., the firefighters, military, police, doctors) are all working together to make us safe (give examples). A review of school safety rules may also be helpful.

- Some students might express hate toward a large group of people. It can be helpful to validate their strong feelings of anger. However, it will be critical to help the students separate thoughts and feelings about the specific people who caused the tragedy from generalizing it to larger groups of people, including their classmates or other people they might know (e.g., all people of Arab descent).

- Young children will process the information about the events at unpredictable times throughout the day. As they try to develop an understanding of what has happened, they may ask questions that may be initially shocking to adults. Try to respond in a calm manner, answering the questions in simple, direct terms and helping the students transition back to their activity.

- Use simple, direct terms to describe what happened. Avoid terms designed to "soften" the information, which inadvertently further confuses children. For example, use the term "died," rather than "went to sleep."

- Students may misunderstand information about the event as they are trying to make sense of what happened. For example, they may blame themselves, believe things happened that did not happen, believe that terrorists are in the school, etc. Gently help students develop a realistic understanding of the event.

• Students may ask the same types of questions repeatedly, which can be confusing and/or frustrating for teachers. Understand that students may need to hear the information multiple times before being able to integrate and understand it. Give the students time to cope with fears.

• Expect some angry outbursts from students. Try to catch students before they "act out," by taking them aside, and helping them calm down and regain control of their behavior.

• Do classroom activities that will reinforce the message that one person can make a difference to help and heal. Activities can include drawing pictures and sending cards or class projects of collecting pennies or aluminum cans.

• Encourage some distraction times, which would include doing school work that that does not require high levels of new learning, as well as enjoyable activities.

• Expect some brief, temporary declines in the students' school performance. Consider reducing homework as the nation heals and the national routine is stabilized (e.g., parents are back to work, no additional threats).

• Provide reassurance to the students that feelings will get smaller and easier to handle over time.

• Expect and understand students, regression (acting younger) and other difficult behaviors that are not typical of the students.

• Protect students from re-exposure to frightening situations and reminders of trauma. This includes limiting teacher-to-teacher conversations about the events in front of students.

• Maintain communication with other teachers, school personnel, and parents to monitor how the students are coping with the demands of school, home, and community activities.

• Remain aware of your own reactions to students' trauma. It is okay to express emotions to your students, such as "I am feeling sad about what happened." However, if you are feeling overwhelmed with emotion, it is important to take care of yourself and seek support from other teachers and staff.

What Can I Do To Help? Guidelines for Parents of Elementary School Students

In addition to the guidelines for teachers of elementary school students (see Teacher Guidelines), the following are ways parents can complement what is being provided in the schools.

- Avoid exposing your child to reminders of the trauma. This includes limiting your child's exposure to the news and other television programs about the tragedy. If you do choose to have your child see this Information on the television, keep it brief, watch it with your child, and talk to your child after to clarify miscommunication. Protecting the children from re-exposure includes limiting exposure to adult conversations about the events—even when you think they are not listening, they often are.

- Maintain the family routines, particularly around sleeping, eating, and extracurricular activities (e.g., sports, church, dance). Be sure the bedtime routine includes safely tucking them in at night. Young children may want a night light again. Make sure your child is receiving a balanced diet and enough rest.

- Avoid unnecessary separations from important caregivers.

- Expect temporary regression in your child's behaviors (e.g., starting to babytalk, wetting the bed). Do not panic, as your child is likely to return to previous functioning with time and support.

- Provide soothing activities, such as reading books, listening to music, taking a walk, riding bikes, etc.

- Increase patience with your child and with yourself. Give your family time to cope. Find ways to emphasize to the children that you love them.

What Can I Do To Help? Guidelines for Parents of Middle School Students

In addition to the guidelines for teachers of middle school students (see Teacher Guidelines), the following are ways parents can complement what is being provided in the schools.

- Avoid exposing your child to reminders of the trauma. This includes limiting your child's exposure to the news and other television programs about the tragedy. If you do choose to have your child see this information on the television, keep it brief, watch it with your child, and talk to your child after to clarify miscommunication. Protecting the children from re-exposure includes limiting exposure to adult conversations about the events—even when you think they are not listening, they often are.

- Maintain the family routines, particularly around sleeping and eating and extracurricular activities (e.g., sports, church, dance). Make sure your child is receiving a balanced diet and enough rest. Extra time with friends who are supportive and meaningful to him/her may be needed.

- Avoid unnecessary separations from important caregivers.

- Provide soothing activities, such as reading books, listening to music, taking a walk, riding bikes, etc. Some middle school students benefit from writing their thoughts and feelings in a journal.

- Address acting-out behavior involving aggression or self-destructive activities quickly and firmly with limit setting. If this behavior is severe or persists, seek professional help.

- Increase patience with your child and with yourself. Give your family time to cope. Find ways to emphasize to the children that you love them.

What Can I Do To Help? Guidelines for Parents of High School Students

In addition to the guidelines for teachers of high school students (see Teacher Guidelines), the following are ways parents can complement what is being provided in the schools.

- Avoid exposing your teen to reminders of the trauma. This Includes monitoring your teen's exposure to the news and other television programs about the tragedy. When you can, watch it with your teen, and talk to your teen after to clarify their understanding of the events and the images seen. Be aware that your teens are often listening when adults are discussing the events. Protect your teen from re-exposure includes limiting exposure to adult conversations, however, find time to include them in age appropriate discussions about the events and resulting thoughts and feelings.

- Maintain the family routines, particularly around sleeping and eating and extracurricular activities (e.g., sports, church, dance). Make sure your teen is receiving a balanced diet and enough rest. Extra time with friends who are supportive and meaningful to him/her may be needed.

- Avoid unnecessary separations from important caregivers.

- Provide soothing activities, such as reading books, listening to music, taking a walk, riding bikes, etc. Some high school students benefit from writing their thoughts and feelings in a journal.

- Address acting-out behavior involving aggression or self-destructive activities quickly and firmly with limit setting. If this behavior is severe or persists, seek professional help.

- Encourage your teen to delay making big decisions.

- Increase patience with your teen and with yourself. Give your family time to cope. Find ways to emphasize to your teen that you love them.

From: APA Online Practice
© PsycNET 2001 American Psychological Association

10

Terror, Disaster, and War: How Can We Help Our Children?

John E. LeCapitaine

To be safe. To be secure. To be healthy. To be housed. To be fed . . . and possibly to have a parent, aunt, uncle, brother, sister, and precious others. The vital needs of children initially appear to be basic. These needs are essential to a healthy foundation for personal and psychological development, and should be the raison d'être of education. Of course, serious attention must also be given to ethnographic, economic, cultural, and other contextual experiences with which the child is absorbed, if not sometimes held hostage by them—experiences that include terror, disaster, and war. All of these need to be addressed vigorously and ambitiously, aptly and now, by parents, educators, and communities. This chapter provides educators and parents-as-educators with strategies for recognizing terrorized children and helping them cope with terror, disaster, and war. Further, educators should be drawn to the sections focused on strengthening critical strands of development.

RATIONALE

The terror of September 11, 2001, is ongoing. The United States is in a state of war, and this is particularly difficult because there is no end in sight. This could go on for a long, long time. For children and adolescents, this unknown is especially scary. They have not been through anything like this before. They do not know what might happen next, and this causes significant fear and stress, expressed in many different ways.

Understanding various strands of developments from early childhood and preschool age through adolescence is vital in treating fear, stress, and anxiety. Each age group might manifest these emotional "monsters" in a different way.

PURPOSE

This chapter examines core reactions and developmental attributes of children, preadolescents, and adolescents with respect to terrorism, disaster, and war. Strategies for parents, teachers, and other significant persons are presented in such a way that they may study and implement such ideas and positive ways of helping children and adolescents in times of real or perceived trauma.

Its purpose is to implore readers, especially educators, to wholeheartedly address personal and psychological development. The chapter provides relevant stage theory and foundations for stage transformations, the *sine qua non* of development and maturity. The critical developmental theories address emotional development, moral/ethical development, ego-identity development, and perspective-taking.

PERSONAL AND PSYCHOLOGICAL DEVELOPMENT

Taking Dewey's (1963) notion of development as the aim of education a step further, personal and psychological development *must* be the aim of education. Personal and psychological curricula may help to maturate the basic strands of human development, including emotional, ethical/moral, ego, social, cognitive, and aesthetic development. These strands, woven together, form stage development models. Combining these parts, *all* persons may have the opportunity to grow and to develop positively. Children may begin to construct and develop their own emotions, moral/ethical reasoning, and ego identity—all constructs much more critical than academic achievement (LeCapitaine, 1999, 2000, 2001).

How do children and adolescents develop, personally and psychologically? They do so primarily by engaging in *meaningful interactions* and *experiences,* by *doing,* through cognitive *dissonance* (dilemmas); through critical, reflective thinking; and through maturation and physical growth.

How do we make the "hidden curriculum" visible and viable, to foster personal and psychological development? Mosher and Sprinthall advocated "deliberate psychological education . . . the deliberate development of positive psychological growth for all children" (1970, pp. 911–924). Not only is the curriculum then explicit, but it is for everyone—it is development for all. And it should be a community response (LeCapitaine, 1999), provided not only by teachers but also by counselors, school psychologists, social workers, and community developmental clinics.

Schools as Developmental Clinics

In the article "Schools as Developmental Clinics: Overcoming the Shadow's Three Faces" (LeCapitaine, 1999), a "shadow" in education is described as having three major faces. Two of these are: (1) the hidden curriculum, which often inculcates inconsistent, random, hidden values and beliefs; and (2) the not-so-hidden curriculum, which preaches a narrow list of academic subjects, at any price, as long as its students remain tied to national standards of achievement, as measured by standardized tests in an exclusive number of academic areas.

What good is it to graduate the mind but to lose the person (LeCapitaine, 2001)? In order for schools to be truly transformative, they must be developmental clinics, which have personal and psychological development as a passion (LeCapitaine, 1999, 2000).

"For all" is a critical term in personal and psychological development. In many schools, the two primary service modalities for teachers, counselors, social workers, and school psychologists are crisis intervention (usually for one student at a time) and remedial programming, for students who need to "catch up" in one academic area or another. Some schools offer preventative programs for teen pregnancy, drug usage, conflict, etc.—but only when the need arises. Very few, if any, schools offer true developmental services, such as clinics that foster positive, age-appropriate lessons for everyone, assisting in personal and psychological development.

These are the very services that actively assist in preventing and treating excessive fear, terror, and other outcomes of war and disaster. It is through these systematic, well-derived, personally meaningful curricular experiences that a child's person and psychology mature.

Myna Shure explains, "We have found in our research that often kids who fail in math don't need more math. They need the ability to concentrate on the math they're getting. They're impeded by emotional blockage" (Sleek, 1997). In *Rethinking Our Classrooms*, Christensen flatly states, "Life's most important lessons are rarely taught in school" and goes on to lament that the terms "joy of schooling" and "thrill of discovering something new" have been replaced by "rigor" and "getting tough" (Bigelow, Christensen, Karp, Miner, & Peterson, 1994, p. 12). If this is the case, the fearful and the terrorized will have justification for the continued dread of being "monsterized."

"Good teachers move between moments of interventions and withdrawal, critique and encouragement" (Kohn, 1994, p. 506). Ralph Mosher (1979) spoke of the "cycle" of curriculum development in which "we think about the students, what we want them to know or become, designing a systematic set of educational experiences, trying out those experiences . . . and evaluating the effect of the curriculum . . . on the students' knowledge, skills, or growth." Then the cycle begins anew with the knowledge of what works and what does not work. In this way, the educator and the community providers develop and implement personal and psychological programs to engender emotional, social, ego, and ethical/moral growth.

EXPRESSIONS OF FEAR AND STRESS

Children at different age and stage levels will express their terror, fears, and stresses in varying ways. Preschoolers may regress in toileting behavior, bed wetting, clinging to parents, or sucking thumbs. Elementary school children may have nightmares, avoid school, or be aggressive. Young adolescents may have physical complaints, problems with parents, poor school performance, or poor sleeping behavior. Older adolescents may be agitated, depressed, irresponsible, and have nightmares or physical complaints (Waddell & Thomas, 1999). Such fears and stresses can in turn terrorize parents and educators.

WHAT YOU CAN DO TO HELP

In helping children deal with fear and stress, three elements seem paramount. The first is to emphasize their immediate safety and security, with repeated assurances. Be honest, without underestimating the gravity of what happened. Children need to hear that they are safe. They can be reminded that nothing has happened where they live, if this is the case. Some children need constant reassurances that they are safe and secure. Children can be taught ways to relax, including using breathing techniques, yoga or exercise; and they may wish to visit a synagogue, church, temple, or mosque.

The second element is to allow children to tell *their* stories and to verbalize their emotions, if possible. If they find it difficult to talk about these thoughts and feelings, play therapy techniques work well and may help young children shape what they are feeling into words. Use concrete terms to question the events: What day was it? What time was it? Who did what? Summarize what the child has said and validate it . . . really listen, reflect on what was said, and put it into perspective.

The third point is to work with the emotions and feelings that the children express. They have to deal with the physical reactions that occur in their bodies, as well as how they are actually thinking about what happened. They also have to recognize and deal with the actions they are taking in response to the emotions, such as angry outbursts and aggression. Kids (and adults) need to be aware of a variety of emotions that they may have. It helps to talk. These emotions may be complex. Sometimes, children experience various emotions that are conflicting, and this is normal.

It is also important to emphasize hope when talking with children about terror. Look at the world's response to terrorism. Most of the world wants it to end. These terrible incidents may have made some families closer; may have even brought the world community closer. Perhaps, at some point, there will be no more terrorists because of this.

STRENGTHENING STRANDS OF DEVELOPMENT

How do educators and parents-as-educators help children every day? Again, they do this through deliberate psychological education for personal and psychological development. Schools and teachers, communities and parents actively engage students in lessons that strengthen emotional, moral/ethical, ego-identity development, and perspective. Maturation in these areas will assist children and adolescents in dealing with fear, anger, pain, and the issues of terrorism, war, and disaster. Educators may find the following sections on strengthening critical strands of development enlightening.

Strengthening Emotional Development

In an effort to avert childhood depression, violence, and crime, Goleman urges parents and schools to teach "emotional literacy" to children, beginning at young ages (Sleek, 1997). He also says he can "foresee a day when education will routinely include inculcating essential human competencies such as self-awareness, self-control and empathy, and the arts of listening, resolving conflicts and cooperation" (Sleek, 1997).

Henry Dupont views emotions as person-social constructions comprising three components—a cognitive appraisal, an alteration of affect, and a terminal action—that can change in form over the life span of the individual. Thus, *we construct our own emotions.* For Dupont, it is the interaction within a relationship that is critical. Social experiences (Kitchener, 1996; Van der Veer, 1996; Vygotsky, 1978) are central to emotional development. Further, Dupont's theory of emotional development postulates that "both our feelings and emotions, which are assumed to be constructions, are informed by our needs and values, and . . . our feelings and emotions change considerably in the course of our development" (Dupont, 1994).

Certainly, Dupont provides a foundation on which schools can operate. In *Emotional Development, Theory and Applications* (1994), he provides for the structure, guidelines, measurement, and the many applications of his paradigm. Basically, as far as curricular experiences are concerned, early education can provide children with opportunities to identify feelings; to observe feelings in others; to ask parents, teachers, and peers about feelings; and to discuss and to role-play experiences that focus on needs, values, feelings, and actions. Intermediate experiences would involve opportunities to role-play, to read, to watch pertinent videos, to observe, and to discuss with peers the process of confronting emotional issues (LeCapitaine, 2000, 2001).

The Emotional Development Interview (EDI) may be used to measure the emotional development of children and adolescents (Dupont, 1994). The EDI measures the critical issues related to the core emotions of joy, anger, guilt, sadness, pride, and fear. From the assessment of each emotion, it is possible to identify the stage of emotional maturity. The students' anger, fear, stress, and terror, may be evaluated and treated accordingly.

STRENGTHENING PERSPECTIVE-TAKING AND SOCIAL DEVELOPMENT

Critical to children's friendships and self-understanding—and a necessary condition for emotional, ego, and moral/ethical maturity—are perspective-taking skills. As stated by Santrock (2000), "perspective-taking is the ability to assume another person's perspective and understand his or her thoughts and feelings." But perspective-taking skills are developmental, and the "structure of the levels of perspective can be used to analyze more fully the developmental aspects of the meaning children make of the issues that define their social relationships" (Selman & Schultz, 1990). Further, Selman's theory explains how friendships are developed and, more importantly, valued. His developmental theory includes five stages of perspective-taking.

Children's perspective-taking is associated with Selman's first three stages: 0) an "egocentric viewpoint" where children fail to differentiate their thoughts and feelings from those of others; 1) "social-informational perspective-taking," where children are cognizant that others have a social perspective but tend to focus on their own perspectives; and 2) "self-reflective perspective-taking" where children are able to put themselves in one another's place, but only as a way of assessing others' perspectives and intentions; they have not, yet, attained mutuality (Lickona, 1976; Santrock, 2000; Selman, 1980).

Ascertaining the child's level of perspective-taking is critical to the developmental process. How often do parents or teachers ask children to take on the role of a peer, a parent, or a teacher, without realizing that those children may not be capable of such a task (LeCapitaine, 2001)?

Thus, mature perspective-taking empowers the child or adolescent to empathize with siblings, peers, parents, victims, and others, ensuring powerful identification and a much-needed sense of "what is going on." They are enabled to help others, and to be helped themselves.

STRENGTHENING IDENTITY DEVELOPMENT

Loevinger (1976, 1983, 1997) maintains that the ego is the "keystone" of personality development, giving purpose and meaning to our lives. Further, the ego organizes and synthesizes our experiences, and is said to be the set of implicit understandings about ourselves (Mosher, 1979). The ego changes throughout the course of our existence as a "complexly interwoven fabric of impulse control, character, interpersonal relationships, conscious preoccupations, and cognitive complexity" (Loevinger, 1976, 1997).

Loevinger uses those five constructs in building her stages of ego development and in measuring a person's level of ego development. The two primary stages for children appear to be the "self-protective" stage and the "conformist" stage. In the former stage, children tend to be concerned with short-term rewards and punishments. The milestone lies in the appearance of initial impulse control on the part of the child; the child does not want to "get caught." In the latter stage, the child begins to follow the rules of the group, not out of fear, but because he or she is identifying with the group and is concerned about the welfare of the group. The implications for working with children at these levels are explicit, because certain strategies work more effectively with children or adolescents who are at corresponding stages of ego maturity. Knowing a person's level of ego maturity may well help pinpoint the type of prevention or intervention that will deal most effectively with the pain, anger, fear, and terror within that person.

STRENGTHENING MORAL AND ETHICAL DEVELOPMENT

Lawrence Kohlberg's model of moral development has roots in Piaget's theories of moral and cognitive development. Certain levels of cognitive development are a necessary, but not sufficient, condition for certain stages of moral maturity. In fact, Kohlberg's model is a cognitive reasoning model—a model for reasoning about justice and fairness. For Kohlberg, mature moral reasoning develops from "an active change in patterns of thinking brought about by experiential problem-solving situations that arise from interactions between the organism and the environment" (Hayes, 1994). Thus, there is great potential for using dilemmas to promote such development. Kohlberg "was not really interested in whether the subject said 'yes' or 'no' to the dilemma but in the reasoning behind the answer" (Crain, 2000). Kohlberg was *not* preaching a set of values or morals.

According to Kohlberg, moral maturity progresses through a universal, invariable sequence of six stages. For children, the stages would comprise: 1) "Punishment-Obedience," whereby children obey authorities or rules to avoid punishment—things are "good" or "bad" and consequences are critical; 2) "Instrumental Hedonism" or "Individualism and Exchange" (Crain, 2000), where children act out of self-interest to meet their needs; this is commonly referred to as the "you scratch my back, I'll scratch yours" stage; and 3) "Good-boy–Good-girl" orientation, which most often characterizes older children, or acting according to what is "right," pleasing, and approved of by others.

The features of each childhood stage are explicit and, after presenting a *meaningful* dilemma, the teacher or parent can readily determine a child's moral maturity (LeCapitaine, 2000, 2001). Acknowledging a child's level of moral maturity has many implications for prevention and intervention with respect to terror, disaster, and war. As a person's reasoning about justice and fairness increasingly matures, so will his or her ability to make sense of horrific constructs.

CONCLUSIONS

Children and adolescents need not be held hostage by terror, fear, stress, disaster, war, and their contextual milieus. Communities and schools may serve as developmental clinics, facilitating vital personal and psychological development, in order to prevent—and when necessary to intervene against—those dreaded "monsters" that can delay positive, mature personal growth.

REFERENCES

Bigelow, B., Christensen, L., Karp, S., Miner, B., & Peterson, B. (Eds.) (1994). *Rethinking our classrooms.* Milwaukee, WI: Rethinking Schools Ltd.

Crain, J. (2000). *Theories of development.* Upper Saddle River, NJ: Prentice-Hall.

Dewey, J. (1963). *Experience and education.* New York: Collier.

Dupont, H. (1994). *Emotional development, theory and applications: A neo-Piagetian perspective.* Westport, CT: Praeger Press.

Hayes, R. (1994). The legacy of Lawrence Kohlberg: Implications for counseling and human development. *Journal of Counseling and Development, 72,* 261–267.

Kitchener, R. (1996). The nature of the social for Piaget and Vygotsky. *Human Development, 39,* 243–249.

Kohn, A. (1994, March/April). The case against rewards and praise: A conversation with Alfie Kohn. *Harvard Educational Letter,* 5–6.

LeCapitaine, J. (1999, Summer). Schools as developmental clinics: Overcoming the shadow's three faces. *Education, 119,* 588–597.

LeCapitaine, J. (2000, Fall). The role of the school psychologist in the treatment of high-risk students. *Education, 121,* 73–79.

LeCapitaine, J. (2001). Promoting personal and psychological development in children: Of what good is it to graduate the mind but to lose the person? *Education, 121,* 459–469.

Lickona, T. (1976). *Moral development and behavior.* New York: Holt, Rinehart, and Winston.

Loevinger, J. (1976). *Ego development.* San Francisco: Jossey-Bass.

Loevinger, J. (1983). Personality: Stages, traits, and the self. *Annual Review of Psychology, 34,* 195–222.

Loevinger, J. (1997). Stages of personality development. In R. Hogan, J. Johnson, & S. Briggs (Eds.), *Handbook of personality psychology.* San Diego, CA: Academic Press.

Mosher, R. (1979). Funny things happen on the way to curriculum development. In R. Mosher (Ed.), *Adolescent development: A Janus knot.* Berkeley, CA: McCutchen Press.

Mosher, R., & Sprinthall, N. (1970). Psychological education in secondary schools: A program to promote individual and human development. *American Psychologist, 25,* 911–924.

Santrock, J. (2000). *Children.* Boston: McGraw-Hill.

Selman, R. L. (1980). *The growth of interpersonal understanding: Developmental and clinical analysis.* New York: Academic Press.

Selman, R. L., & Schultz, L. H. (1990). *Making a friend in youth: Developmental theory and pair therapy.* Chicago: University of Chicago Press.

Sleek, S. (1997). Can "emotional intelligence" be taught in today's schools? *APA Monitor, 28(6).*

Van der Veer, R. (1996). Vygotsky and Piaget: A collective monologue. *Human Development, 39,* 237–242.

Vygotsky, L. S. (1978). *Mind in society: The development of higher mental processes* (M. Cole, V. John-Steiner, S. Scribner, & E. Souberman, Eds.). Cambridge, MA: Harvard University Press. (Originally published 1930)

Waddell, D., & Thomas, A. (1999). *Disasters: Developing a crisis response plan.* Bethesda, MD: National Association of School Psychologists.

SUPPLEMENTARY BIBLIOGRAPHY

American Association for Counseling and Development (1991). Multiculturalism as a fourth force in counseling. *Journal of Counseling and Development, Special Issue 70 (1).* Alexandria, VA: AACD Press.

Anderson, B. (Ed.) (1995). *Taking back tomorrow: A school leader's guide to violence, security and safeguarding our school children.* Alexandria, VA: National School Boards Association.

Arnold, M. (1960). *Emotions and personality: Vol. 1, Psychological aspects.* New York: Columbia University Press.

Belenky, B., Clinchy, N., Goldberg, N., & Taruler, J. (1986). *Woman's ways of knowing.* New York: Basic Books.

Benson, C. (1989). Aesthetics, development and cognitive science. *Irish Journal of Psychology, 10,* 247–260.

Blasi, A. (1993). The theory of ego development and the measure. *Psychological Inquiry, 4,* 17–19.

Blumenkrantz, D. (1992). *Fulfilling the promise of children's services: Why primary prevention efforts fail and how they can succeed.* San Francisco: Jossey-Bass.

Brock, S. E., Sandoval, J., & Lewis, S. (1996). *Preparing for crises in the schools: A manual for building school crisis response teams.* New York: Wiley.

Brown, L., & Gilligan, C. (1993). Meeting at the crossroads: Women's psychology and girls' development. *Feminism and Psychology, 3,* 11–35.

Canter, A., & Carroll, S. (Eds.) (1998). *Helping children at home and school: Handouts from your school psychologist* (Section 8: Safety and Crisis). Bethesda, MD: National Association of School Psychologists.

Corrigan, D., & Udas, K. (1997). Creating collaborative, child-and-family centered education, health, and human service systems. In J. Sikula, T. Buttery, & E. Guyton (Eds.), *Handbook of research on teacher education* (2nd ed., pp. 893–921). New York: Simon & Schuster/Macmillan.

D'Andrea, M., & Daniels, J. (1992). Measuring ego development for counseling practice: Implementing developmental eclecticism. *Journal of Humanistic Education and Development, 31*, 12–21.

Darling-Hammond, L. (1993). Reframing the school reform agenda: Developing capacity for school transformation. *Phi Delta Kappan, 74 (10)* .

Dryfoos, J. (1994). *Full-service schools: A revolution in health and social services for children, youth, and families.* San Francisco: Jossey-Bass.

Dwyer, K., Osher, D., & Warger, C. (1998). *Early warning, timely response: A guide to safe schools.* Washington, DC: U.S. Department of Education. (Available online at www.ed. gov/offices/OSERS/OSEP/earlywarna.html and www.naspweb.org/center.html)

Eaton, S. (1993, November/December). For most children in poverty, school breakfast is still an unfulfilled promise. *Harvard Educational Letter,* 5–6.

Elkind, D. (1981). *The hurried child.* Reading, MA: Addison-Wesley.

Ellis, A. (1962). *Reason and emotion in psychotherapy.* New York: Lyle Stewart.

Fagan, F., & Wise, P. (1994). *School psychology: Past, present, and future.* New York: Longman.

Flavell, J. H. (1963). *The developmental psychology of Jean Piaget.* New York: Van Nostrand Reinhold.

Flavell, J. H., Botkin, P. T., Fry, C. L., Wright, J. W., & Jarvis, P. E. (1968). *The development of role-taking and communication skills in children.* New York: John Wiley.

Furlong, M. J., & Smith, D. C. (Guest Eds.). (1998). Addressing anger and aggression in the school settings. *Psychology in the Schools (Special Issue), 35* (3).

Franklin, M. (1994). *Development and the arts: Critical perspectives.* Hillsdale, NJ: Lawrence Erlbaum.

Gardner, H. (1991). The course of creative growth: A tribute to Joachim Wohlwill. In *Visions of aesthetics, the environment and development: The legacy of Joachim F. Wohlwill* (pp. 23–43). Hillsdale, NJ: Lawrence Erlbaum.

Gilligan, C. (1991). Women's psychological development: Implications for psychotherapy. *Woman and Therapy, 11* (Special issue: *Women, girls and psychotherapy: Reframing Resistance*), 5–31.

Gilligan, C. (1996). The centrality of relationship in human development: A puzzle, some evidence and a theory. In *Development and vulnerability in close relationships. The Jean Piaget Symposium Series* (pp. 237–261). Mahwah, NJ: Lawrence Erlbaum.

Goldstein, A., & Conoley, J. (1997). *School violence prevention: A practical handbook.* New York: Guilford.

Goodlad, J., & Keating, P. (Eds.) (1990). *Access to knowledge: An agenda for our nation's schools.* New York: College Entrance Examination Board.

Hanford, J. (1991). The relationship between faith development of James Fowler and moral development of Lawrence Kohlberg: A theoretical review. *Journal of Psychology and Christianity, 10,* 306–310.

Herring, R. D. (1998). *Career counseling in schools: Multicultural and developmental perspectives.* Washington, DC: American Counseling Association.

Hixton, J., & Tinzman, M. (1990). *Who are the "at risk" students of the 1990's?* Oak Brook, IL: NCREL.

Klein, P. (1994). *Mediating the cognitive, social, and aesthetic development of precocious young children.* Ramat Gan, Israel: Bar-Ilan University.

Kohlberg, L. (1994). *Kohlberg's original study of moral development*. New York: Garland Publishing.

Kohlberg, L. (1994). Stage and sequence, the cognitive-developmental approach to socialization. In B. Puka (Ed.), *Moral development: A compendium* (Vol. 1, pp. 1–134). New York: Garland Publishing.

Kohlberg, L., & Mayer, R. (1972). Development as the aim of education. *Harvard Educational Review, 42*, 451–496.

Lazarus, R. (1991). Progress on a cognitive-motivational-relational theory of emotions. *American Psychologist, 46*, 819–834.

LeCapitaine, J. (2002). *Personal and psychological maturity: A developmental model*. River Falls, WI: Steinway Press.

Loevinger, J. (1993). Ego development: Question of method and theory. *Psychological Inquiry, 4*, 56–63.

Loevinger, J. (1994). In search of grand theory. *Psychological Inquiry, 5*, 142–144.

Manning, M., & Baruth, L. (1995). *Students at risk*. New York: Bacon.

Paisley, P., & Hubbard, G. (1994). *Developmental school programs: From theory to practice*. Alexandria, VA: American Counseling Association.

Parr, G., & Ostrovsky, M. (1991). The role of moral development in deciding how to counsel children and adolescents. *The School Counselor, 39*, 14–19.

Parsons, M., & Durham, M. (1979). A cognitive-developmental approach to aesthetic experience. In R. Mosher (Ed.), *Adolescent development: A Janus knot*, 209–235. Berkeley, CA: McCutchen Press.

Piaget, J. (1959). *The language and thought of the child* (M. Gabain, Trans.). London: Routledge and Kegan Paul. (Originally published 1923)

Piaget, J. (1963). *The child's conception of the world* (J. & A. Tomlinson, Trans.). Savage, MD: Littlefield, Adams and Co. (Originally published 1926)

Piaget, J. (1964). *Six psychological studies* (A. Tenzer & D. Elkind, Trans.). New York: Vintage Books.

Piaget, J. (1965). *The moral judgment of the child* (M. Gabain, Trans.). New York: Free Press. (Originally published 1932)

Piaget, J. (1974). *The origins of intelligence in children* (M. Cook, Trans.). New York: International Universities Press. (Originally published 1936)

Piaget, J. (1983). Piaget's theory. In P. H. Mussen (Ed.), *Handbook of Child Psychology* (4th ed.) (Vol. I, W. Kessen, Ed.). New York: John Wiley. (Originally published 1970)

Piaget, J., & Inhelder, B. (1956). *The child's conception of space* (F. J. Langdor & J. L. Lunzer, Trans.). London: Routledge & Kegan Paul. (Originally published 1948)

Piaget, J., & Inhelder, B. (1966). *The psychology of the child* (H. Weaver, Trans.). New York: Basic Books.

Piaget, J., & Szeminska, A. (1941). *The child's conception of number* (C. Cattegno & F. M. Hodgson, Trans.). New York: W. W. Norton & Co.

Piatelli-Palmarini, M. (Ed.) (1979). *Language and learning: The debate between Jean Piaget and Noam Chomsky*. Cambridge, MA: Harvard University Press, 1980.

Pitcher, G., & Poland, S. (1992). *Crisis intervention in the schools*. New York: Guilford.

Puka, B. (1994). *Fundamental research in moral development*. New York: Garland Publishing.

Selman, R. K. (1976). Social-cognitive understanding: A guide to educational and clinical practice. In T. Lickona (Ed.), *Moral development and behavior*. New York: Holt, Rinehart & Winston.

Sigelman, C. K. (1999). *Life-span human development* (3rd ed.). Pacific Grove, CA: Brooks/Cole Publishing.

Super, D. E. (1984). Perspectives on the meaning and value of work. In N. C. Gysbers (Ed.), *Designing careers: Counseling to enhance education, work, and leisure*. San Francisco: Jossey-Bass.

Super, D. E. (1990). A life-span, life-space approach to career development. In D. Brown & L. Brooks (Eds.), *Career choice and development: Applying contemporary theories to practice* (pp. 197–261). San Francisco: Jossey-Bass.

Tiedeman, D. V., & Miller-Tiedeman, A. (1984). Career decision-making: An individualistic perspective. In D. Brown & L. Brooks (Eds.), *Career choice and development: Applying contemporary theories to practice*. San Francisco: Jossey-Bass.

Tomkins, S. (1962). *Affect, imagery, consciousness: Vol. 1: The positive effects*. New York: Springer Press.

Tudge, J., Putnam, S., & Valsiner, J. (1996). Culture and cognition in developmental perspective. In R. B. Cairnes, G. H. Elder, Jr., & E. J. Costello (Eds.), *Developmental science*. New York: Cambridge University Press.

Vygotsky, L. S. (1962). *Thought and language* (E. Hanfmann & G. Vakar, Eds. & Trans.). Cambridge, MA: MIT Press. (Originally published 1934)

Walker, H. M., & Gresham, F. M. (1997). Making schools safer and violence free. *Intervention in School and Clinic, 32*, 199–204.

Young, M. A. (1998). *Community crisis response team training manual* (2nd ed.). Washington, DC: National Organization for Victim Assistance.

Zabriske, J. (February, 1999). APA teams with MTV to prevent violence. *APA Monitor*.

Zweig, C., & Abrams, J. (1991). *Meeting the shadow: The hidden power of the dark side of human nature*. Los Angeles: Jeremy P. Tarcher.

NOTE

Dedicated to Lauren Astley, Amalia and Alejandro Fuentes, Maya Hampsey, Katie LeCapitaine, Benjamin Weissman, and to children everywhere.

Afterword

Harvey Langholtz
Series Editor
Psychological Dimensions to War and Peace

In the four edited volumes of the *Psychology of Terrorism,* Dr. Chris Stout and forty-three contributing authors have explored terrorism from the perspectives of psychological theory, therapy, history, sociology, political science, international relations, religion, anthropology, and other disciplines. These authors have brought differing viewpoints and they offer different views. In some cases the reader might even wonder if these authors have been addressing different subjects and different realities.

But this is the fundamental anomaly in the study of terrorism. On the one hand, it is easy to oversimplify and explain terrorism. On the other hand, recent events show us how difficult it is truly to understand terrorism, much less to know how to deal with it both reasonably and effectively. There is no universally agreed-upon definition of terrorism. Views on terrorism are often politically driven and it seems to be easier to cloud the discussion than to agree on an understanding. The issue urgently demands immediate solutions but these solutions appear to be a long way off.

As we look back over the ten years that preceded September 11, 2001, it seems we all missed the signals—the bombing of the Khobar Towers in Saudi Arabia, the U.S. embassies in Kenya and Tanzania, the USS *Cole,* and the federal building in Oklahoma City; the gas attack on the Tokyo subway; and of course the 1993 attack on the World Trade Center itself. Did our world actually change on that one day or were we only coming to realize as we watched the events in helpless disbelief that our understanding of the world had been wrong?

In the long view of history, September 11 will be remembered as a day when we were forced in fear and pain to reexamine some of our fundamental assumptions. And in this long view scholars will look to see what the serious and well-considered reactions were in the months following the event as psychologists and others took the time to reflect on the events of the day. That is what the contributing authors to these four volumes have sought to do in the immediate aftermath of the event: To consider terrorism, the causes of terrorism, people's reactions to terrorist acts, interventions to prevent or contain terrorism, and the possible role psychologists can play in understanding, explaining, and limiting terrorism and its effects.

Index

Adolescence: defined, 132; identity and attitude formation in, 132–33; and media modeling, 133; peer relations and ingroup/outgroup dynamics in, 134; role models and social learning of, 134; self-reflection and egocentrism in, 132

Adolescent interventions: for anger management, 138–39, 140–44; controlled intergroup contact and, 137–38; curricular, 140–44; psychology education in, 131–32, 137, 144–50; for reducing prejudice, 137–38; societal and educational, 134

Adolescents, as perpetrators and victims of violent crime, 158. *See also* Juvenile violence

Affect, of potential terrorist, 25

Afghanistan: perceptions of U.S. interventions in, 64; psychology education in, 48; U.S. militarization of, 70

Africa, local/internal terrorism in, 30. *See also* South Africa

African National Congress (ANC): banning and militarization of, 5, 6; Inkatha Freedom Party (IFP) and, 13–16

Aggression: American rhetoric of, 96; and anger, 95–98; collective, denial of, 106–9; as conscious choice, 98; cultural context of, 94–112; definitions of, 41; as emotional state, 97–98; environmental conditions for, 41; individual, media

focus on, 109; intergroup norms of, 43; multiple meanings of, 97; negative projection and, 103–4; normalization and desirability of, 43, 96, 97; paradigm of individualism and, 99–100; parenting and, 158; and perceived threat of attack, 40–41, 43–44; political ideology and, 43–44; proactive, prevalence of, 158; psychological factors and processes in, 42, 95, 111; role of power in, 109–10; shame and, 101–3; and shame/counter-shame cycle, 102; and social learning theory, 42–43. *See also* Child aggression; Juvenile violence

al-Qaeda, enemy images of, 60

American culture: of aggression, 43, 96, 97; individualism and power distance in, 29, 99–100; victimization and shame in, 102–3

American Psychological Association (APA), Global Psychology Project of, 144–50

Anger: and aggression, 95–98; management, 138–39, 140–44; as shame reaction, 98, 101

Antisocial behavior: onset patterns of, 159; psychological processes in, 42

Arab world, perceptions of United States in, 61–65

Arab-Israeli conflict, United States' role in, 62–63

About the Editor and Advisory Board

CHRIS E. STOUT is a clinical psychologist who holds a joint government and academic appointment in the Northwestern University Medical School, and serves as the first Chief of Psychological Services of the state of Illinois. He served as an NGO Special Representative to the United Nations, was appointed by the U.S. Department of Commerce as a Baldrige Examiner, and served as an advisor to the White House for both political parties. He was appointed to the World Economic Forum's Global Leaders of Tomorrow. He has published or presented more than three hundred papers and twenty-two books. His works have been translated into five languages. He has lectured across the nation and in sixteen countries and has visited more than fifty nations. He has been on missions around the world and has reached the top of three of the world's Seven Summits. He was Distinguished Alumni of the Year from Purdue University and Distinguished Psychologist of the Year, in addition to receiving more than thirty other postdoctoral awards. He is past President of the Illinois Psychological Association and is a member of the National Academy of Practice. He has been widely interviewed by the media, including CNBC, CNN, Oprah, *Time*, the *Chicago Tribune*, and the *Wall Street Journal*, and was noted as "one of the most frequently cited psychologists in the scientific literature" by Hartwick College. A distinct honor was his award as one of ten Volunteers of the Year in Illinois, and both the Senate and House have recognized his work by proclamation of "Dr. Chris E. Stout Week."

DANA ROYCE BAERGER is a practicing clinical and forensic psychologist in Chicago. She specializes in issues related to children, families, mental health, and the legal system. She is on the clinical faculty of the Department of Psychiatry and Behavioral Sciences at Northwestern University Medical School, and is also a staff member of the Children and Family Justice Center at Northwestern University Law School. In her private practice she provides psychotherapy services to individuals, couples, and groups; consults with attorneys regarding clinical and forensic practice standards; and consults with mental health professionals regarding ethical and risk management issues.

TERRENCE J. KOLLER is a practicing clinical psychologist in Chicago. He also serves as Executive Director and Legislative Liaison of the Illinois Psychological Association. He is Clinical Assistant Professor of Psychology in the Department of Psychiatry at the University of Illinois Medical School in Chicago. His areas of expertise include attachment and loss, parent-child interaction, and ethical and legal issues relating to the practice of psychology. He was the 1990 recipient of the Illinois Psychological Association's Distinguished Psychologist Award, and received an honorary doctor of humane letters degree from the Chicago School of Professional Psychology in 1995.

STEVEN P. KOURIS is associate chairman of the Department of Psychiatry at the University of Illinois College of Medicine in Rockford and medical director of the Jack Mabley Developmental Center in Dixon, Illinois. A medical graduate of Des Moines University, he interned at the Mayo Clinic and served clinical residencies at the University of Michigan and Detroit Medical Centers. He also completed an epidemiology research fellowship at the Minnesota Department of Health, and earned degrees in environmental health from the University of Minnesota and in preventive medicine from the University of Wisconsin. An accomplished clinician, teacher, and researcher, he is certified in multiple areas of psychiatry and medicine, and specializes in pediatric and developmental neuropsychiatry.

RONALD F. LEVANT is Dean and professor of psychology at the Center for Psychological Studies at Nova Southeastern University. He chairs the American Psychological Association (APA) Committee on Psychology's Response to Terrorism, and is a Fellow of APA Divisions 1, 12, 17, 27, 29, 31, 39, 42, 43, and 51. He has served on the faculties of Boston University, Harvard Medical School, and Rutgers University. He has authored or edited thirteen books and more than one hundred refereed journal articles and book chapters. He has served as Editor of the *Journal of Family Psychology*, is an Associate Editor of *Professional Psychology: Research and Practice*, and is an advisory editor or consulting editor to the following journals: *American Journal of Family Therapy, Journal of Marriage and Family Therapy, Men and Masculinities, Psychology of Men and Masculinity, Journal of African American Men, Journal of Trauma Practice, In Session: Psychotherapy in Practice*, and *Clinical Psychology: Science and Practice*.

MALINI PATEL is clinical associate professor of psychiatry and behavioral sciences at Finch University of Health Sciences/Chicago Medical School, and Acting Medical Director at a state psychiatric facility. She is board certified with added qualifications in addiction psychiatry. She is actively involved in resident and medical student training programs and has received awards for her teaching and contributions to psychiatric education. She also practices in a community mental health clinic where she sees patients in the Dual Diagnosis and Assertive Community Treatment Programs. She has published and presented on topics related to court-ordered treatment, administrative psychiatry, and substance abuse.

About the Contributors

SHARIF ABDULLAH is an adjunct faculty member at Marylhurst University and Portland State University. An author, proponent, and catalyst for inclusive social, cultural, and spiritual transformation, his work as a humanistic globalist has taken him to more than two dozen countries and to every continent. He received a B.A. in psychology from Clark University and a J.D. from Boston University. He has appeared on several international globalization forums. His writings include *The Power of One: Authentic Leadership in Turbulent Times.* He is founder and president of Commonway Institute in Portland, Oregon.

RUBÉN ARDILA is Professor of Psychology at the National University of Colombia (Bogota, Colombia). He has published twenty-three books and more than one hundred and fifty scientific papers in different languages, mainly Spanish and English. He founded the *Latin American Journal of Psychology* and has been the editor of this journal for several years. His main areas of research are the experimental analysis of behavior, social issues, peace psychology, and international psychology. He has been a visiting professor in the United States, Germany, Spain, Argentina, and Puerto Rico. He is a member of the executive committee of the International Union of Psychological Science.

BENJAMIN BEIT-HALLAHMI received his Ph.D. in clinical psychology from Michigan State University in 1970. Since then he has held clinical, research, and teaching positions in the United States, Europe, and Israel. He is the author, coauthor, editor, or coeditor of seventeen books and monographs on the psychology of religion, social identity, and personality development. In addition, he has a special interest in questions of ethics and ideology in psychological research and practice. In 1993, he was the recipient of the William James Award for his contributions to the psychology of religion.

FRED BEMAK is currently a Professor and the Program Coordinator for the Counseling and Development Program at the Graduate School of Education at George Mason University. He has done extensive work in the area of refugee and immigrant psychosocial adjustment and mental health. He has given seminars and lectures and conducted research throughout the United States and in more than thirty countries in the areas of cross-cultural psychology and the psychosocial adjustment of refugees and immigrants. He is a former Fulbright Scholar, a Kellogg International Fellow, and a recipient of the International Exchange of Experts and Research Fellowship through the World Rehabilitation Fund. He has been working nationally and internationally in the area of refugee adjustment and acculturation for the past twenty years as a researcher, clinician, and clinical consultant and has numerous publications in the area. He has recently written a book in collaboration with Rita Chi-Ying Chung and Paul Pedersen, *Counseling Refugees: A Psychosocial Approach to Innovative Multicultural Interventions*, published by Greenwood Publishing.

BRENDA ANN BOSCH is Clinical and Research Coordinator, Senior Clinical Psychologist, and Lecturer in the Department of Medically Applied Psychology, Nelson R. Mandela School of Medicine, University of Natal, Durban, South Africa. She is a member of several scientific organizations and professional societies. She is a consultant in clinical neuropsychology/disability, dissociative disorders in forensic psychology, traumatic stress, and peer supervision. Her current research and publication thrusts include the relationship between stress and neuropsychological deficits, stress and psycho-oncology, the intensive care unit, and mortuaries/law enforcement.

HENRY BREED has worked more than a decade in the United Nations, having been a Humanitarian Affairs Officer, Assistant to the Under-Secretary-General for Peacekeeping, and Assistant to the Special Representative of the Secretary-General to the former Yugoslavia and to the North Atlantic Treaty Organization. He is currently Political Affairs Officer in the Office of the Iraq Programmed. In past posts, he has been called upon to go to Mozambique, Rwanda, and the former Yugoslavia. In his current post, he has been closely involved in a broad range of international activities within Iraq. He has worked as a consulting editor for UNESCO on issues including education, development, and cultural preservation, and he has been actively involved in a range of environmental activities related to the Earth Summit. Born in Norway and raised in New York, he received undergraduate degrees in music and fine arts from Indiana University in Bloomington. He also holds a master's degree in public administration from Harvard University, a diplôme in international history and politics from the Graduate Institute of International Studies in Geneva, and a master's in international affairs from Columbia University. A member of the Council on Foreign Relations and of the International Institute of Strategic Studies, he was awarded the Beale Fellowship at Harvard and was admitted to the academic fraternity Pi Kappa Lambda at Indiana University. He is also a Fulbright Scholar, a "boursier de la Confédération Suisse," and a Regents Scholar. He lives in New York.

GIOVANNI CARACCI is a Clinical Associate Professor of Psychiatry at the Mount Sinai School of Medicine and Director of Residency Training and Medical Student Education at the Mount Sinai School of Medicine (Cabrini) Program. He is the Chair of the World Psychiatric Association on Urban Mental Health and a member of the Commission on Global Psychiatry of the American Psychiatric Association. He represents the World Psychiatric Association at the United Nations in New York, where he is Chair of the Non Governmental Organizations Executive Committee on Mental Health and Treasurer of the NGO Executive Committee of HABITAT (Center for Human Settlement). His main fields of expertise are international mental health, education, and cultural issues in mental health.

RITA CHI-YING CHUNG received her Ph.D. in psychology at Victoria University in Wellington, New Zealand. She is currently an Associate Professor in the Counseling and Development Program in the Graduate School of Education at George Mason University. She was awarded a Medical Research Council (MRC) Fellowship for postdoctoral work in the United States. Following the MRC fellowship, she remained as a Project Director for the National Research Center on Asian American Mental Health at the University of California, Los Angeles. In addition, she has been a visiting professor at the Federal University of Rio Grande do Sul in Brazil, Johns Hopkins University, and George Washington University, and a consultant for the World Bank. She has conducted research and written extensively on Asian immigrants and refugee mental health and has worked in the Pacific Rim, Asia, Europe, and Latin America. She has recently written a book in collaboration with Fred Bemak and Paul Pedersen, *Counseling Refugees: A Psychosocial Approach to Innovative Multicultural Interventions*, published by Greenwood Publishing.

JOHN M. DAVIS is Professor of Psychology at Southwest Texas State University. He completed advanced work at two German universities and received his Ph.D. in experimental/social psychology from the University of Oklahoma. He has lived and worked as a psychologist in Germany, China, England, and the United States. He has researched and published in the areas of interpersonal relations, refugee stress/adaptation, health psychology, and international psychology. Recent publications include a book chapter (1999) on health psychology in international perspective and an invited article (2000) on international psychology in the prestigious *Encyclopedia of Psychology* (APA/Oxford University Press). His current research interests include international terrorism from the perspectives of social and international psychology, and the influences of ethnic self-identity and attitude similarity on interpersonal and intergroup attraction.

ARTHUR A. DOLE is Professor Emeritus at the University of Pennsylvania Graduate School of Education, and former Chair of the Psychology in Education Division. He is a member of the Board of Directors of AFF, a nonprofit organization that encourages education and research about abusive groups, and a consulting editor of the *Cultic Studies Journal.* His research has focused on the harmfulness of cultic groups.

BORIS DROZDEK is a psychiatrist working at the GGZ Den Bosch/Outpatient and Daytreatment Centre for Refugees, the Netherlands. He is researching, publishing, and teaching in the field of psychotrauma and forced migration.

JONATHAN T. DRUMMOND is a doctoral student in social psychology at Princeton University. Prior to beginning doctoral work, he taught at the United States Air Force (USAF) Academy in the Department of Behavioral Sciences and Leadership as a major in the USAF. His research interests include psychological construction and attributions of legitimacy about political and judicial institutions in the United States and South Asia, retaliatory violence, white separatism, and divergent Aryan identity narratives (present and historical) in Indian Hindutva, Sinhalese Buddhism, and Euro-American Wotanism.

SOLVIG EKBLAD, a clinical psychologist, is Adjunct Associate Professor in Transcultural Psychology at the Karolinska Institutet, Department of Neurotec, Section of Psychiatry, Stockholm, Sweden. She is also Head of the Unit for Immigrant Environment and Health at the National Institute of Psychosocial Factors and Health, Solna, Sweden. She is in charge of the research group "Transcultural Psychology" and supervises Ph.D. and master's level students. At present, she has research grants from the National Swedish Integration Office, the European Refugee Fund, and the Stockholm County Council. She is collaborating with several foreign and local research teams. She is Co-Chair for the International Committee of Refugees and Other Migrants (ICROM), World Federation for Mental Health. She has written many articles and book chapters and has presented papers at international and national conferences in the field of migration and mental health.

SALMAN ELBEDOUR received his Ph.D. in school psychology from the University of Minnesota. After working at Ben-Gurion University, Israel, for six years, and at Bir Zeit University in the Palestinian Authority, he joined the School of Education at Howard University. He is currently an Associate Professor and the Coordinator of the School Psychology Program. His research and clinical interests are focused on psychopathology, maltreatment, child abuse, and neglect. He has published in the areas of cross-cultural and developmental studies of young children and adolescents placed at risk, specifically children exposed to political unrest, family conflict, and school violence. He has published extensively on the impact of the Israeli-Arab conflict on the development and socialization of children in the region. His Ph.D. thesis, "Psychology of Children of War," investigated the traumatic risk, resilience, and social and moral development of Palestinian children of the uprising, or *intifada.*

J. HAROLD ELLENS is a retired Professor of Philosophy, Theology, and Psychology, as well as the author, coauthor, and/or editor of 68 books and 148 professional journal articles. He spent his professional life on the issues involved in the interface of psychology and theology, served for fifteen years as Executive Director of the Christian Association for Psychological Studies, and as Founding Editor and Editor-in-Chief of the *Journal of Psychology and Christianity.* He holds a Ph.D. from Wayne State University in the psychology of human communication, a Ph.D. from the University of Michigan in Biblical and Near Eastern Studies, and master's degrees from Calvin Theological Seminary, Princeton Theological Seminary, and the University of Michigan. His publications include *God's Grace and Human Health* and *Psychotheology: Key Issues,* as well as chapters in *Moral Obligation and the Military, Baker Encyclopedia of Psychology, Abingdon Dictionary of Pastoral Care,* and *Humanistic Psychology.* He is currently a research scholar at the University of Michigan, Department of Near Eastern Studies. He is also a retired Presbyterian theologian and minister, and a retired U.S. Army Colonel.

TERI L. ELLIOTT is a clinical psychologist in New York City, specializing in children and adolescents. She is an Assistant Professor at the Disaster Mental Health Institute (DMHI), where she focuses on children and violence, bullying interventions, disaster response and preparedness, and psychological responses to weapons of mass destruction. She teaches and consults nationally and internationally on topics including children and trauma, crisis intervention, psychological support, and refugee mental health.

STEPHEN D. FABICK is a consulting and clinical psychologist in Birmingham, Michigan. He is past President of Psychologists for Social Responsibility (PsySR), past Chair of the PsySR Enemy Images program, and current Chair of its Conflict Resolution Action Committee. He is also Chair of the Conflict Resolution Working Group of the Society for the Study of Peace, Conflict and Violence (Division 48 of the American Psychological Association). His interest has been in conflict transformation and prejudice reduction. He authored *US & THEM: The Challenge of Diversity,* a Workshop Presenter's Manual. The program was included in President Clinton's Initiative on Race Relations and selected by the Center for Living Democracy as a model program in their book *Bridging the Racial Divide.* The program focuses on transforming group prejudice and conflict.

DON J. FEENEY, JR., is a clinical psychologist and Executive Director of Consulting Psychological Services in Chicago. In practice for more than twenty-five years, he has authored books including *Entrancing Relationships* (Praeger, 1999) and *Motifs: The Transformative Creation of Self* (Praeger, 2001).

RONA M. FIELDS is a clinical psychologist and Senior Associate at Associates in Community Health and Development and Associates in Community Psychology, in Washington, D.C. She has been an Assistant Professor at California State University, a Professor at the California School of Professional Psychology, and an Adjunct Professor at George Mason University and the American School of Professional Psychology. Her research includes studies of terrorism, violence and prejudice, peace-keeping operations and hostage negotiations, and treating victims of torture.

TIMOTHY GALLIMORE is a certified mediator, facilitator, and third-party neutral in conflict resolution. He researches and writes on trauma healing and reconciliation and on violence prevention. He earned a Ph.D. in mass communication from Indiana University in 1992. He was a consultant to the United Nations Development Program for Women and on the USAID Rwanda Rule of Law project to institute a community restorative justice system for trying genocide suspects.

TED G. GOERTZEL is Professor of Sociology at Rutgers University in Camden, New Jersey. His books include *Turncoats and True Believers, Linus Pauling: A Life in Science and Medicine,* and *Fernando Henrique Cardoso: Reinventing Democracy in Brazil.* His articles include "The Ethics of Terrorism and Revolution" and "Myths of Murder and Multiple Regression," and can be found on his Web site at http://goertzel.org/ted.

EDITH HENDERSON GROTBERG, a developmental psychologist, works for the Civitan International Research Center at the University of Alabama, Birmingham, and with the Institute for Mental Health Initiatives, George Washington University, Washington, D.C. Through the International Resilience Research Project (IRRP), she found many answers to the role of resilience in understanding and enhancing human health and behavior. Her articles have been published in *Ambulatory Child Health* and *The Community of Caring,* and some of her books on resilience have been translated into other languages.

RAYMOND H. HAMDEN is a clinical psychologist and Director of Psychology Services at the Comprehensive Medical Center in Dubai, United Arab Emirates. Born in the United States, he was a 1986 Visiting Fellow at the University of Maryland, College Park, Center for International Development and Conflict Management. His research and consultations focused on the psychology of the terrorist and hostage situations. He earned a Ph.D. at Heed University, Department of Psychology, and continued postgraduate study in psychoanalysis at the Philadelphia School of Modern Psychoanalysis. In 1990, he moved to the United Arab Emirates and established his own practice. He holds adjunct faculty positions at institutions including the University of Indianapolis, and has taught at the American Universities in Dubai and Sharjah. He holds Diplomate and Fellow status at the American College of Forensic Examiners and the American Academy of Sexologists. He is licensed by the Dubai Department of Health and Medical Services, as well as by the Board of Psychology Examiners in Washington, D.C. He is also a member of the International Society for Political Psychology and the International Council of Psychologists. He is an ACFE Diplomate, American Board of Psychological Specialties.

FADEL ABU HEIN is a community and clinical psychologist on the faculty of Al Aksa University in Gaza. He was for many years the senior psychologist at the Gaza Community Health Center, where he developed the research program and also instituted a broad outreach service for a traumatized population that had no other mental health resource. He has more recently established his own clinical practice in Gaza in conjunction with his teaching responsibilities at Al Aksa University.

CRAIG HIGSON-SMITH is a research psychologist employed in the Child, Youth and Family unit of the Human Sciences Research Council of South Africa. He is a specialist researcher in the fields of violence and traumatic stress. Previously, he cofounded and managed the KwaZulu-Natal Programme for Survivors of Violence, a nongovernment organization dedicated to supporting communities ravaged by civil conflict in Southern Africa. More recently, he cofounded the South African Institute for Traumatic Stress.

J. E. (HANS) HOVENS is a clinical psychologist and psychiatrist. He has published extensively on the subject of post-traumatic stress disorder. Currently, he is a lecturer on psychiatry at the Delta Psychiatric Teaching Hospital in Poortugaal, the Netherlands.

NIRA KFIR is a clinical psychologist who received her Ph.D. in social psychiatry at the Université de Paris, Sorbonne, Center for Social Psychiatry. She is the Director of Maagalim-Institute of Psychotherapy and Counseling in Tel Aviv. In 1973, she developed a Crisis Intervention program adopted by the Israeli Ministry of Defense, and it is still in use for group work with bereaved families. She developed the psychotherapeutic diagnostic system of Personality Impasse/Priority Therapy.

OLUFEMI A. LAWAL is a Ph.D. candidate at the University of Lagos, Akoka-Yaba, Lagos, Nigeria. He has been a teacher and coordinator at St. Finbarr's College in Lagos, and is now an instructor at Quantum Educational Services, Ilupeju, Ibadan, Oyo.

JOHN E. LeCAPITAINE is Professor and former Chair of the Department of Counseling and School Psychology, University of Wisconsin, River Falls. He has a doctorate in counseling psychology (Boston University), a doctorate in metaphysics, a master of science in school psychology, and a bachelor of science in mathematics. He is a Diplomate Forensic Psychologist and a member of the International Council of Psychologists, the American Psychological Association, the American College of Forensic Examiners, the Institute of Noetic Sciences, the National Association of School Psychologists, and *Who's Who in the World.* He has written a number of articles, receiving the Special Merit award from *Education* for *Schools as Developmental Clinics: Overcoming the Shadow's Three Faces.*

JOHN E. MACK is a Pulitzer Prize–winning author and Professor of Psychiatry at Harvard Medical School who has explored how cultural worldviews may obscure solutions to social, ecological, and spiritual crises. He is the founder of the Center for Psychology and Social Change. He also founded the Department of Psychiatry at the Cambridge Hospital in 1969. In 1983 he testified before Congress on the psychological impact of the nuclear arms race on children. He is the author or coauthor of ten books, including *A Prince of Our Disorder*, a Pulitzer Prize–winning biography of T. E. Lawrence, and, most recently, *Passport to the Cosmos.*

SHERRI McCARTHY is an Associate Professor of Educational Psychology at Northern Arizona University's Yuma campus. She has published research in international journals on a variety of topics, including developing critical thinking skills, anger management training, substance abuse counseling, and the role of psychology in improving society. She has also written books in the areas of special education and grief and bereavement issues. She is active in the International Council of Psychologists' Psychology and Law interest group. She is also active in the American Psychological Association, serving as the Division 2 Teaching of Psychology liaison to the Council on International Relations in Psychology and as the leader of the P3 Global Psychology Project.

CLARK McCAULEY is a Professor of Psychology at Bryn Mawr College and serves as a faculty member and Co-Director of the Solomon Asch Center for Study of Ethnopolitical Conflict at the University of Pennsylvania. He received his Ph.D. in social psychology from the University of Pennsylvania in 1970. His research interests include stereotypes and the psychology of group identification, group dynamics and intergroup conflict, and the psychological foundations of ethnic conflict and genocide. His recent work includes a new measure of intergroup contact, "the exposure index."

STEVE S. OLWEEAN is a psychotherapist with a degree in clinical psychology from Western Michigan University. He is President of the Association for Humanistic Psychology (AHP), and Founding Director of Common Bond Institute. Since 1990, he has served as AHP International Liaison and Coordinator of International Programs. His principal treatment area is trauma and abuse recovery and reframing negative belief systems. His primary international focus is conflict transformation, forgiveness, reconciliation, and humanitarian recovery efforts. He cofounded and each year coordinates the Annual International Conference on Conflict Resolution held in St. Petersburg, Russia. He also developed an integrated Catastrophic Trauma Recovery (CTR) treatment model for treating large populations experiencing trauma due to war, violence, and catastrophe.

DIANE PERLMAN is a clinical psychologist in Pennsylvania, with a special interest in political psychology. She is Co-Chair of the American Psychological Association Committee on Global Violence and Security within Division 48, the Society for the Study of Peace, Conflict, and Violence. She is also a research associate with the Citizens Panel on Ultimate Weapons at the Center on Violence and Human

Survival. She is Vice President of the Philadelphia Project for Global Security, and Liaison to the psychology community for the Global Nonviolent Peace Force. She is also Founding Member of and a research associate for the Transcending Trauma Project, studying adaptation of Holocaust survivors and their children. She is a Fellow of the Solomon Asch Center for Study of Ethnopolitical Conflict at the University of Pennsylvania and was a speaker for two decades for Physicians for Social Responsibility.

MARC PILISUK is a clinical and social psychologist. He is Professor Emeritus of the University of California and a Professor at the Saybrook Graduate School and Research Center in San Francisco. He is a past President of APA Division 48, the Society for the Study of Peace, Conflict, and Violence; a member of the steering committee of Psychologists for Social Responsibility; and one of the founders of the first teach-in.

JERRY S. PIVEN is a Professor of Psychology at New School University and New York University, where his courses focus on the psychology of religion, death, and sexuality. He is a member of the National Psychological Association for Psychoanalysis and author of *Death and Delusion: A Freudian Analysis of Mortal Terror*. He is editor of the series Psychological Undercurrents of History and is presently working on a psychoanalytic exploration of the madness and perversion of Yukio Mishima.

WILLIAM H. REID is a Clinical and Adjunct Professor of Psychiatry at the University of Texas Health Science Center, Texas A&M College of Medicine, and Texas Tech University Medical Center. He is past President of the American Academy of Psychiatry and the Law. He is a fellow of the Royal College of Physicians, American College of Psychiatrists, and American Psychiatric Association. He is also past Chair of the National Council of State Medical Directors, and a U.S. Observer for the Board of Presidents of the Socialist Countries' Psychiatric Associations, Sofia, Bulgaria. He was U.S. Representative, Ver Heyden de Lancey Conference on Psychiatry, Law, and Public Policy at Trinity College, Cambridge University, as well as visiting lecturer, Hunan Medical College, Changsha, Hunan.

LOURENS SCHLEBUSCH is Professor and Head of the Department of Medically Applied Psychology, Nelson R. Mandela School of Medicine, University of Natal, Durban, South Africa. He is a suicidologist, stress management and medico-legal/disability consultant, Chief Clinical Psychologist for the Hospital Services of the KwaZulu-Natal Provincial Administration, and Chief Consultant in Behavioural Medicine at various hospitals in Durban, South Africa. He is a member of many scientific editorial boards, organizations, and societies, and is a reviewer of scientific publications both nationally and internationally. He has many professional listings, honors, and awards. He has made many significant research contributions to his field and has published widely. He is currently researching various aspects of traumatic stress and suicide prevention.

KLAUS SCHWAB is Founder and President of the World Economic Forum, an organization committed to improving the state of the world, and based in Geneva, Switzerland. He has worked in several high-level roles with the United Nations and is now a Professor at the University of Geneva. He studied at the Swiss Federal Institute of Technology, the University of Fribourg, and the John F. Kennedy School at Harvard University.

KATHY SEXTON-RADEK is Professor of Psychology at Elmhurst College and Director of Psychological Services, Hinsdale Hospital/Suburban Pulmonary and Sleep Associates. She has designed conflict resolution and stress management curriculums for elementary and secondary school children and has implemented these programs with inner-city students at risk for violence and substance abuse. She has also constructed and taught anti-violence workshops for teachers. She is the author of more than thirty peer-reviewed articles in the areas of behavioral medicine, applied cognitive behavior theory in school settings, and psychology pedagogy. She is an elected member of her local school board, and a member of the American Psychological Association, Sigma Xi, and the Sleep Research Society.

ERVIN STAUB is Professor of Psychology at the University of Massachusetts at Amherst. He has published many articles and book chapters and several books about the influences that lead to caring, helping, and altruism, and their development in children. His upcoming book is *A Brighter Future: Raising Caring and Nonviolent Children.* He has also done extensive research into and writing about the roots and prevention of genocide and other group violence, including his book *The Roots of Evil: The Origins of Genocide and Other Group Violence.* Since 1999, he has been conducting, with collaborators, a project in Rwanda on healing, reconciliation, and other avenues to the prevention of renewed violence. His awards include the Otto Klineberg International and Intercultural Relations Prize of the Society for the Psychological Study of Social Issues. He has been President of the Society for the Study of Peace, Conflict, and Violence (Division 48 of the American Psychological Association) and of the International Society for Political Psychology.

MICHAEL J. STEVENS is a Professor of Psychology at Illinois State University in Normal. He is a Fellow of the American Psychological Association, serving as Chair of the Committee for International Liaisons of the Division of International Psychology. He is also a member of the Advisory Board of the Middle East Psychological Network. He is an honorary professor at the Lucian Blaga University of Sibiu, Romania, where he completed Fulbright and IREX grants. In 2000, he received the Recognition Award from the American Psychological Association for his work in international psychology.

TREVOR STOKES is Professor of Child and Family Studies, Professor of Psychology, Professor of Psychological and Social Foundations of Education, and Professor of Special Education at the University of South Florida, Tampa. He received his bachelor's degree with first-class honors in psychology at the University of Western

Australia, a Ph.D. in developmental and child psychology from the University of Kansas, and Ph.D. Clinical Psychology Augmentation at West Virginia University. His research, teaching, and clinical activities involve the behavior analysis and developmental assessment of aggression within families, with a focus on techniques for interception of violent repertoires by children.

TIMOTHY H. WARNEKA treats adolescents and children in a community mental health center near Cleveland, Ohio. He specializes in working with sexually aggressive and/or aggressive juveniles. He has studied the martial art of aikido for more than twelve years and incorporates aikido principles into his psychotherapeutic work. He is President of Cleveland Therapists, Ltd. (www.clevelandtherapists. com), a referral site for mental health professionals. He is President of Psyche & Soma Consulting, Ltd., an organization that offers training and consultation on a variety of mental health subjects.

MICHAEL WESSELLS is Professor of Psychology at Randolph-Macon College and Senior Technical Advisor for the Christian Children's Fund. He has served as President of the Division of Peace Psychology of the American Psychological Association and of Psychologists for Social Responsibility. His research examines psychology of terrorism, psychosocial assistance in emergencies, post-conflict reconstruction, and reintegration of former child soldiers. In countries such as Angola, Sierra Leone, East Timor, Kosovo, and Afghanistan, he helps to develop community-based, culturally grounded programs that assist children, families, and communities affected by armed conflict.

ANGELA WONG is a University of California student in sociology and social welfare. She is a research assistant and an intern providing assistance at homeless shelters.